35 MILES
FROM SHORE

The Ditching and Rescue
of ALM Flight 980

Published by Odyssey Publishing, LLC

Library of Congress 2006902232

ISBN: 978-0-9778971-0-0

Publisher's Cataloging-in-Publication Data

Corsetti, Emilio.
    35 miles from shore: the ditching and rescue of ALM flight 980/
    Emilio Corsetti III.
    p. cm.
    Includes bibliographical references.
    ISBN 9780977897100

1. Aircraft accidents—Investigations—Virgin Islands of the United States.
2. Survival after airplane accidents, shipwrecks, etc. I. Thirty-five miles from
shore : the ditching and rescue of ALM flight nine hundred eighty. II.Title.

TL553.5.C66 2007
363.124—dc22   2006902232

35 MILES FROM SHORE

The Ditching and Rescue of ALM Flight 980

Emilio Corsetti III

"3 63
.1246
5
C 826

ODYSSEY PUBLISHING, LLC
Lake St. Louis, MO

For the missing

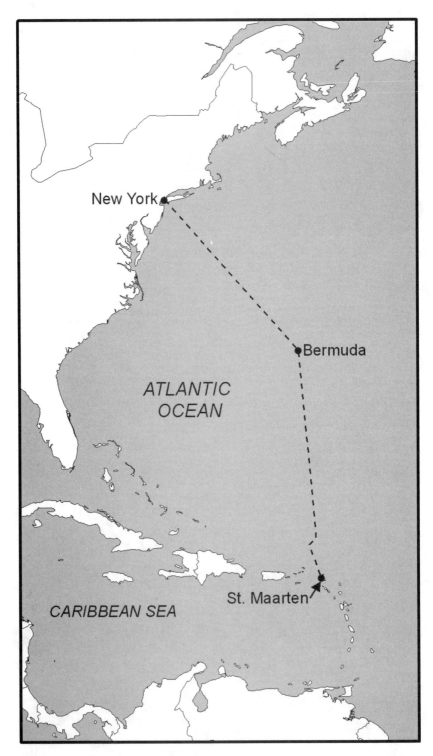

Figure 1. Route map.

Passengers & Crew

Crew

1. Captain Balsey D. DeWitt
2. First Officer Harry E. Evans II
3. Navigator Hugh H. Hart
4. Stewardess Margareth A. Abraham*
5. Steward Tobias (Tito) G. Cordeiro
6. Purser Wilford J. Spencer

Passengers: (This list was taken from newspaper accounts. Errors in names have been corrected where known.)

1. Barbara Adler
2. Jerome Adler*
3. Edward Alexander
4. Rick Arnold
5. Elaine Babb
6. B. Bernitt*
7. G. Bessi*
8. Jacinth M. Bryanth
9. Gloria Caldwell
10. Jennifer Caldwell*
11. Kristin Caldwell*
12. William Caldwell*
13. H. Carey*
14. Mildred Carey
15. Christine Cromwell
16. A. Edwards*
17. Ethel Eisenberg
18. Julius Eisenberg+
19. Frances Ellison
20. Wilma Evans
21. Winston Evans
22. Allen Grant
23. Gene Gremelsbacker*
24. Loretta Gremelsbacker

(Passenger list continued)

25. Walter Hodge
26. Esther Holmes
27. Arthur Johnson
28. Sybil Johnson
29. George Kellner
30. Martha Kellner
31. Israel Kruger
32. Toby Kruger
33. J. Kurtz*
34. Mrs. Kurtz*
35. Jeannie Larmony
36. Alex McCauley*
37. Mrs. Paris*
38. William Paris
39. Mrs. Marion Parmentier*
40. Mr. Robert Parmentier*
41. C. Phillips*
42. Margaret Phillips
43. Hedwig (Hedi) Razzi*
44. James Razzi
45. Vivian Rosoto
46. Giancafo Rossini
47. Jane Schmidt
48. Roger Schmidt
49. David Schwartz
50. Sylvia Schwartz
51. Jacques Urighere*
52. Sylvia Urighere*
53. Emerson Ussery
54. Yvonne Vulliemoz
55. Philip Winslow
56. V. Zangara*
57. Mrs. E. Zipkin*

* Missing
+ Pronounced dead upon arrival at the St. Croix hospital

Rescuers

Crew of Pan Am 454 (Boeing 727)
Captain – William Pash
First Officer – William M. Hall
Flight Engineer – James L. Phillips

Antilles Airboat 62C
Crew unknown

Crew Of Skyvan N33BB
Pilot – Bill Bohlke Jr.
Co-Pilot – George Johnson
Paul Wikander
Andy Titus
George Stoute

Crew of HU-16 Albatross 7245
Pilot – Lieutenant Thomas E. Blank
Co-Pilot – Lieutenant (j.g.)
Richard Evans
Radio operator – Barkley
Remainder of crew unknown

US Coast Guard HH-52A Helicopters from San Juan

Crew of Helicopter 1463
Pilot – Lieutenant (j.g.) William Shields
Co-Pilot – Lieutenant (j.g.) Carmond C. Fitzgerald
Third crewmember unknown

Crew of Helicopter 1426
Pilot – Lieutenant Commander Jim Brawley
Co-Pilot – Captain Charles Mayes

Crew of U.S. Navy SH-3A (Sea King) helicopter from Roosevelt Roads Puerto Rico
Fleet Composite Squadron (VC-8) GF-15
Pilot – Lieutenant Commander LCDR James E. Rylee
Co-Pilot – Lieutenant (j.g.) Donald G. Hartman
Chief Aviation Machinist's Mate – William A. Brazzell
Aviation Machinist's Mate – Calvin V. Lindley

Marine Medium Helicopter Squadron 261 (HMM-261)
Marine Aircraft Group 26, 2nd Marine Aircraft Wing, FMF, Atlantic Marine Corps Air Station (Helicopter) New River, Jacksonville, NC

Crew of EM-15
Pilot – Major Dennis Beckman
Co-Pilot – Lieutenant Ken Bradley
Rest of crew unknown

Crew of EM-13
Pilot – Captain Art Nash
Co-Pilot – Captain Bill Murphy
Crew Chief – Corporal John D. Barber
Corporal Vince Perron
Captain Randy Logan

(Rescuers continued)

Crew of EM-16
Pilot – Captain Charles Crookall
Rest of crew unknown

EM-14
Crew unknown

EM-07
Pilot – Captain Glen C. Warren
Co-Pilot – Captain Ned J. Lemoine
Crew Chief – Sergeant Gary
Bockman
First Mechanic – Lance Corporal
William S. Schrader
Rest of crew unknown

EM-01
Pilot – Captain Gordon Tubesing
Rest of crew unknown

Crew of U.S.C.G. Cutter *Point Whitehorn*
Commander – Billy C. Cobb
Boatswain Mate First Class –
Kenneth P. Borrego
Commisaryman Second Class –
G. E. Baez
Fireman – Paul Molignoni
Seaman – Earl Floyd
Seaman – R.C. Sass
Remainder of crew unknown

Investigators, Airline Personnel, and Other Interested Parties

NTSB

George R. Baker – Investigator In Charge

Gerrit Walhout – Survival Factors Group

Isabel A. Burgess – Chairman for the hearings

Technical Panel

Dr. John H. Fahrni – Human Factors Group – Co-Chairman

Martin A. Speiser – Operations Group Chairman

Francis X. Graves – Air Traffic Control Group

FAA

Carl Morgan – FAA man in charge of ONA

Mack Wood – Flight Standards Office FAA in San Juan

ONA

G. F. Steedman Hinckley – President and CEO

J. W. Bailey – Executive Vice President and General Manager

Malcolm E. Starkloff – Director of Operations

Edward Veronelli – Assistant DC-9 Chief Pilot

Vince Duffy – Marketing Vice President for ONA

George Chopay – ONA Maintenance Representative

Kristina Linder – Flight Attendant Instructor

Edwin A. Leiser – Superintendent of Maintenance

John P. O'Brien – ALPA Lawyer

Stephen R. Lang – ONA lawyer

Robert E. Wagenfeld – Assistant Vice President-Legal

ALM

Ciro Octavio (Tawa) Irausquin – President

Max Waas – Chief Purser

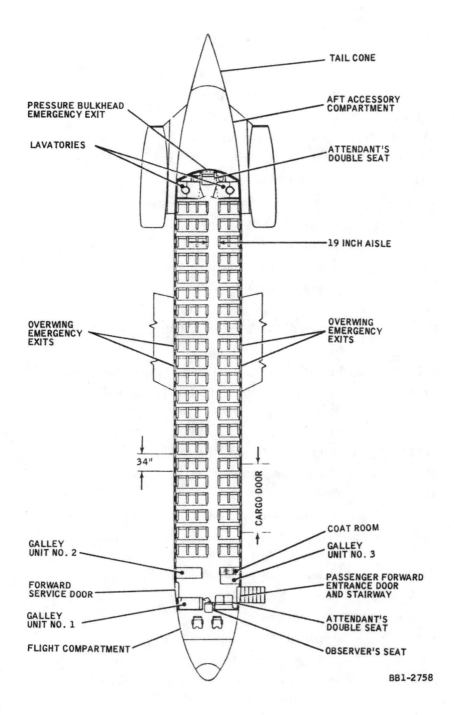

Figure 2. DC-9 seating diagram.

Abbreviations

ALM	Antilliaanse Luchtvaart Maatschappij, the official airline of the Netherlands Antilles
ALPA	Airline Pilots Association
AMVER	Automated Merchant Vessel Reporting System
ARTCC	Air Route Traffic Control Center
CAB	Civil Aeronautics Board
COMGANTS	Commander Greater Antilles Section
DACO	Douglas Aircraft Company
ETA	Estimated Time of Arrival
FAA	Federal Aviation Administration
FAR	Federal Aviation Regulations
FL	Flight Level
ICS	Intercom Communication System
IFR	Instrument Flight Rules
JFK	Identifier for John F. Kennedy International Airport
KLM	Koninklijke Luchtvaart Maatschappij, Royal Dutch Airlines
KTS	Knots
LORAN	Long Range Navigation
MATS	Military Air Transport Service
MEC	Master Executive Council
MEL	Minimum Equipment List
NDB	Non-Directional Beacon, also known as an ADF (navigation aid)
NTSB	National Transportation Safety Board
ONA	Overseas National Airways
Pan Am	Pan American Airways
SAR	Search and Rescue
SJU	Identifier for San Juan International Airport
SXM	Identifier for St. Maarten Princess Juliana Airport, Netherlands Antilles
VOR	A ground-based navigation aid

Prologue

THIRTY-FIVE MILES OFF THE COAST OF ST. CROIX, SIT-
TING beneath some five thousand feet of
water, lies the most unlikely of deep-sea wrecks. It is not the wreck
of an ocean liner or a Spanish galleon or a fishing boat caught in an
unexpected storm. This wreck is that of a passenger jet. The exact
condition of the aircraft is unknown. It has remained unseen in the
dark depths of the Caribbean Sea for more than thirty-five years.
What is known is the condition of the aircraft before it sank.

The plane remained afloat and intact for at least five to ten minutes. The galley door and two of the four overwing exits had been
opened. There was a hole in the forward cargo compartment large
enough to allow several aircraft tires to float free. Witnesses reported
watching the plane bank to the right, then sink nose first. From
there it would have continued its mile-long dive until finally hitting
the sea bed.

No attempts have ever been made to recover the aircraft or any
of the flight recorders. The cost of recovery simply outweighs the
value of what might be retrieved. Treasure seekers might find a few

items of interest. There is a blue suitcase discarded by one passenger who claims that the suitcase contained over $135,000 in jewelry. Another passenger claims to have left behind a briefcase containing several hundred thousand dollars in cash. The veracity of these claims has yet to be proved or disproved. Little else of value remains inside the fuselage: a few purses, reading glasses, a wine bottle. There are four twenty-five-man life rafts still secured inside the large bins mounted in the ceiling. Somewhere in the debris inside the cabin are two cameras containing rolls of undeveloped film that captured the last moments of the ill-fated flight. There is something else inside, however, of great importance to a number of people—clues to what might have happened to those who didn't make it out.

The date is May 2, 1970. Low on fuel and flying just hundreds of feet above the ocean's surface, the crew of ALM 980 look out their cockpit window and see a turbulent sea swirling beneath them. Ten- to fifteen-foot swells rise and fall in all directions. The sky above is equally turbulent, with heavy rain and low visibility. Back in the cabin the passengers don their life vests, for they have been told to prepare for a possible ditching. They are obviously concerned, but most consider it nothing more than a precaution. A few passengers refuse to put on their life vests, viewing it as an unnecessary inconvenience. Assisting in the cabin is a purser, a steward, and one stewardess. The stewardess moves through the cabin helping passengers with their cumbersome life jackets. In the front of the cabin, in the galley area just behind the cockpit, the purser, the steward, and a third cockpit crewmember, a navigator, struggle with one of the five life rafts aboard. No one pays much attention to the four life rafts located in the bins mounted in the ceiling just above the four overwing exits.

The lack of concern displayed in the back of the aircraft is not shared by the two men in the cockpit. Their eyes are glued to the digital fuel totalizer, which indicates a figure so low that the number is unreliable. Both men know they are only seconds away from losing both engines due to fuel exhaustion. When the engines finally do quit, there are only seconds left in which to act. The captain flicks the seatbelt and no smoking signs off and on to signal the cabin crew of the impending impact; he doesn't use the passenger address (PA) system because it's not working.

Some of the passengers stand as they put on their life vests. Others sit with their seatbelts unfastened. No one notices the seatbelt and no smoking signs flicker off and on. Nor do they hear the bells that accompany these signs. Even if they had noticed, it wouldn't make much difference. The cabin crew was trained by a different airline, one that didn't use bells to signal an emergency landing. A few people look outside their window and note how close they are to the water. One man sitting near an emergency overwing exit looks around at his fellow passengers; most have no idea that they are just moments away from impact. In the forward section of the cabin, two men stand in the aisle snapping pictures. They are not wearing life jackets. There are shouts from the front of the cabin for everyone to sit down. But the aircraft strikes the water before everyone can take their seats.

Accident investigators often use the term "error chain" when explaining how accidents occur. They know from experience garnered from decades of accident investigations that accidents don't occur in a vacuum. Accidents are usually the end result of a series of mistakes or events. Remove one of the preceding events, or links in the error chain, and the accident does not occur. While we can never totally eliminate errors, we can strive to not repeat them. When I first contacted the captain of the flight, Balsey DeWitt, to inform him of my intention to tell this story, he was reluctant to participate. He finally agreed to be interviewed because he felt that by doing so he might help prevent a similar accident from occurring again, or at least increase the chances of survival should another plane succumb to a similar fate. In the numerous times that I have spoken with the former captain, he has not once shifted blame to another individual. He accepts full responsibility for what took place. But the mistakes he admits to are not the only links in the error chain that led to the ditching of ALM 980.

Part One

PREFLIGHT

Chapter 1

E ARLY ON THE MORNING OF MAY 2, 1970, OVERSEAS National Airways (ONA) mechanic George Chopay began his day with a walk-around inspection of aircraft N935F. The plane had just returned from an all-night flight from Las Vegas, landing at John F. Kennedy airport a little after 7:00 A.M. The DC-9 would have only a couple of hours on the ground before it was once again sent back out for a full day of flying, this time to the Caribbean and back.

It was a quiet morning as George made his way around the like-new jet. Saturday mornings were always a little slow. The normal cacophony of jet engines and spinning propellers was supplanted by the sound of seagulls searching for food along the shores of nearby Jamaica Bay. The ever-present seagulls were a constant reminder of just how close to water JFK actually lies.

After completing the walk-around inspection and clearing two minor maintenance items, George taxied the plane from the north passenger terminal to the international terminal located on the northwest side of the airport. He parked the plane on the ramp.

Passengers would later board using stairs that extended out and down from just under the main cabin door.

Before exiting the cockpit, George called for fuel and requested that the aircraft be topped off. He would later note that the digital fuel totalizer indicated just under 29,000 pounds after the fueling, which was almost 500 pounds more than the stated maximum fuel capacity of the DC-9, the difference attributed to fuel density.

Sometime between 10:10 A.M. and 10:20 A.M. the three flight crewmembers arrived at the aircraft. The flight crew consisted of Captain Balsey DeWitt, First Officer Harry Evans, and Navigator Hugh Hart.[1] George handed the captain the fuel slip and told him about the two write-ups that had been cleared earlier. George knew Captain DeWitt well. Thirty-seven-year-old Balsey DeWitt was a check airman and flight instructor for ONA. George glanced at the other two crewmembers and wondered which one of them was getting a line check. He guessed the first officer by the way he was standing with his hands stuffed in his pockets and his eyes fixed on the pavement. George was glad he wasn't in the first officer's shoes. Balsey had a reputation for being a tough examiner.

With the handover completed, Balsey and Hugh climbed the stairs to the cabin while Harry Evans began an exterior preflight. If Harry had appeared uneasy to George, there was good reason. Harry hadn't flown much in the past three months. And while he wasn't getting a line check this day, he was making his first international flight. It also didn't help that he was flying with a check airman. Regardless of the circumstances, flying with a flight examiner is always stressful.

Inside the aircraft, Balsey and Hugh found the two flight stewards and one stewardess busy with their own preflight checks. There was a brief exchange but no formal briefing. Balsey had flown with purser Wilfred Spencer and stewardess Margareth Abraham before and had confidence in their abilities. Had he not recognized them, he might have spent a little more time with them. As it was, they were already running a little behind schedule. Departure was less than forty-five minutes away.

Balsey took his seat on the left side of the cockpit and started to run through his preflight checks. Pilots use cockpit flows that allow them to perform the necessary checks without reference to a checklist. The flow on the DC-9 starts with the overhead panel, from there down to the glare shield, the center instrument panel, and finally to the center pedestal, where the dials for the communication and navigation radios are located. Balsey and Harry would later go through the checklist item by item to make sure that nothing was missed.

One of the last things Balsey did before the passengers boarded was test the PA system. PA announcements from the cockpit are made through a phone like handset located aft of the center pedestal. Testing the PA was not a checklist item. It was something Balsey did by habit. He picked up the handset and talked into it. He turned around and asked if anyone in back had heard the test. Hugh Hart, who was standing in the forward galley, indicated that all he heard was static and noise. Balsey spoke once more into the handset, and once again Hugh told him it was garbled.

Balsey pulled out the minimum equipment list (MEL) and looked to see if the PA was a mandatory item. The MEL is a list of aircraft components that can be inoperative as long as the inoperative component is repaired within a designated time period. Balsey found that the PA system was listed in the MEL, which meant it didn't have to be working. That was all he needed to know. Had there been more time, he would have written the PA up in the logbook and had George Chopay attempt to fix the problem. George was still inside the international terminal. He normally stayed with the aircraft until it departed the ramp, just in case he was needed. Balsey either didn't know that George was inside or deemed the problem too insignificant to delay the flight. There wasn't that much to talk about flying over the Atlantic anyway. He decided that the problem could be resolved when the plane returned later that evening.

The reason why the cockpit PA system was not a required item was because there were alternative means of communicating with the passengers. The PA system from the back was working normally. Balsey had heard one of the flight attendants checking the cabin PA earlier.[2] There was also a backup procedure for communicating with the flight attendants using bells for in-flight alerts. One bell meant that the flight attendant was to pick up the interphone; two bells meant that the flight attendant should come to the cockpit; three bells signaled an emergency.[3]

Inside the terminal, the passengers lined up by the door as they prepared to board ALM Flight 980 to St. Maarten. There was a normal mix of passengers. The only anomaly was the twenty-six adult women, which was slightly more than typical for this time period. Most were from the New York area, but there were a few from the Caribbean and elsewhere. One passenger, fifty-six-year-old Jeannie Larmony, who was currently living in New York but was originally from St. Maarten, struck up a conversation with another passenger as she stood in line. The passenger was Walter Hodge. Walter was a bus driver for the New York City transit system and a former resident of the Dutch side of St. Maarten.[4] He was headed home for a long awaited visit. The two compared notes on the island as the boarding proceeded.

Balsey, who could see the boarding process from his seat in the cockpit, made a cursory inspection of the passengers as they made their way to the plane. He spotted two little girls traveling with their parents. He guessed the girls were about four or five.

Balsey enjoyed having children on board. He would always assume that it was their first time on an airplane and would make an extra effort to give them a smooth ride. He especially liked it when the kids would come up to the cockpit for a visit. They would usually stand just outside the cockpit door, wide-eyed and mouths agape. Balsey would invite them in for a closer look. Once they realized that Balsey wasn't going to bite their heads off, they would start firing off the questions. *What's that switch for? How fast does this thing go? How do you make the plane go up in the air?* Balsey would patiently answer each question regardless of how late he might be running. If the first officer wasn't in the cockpit, he'd pick them up and plop them down in the co-pilot's seat. He would tell them that if they studied hard and listened to their parents, they could be airline pilots too. That always brought smiles to their faces.

This day, however, there would be no visits to the cockpit. The three flight attendants were doing all they could to keep the flight on schedule. The two little girls and their parents moved quickly past the partially opened cockpit door.

Even with the flight attendants trying to hurry things along, a few passengers hesitated as they approached the stairs leading up to the main cabin door. The plane, not much bigger than a school bus, looked too small for such a long flight. And the markings on the plane said Overseas National.[5] Most were expecting to see a KLM aircraft, the Royal Dutch Airline, the airline from which they had purchased their tickets. They didn't know that the flight they were about to take was the result of an agreement between two airlines, neither of which was KLM.[6] Most would not discover this fact until months later. "Welcome aboard," came the greeting from purser Wilfred Spencer. One by one they climbed the stairs and took their seats.

A few minutes before the flight was scheduled to depart, a final passenger strode briskly across the ramp and up the stairs. He took the first seat he came to as he entered the cabin. The passenger was Emerson Ussery, a general contractor and developer of commercial and residential properties in the Caribbean. He had flown to New York three days earlier from San Juan to meet with a group of investors involved in the construction of a resort on Antigua. He was originally scheduled to return to St. Croix on a Pan Am flight. Earlier in the day, however, Emerson had received a call from one of the investors asking him if he would instead fly to St. Maarten to close a deal on some property for a future hotel and casino. When Emerson arrived at the airport, he was told that he could exchange his Pan Am ticket at the KLM ticket counter. But when Emerson tried to exchange the ticket, the KLM ticket agent refused to accept it. An argument ensued. The argument continued as the boarding began. Emerson was determined to get on the flight; he threw his Pan Am ticket on the counter and proceeded to board the aircraft over the objections of the KLM ticket agent.[*]

The KLM ticket agent immediately called her supervisor. A few minutes later, the supervisor boarded the plane along with a uniformed security officer. Emerson pleaded his case with the supervisor, who finally agreed to accept the Pan Am ticket after talking over the situation with stewardess Margareth Abraham, who happened to be in the forward galley at the time.[7]

Emerson's insistence on getting on the flight had a lot to do with the phone call he had received earlier that morning. Prior to arriving at the airport, he had stopped to pick up two cashier's checks that were to be used for closing the property deal in St. Maarten. In addition to two $150,000 cashier's checks, Emerson also received $350,000 in cash. The deal he was being asked to close was to be

---

[*] Airport security was considerably lax during this time period, even on international flights.

an "under the table" deal, one intended to usurp taxes and other restrictions. The money was in a briefcase that he quietly stuffed under his seat.[8]

With everyone boarded and accounted for, the stairs were raised and the cabin door was closed. If there were any concerns about the flight, chances are they had more to do with the possibility of being hijacked than of being involved in an aircraft ditching. In 1970, a hijacking took place somewhere in the world on average of once every eight days.[9] The day before, a British West Indies Airways Boeing 727 had been hijacked on a flight from Kingston, Jamaica to Grand Cayman Island. The plane was diverted to Havana, Cuba, where the two hijackers were taken into custody.[10]

At 11:02 A.M. Eastern Daylight Time, ALM 980 taxied from the international ramp. It was a perfect spring day with partly cloudy skies, a light southeast wind, and a temperature of 64 degrees. Purser Wilfred Spencer gave the first passenger briefing from the front of the plane while reading from a briefing card. Stewardess Margareth Abraham stood in the aisle near the front, and steward Tobias Cordeiro was positioned toward the rear of the plane. Wilfred began with a welcome aboard announcement that included information about the estimated flight time and the planned cruising altitude. He then gave the standard emergency briefing covering the seatbelts and emergency exits. This was done in both English and Dutch. He also instructed the passengers to review the emergency briefing cards in the seat pockets in front of them. There was no demonstration of the oxygen masks or the life vests, despite the fact that the flight would be flown over water almost from the moment of liftoff until touchdown. It was common practice at that time to wait until after takeoff to brief the passengers on those items so as not to delay the departure. Not that it mattered; the majority of the passengers paid little attention to what was being said or demonstrated.[11]

Traffic was light at JFK as ALM 980 taxied to runway 13R. The flight was cleared for takeoff at 11:14 A.M. Both the captain and the first officer noted that the fuel totalizer indicated 28,450 pounds of fuel as the power was brought up for takeoff.[12] It was a number that both would later be asked to recall.

Shortly after takeoff, Wilfred gave the oxygen mask and life vest briefing. Once again he read from a briefing card while Margareth and Tobias demonstrated the procedures. There was no mention of life rafts.[13]

Chapter 2

CLIMBING OUT FROM JFK, ALM 980 BANKED TO the right and took up a southerly course. The plane was over water and would remain so for the duration of the flight, except for a minute or two when it would pass over Bermuda. Passengers on the right side of the aircraft could still see the coast and the hundreds of small boats that dotted the waters close to shore. Those on the left side of the aircraft might have caught a glimpse of a large tanker or a lone sailboat in search of less-crowded seas. From this altitude the water looked peaceful, almost inviting.

As ALM 980 thundered into an azure sky, the president and CEO of Overseas National Airways, thirty-eight-year-old Steedman Hinckley, was at a family gathering in Virginia.[1] It was a much needed break for Steedman. He had been working non-stop for months and had been looking forward to getting away from New York for a few days. He spent the afternoon relaxing with his family and enjoying the warm spring weather while his parents doted on

15

his one-and-a-half-year-old daughter Annalisa. It would turn out to be a short reprieve. Before the day was through, Steedman would be consumed with concerns over the fate of the passengers and crew aboard ALM 980, the future of his airline, and the role a business decision he had made weeks earlier might have played in the tragedy that was to take place that afternoon.

In aviation circles, Steedman Hinckley was considered to be something of a phenom, an airline whiz-kid who was just thirty-three when he started ONA, or more accurately, resurrected it, like a phoenix rising from the ashes. Steedman was an innovator along the lines of Herb Kelleher of Southwest Airlines and Richard Branson of Virgin Atlantic Airways. And while he wasn't as flamboyant as those two better known airline CEOs, he shared their sense of adventure and ability to see opportunities long before the competition.

Steedman's interest in aviation can be traced back to his father, who had served in the Army Air Corps and later as a colonel in the Air Force.[2] His father was also a successful stockbroker who had done well enough in that pursuit that he was able to purchase a single engine Cessna. The small plane was housed in a hangar built right on the family farm. Steedman learned to fly in his dad's plane.

At fourteen, Steedman attended the renowned Phillips Exeter Academy, a private New England boarding school. Steedman flourished in the college like atmosphere at Exeter. He busied himself with his class work and played intramural sports during his free time. If there was one drawback at Exeter, it was the fact that there were no female students, which may have been the reason his parents had sent him there in the first place.[3] Absent the normal distractions facing most teenagers, Steedman excelled academically. By the time he moved on to Princeton, he was light-years ahead of his classmates.

The normal course for someone with Steedman's background would have been to go directly into the corporate world, where promotions and pay increases would have come quickly and easily. Steedman, however, had fallen in love with flying. He flew every chance he got, usually during the holidays or during his summer breaks from Exeter and Princeton. When he graduated from Princeton in 1953 with a degree in English, Steedman put his corporate prospects on hold and enlisted in the Air Force. He had hoped to contribute to the Korean War effort, but the war ended before he completed his flight training. Instead of flying fighter jets over North Korea as he had hoped, he was put to work flying long supply flights between military bases in the U.S. and abroad. He saw most of the U.S. and much of Europe from the cockpit of a DC-6.

Upon the completion of his military commitment, Steedman took a job with the Aerospace Division of Chrysler. His work involved the Red Stone Missile Arsenal in Huntsville, Alabama. It was just the type of job that his father had hoped Steedman would seek. But Steedman disliked the job. Sitting behind a desk to him was akin to a sailor being adrift in a calm sea. He was still flying part time in the Air Force Reserve, but that only made his job at Chrysler even more unbearable. When he learned of an opening with a New York-based charter airline called Overseas National Airways, he jumped at the chance to get back into the air on a full time basis.

The flying at ONA was not that far removed from the flying that he had done in the Air Force. ONA was primarily a Military Air Transport Service (MATS) carrier. Not only was he flying the same type of aircraft, but he was flying into and out of the same military bases. His familiarity with the aircraft and routes allowed him to move up the ladder quickly at ONA. He went from line pilot to the training department to assistant chief pilot. He worked in sales and promotions. He so impressed the management of ONA that it paid the cost of sending him to the middle management program at Harvard Business School.

At its peak in 1960, ONA was one of the largest MATS carriers in the country, with a fleet of DC-4s, DC-6s, and DC-7s and operations on both coasts. ONA's dominance in the military market, however, came at the expense of its competitors, which it consistently underbid, sometimes at a loss. When a new bidding process was implemented in 1961, the airline saw its contracts drop drastically. Adding to its difficulties was increased competition from the major airlines, which had begun bidding on MATS contracts using more efficient jet aircraft. Unable to purchase its own jet aircraft, financially strapped ONA was forced to cease operations in the fall of 1963.

By this time, Steedman had taken an interest in the business side of running an airline. He had some savings and some money in a trust fund that had been set up by his grandparents. He used those funds to purchase twenty percent of the stock of Saturn Airways, a competing supplemental carrier.[4] He also went to work for Saturn as an executive vice president.

While there was plenty of opportunity at Saturn, Steedman was often at odds with upper management, which he saw as resistant to change and profligate in its spending. When Saturn began talks for a possible merger with a smaller rival, Steedman decided that the time was right to set out on his own.

Rather than undertake the time and expense of starting an airline from scratch, Steedman approached the former owners of ONA with a proposal to purchase the airline's operating certificate. ONA existed only on paper at the time; there were no aircraft or employees. But the airline still had authority to fly. Steedman was confident that the ONA name still had clout in the military market. The Vietnam War was just starting to heat up. The promise of one or two military contracts was all he would need to lure financial backers. In return for a seat on the board of the new airline, George Tompkins, the former president and founder of ONA, agreed to sell the operating certificate to Steedman for just one dollar.

Unlike the previous owners, who had focused primarily on military charters, Steedman planned to expand into the commercial charter market. He had seen firsthand how the former owners' total dependence on military contracts had led to the airline's demise. But there were several other factors driving his decision. First, there was the introduction of the jet aircraft, which was revolutionizing air travel. Jet aircraft were faster, quieter, and more comfortable than the piston aircraft that made up the majority of the airline fleets in 1965. Their size and efficiency also helped to make air travel more affordable.

Another important development in 1965 was the first widespread use of credit cards, which for the first time major banks began issuing to hundreds of thousands of customers. The combination of easy credit and the novelty of the jet aircraft jumpstarted an ailing airline industry. A whole new market segment was created — the leisure traveler. Major airlines scrambled to replace their older piston aircraft with new Boeing 707s and Douglas Aircraft DC-8s and DC-9s.

The rush to convert to jet aircraft created a glut of piston aircraft. Steedman picked up two bargain-priced DC-7s and put them to work flying MATS flights. He also secured the help of several financial backers who provided the funding needed to place orders for two new DC-8s.[5]

With two jets on the way and plans for purchasing additional aircraft, Steedman set out for Sweden to hire stewardesses. He was planning on doing a lot of international flying and wanted stewardesses who could speak several languages. It was during this visit that Steedman met a young Swedish girl named Ingrid.

Ingrid was among a large group of attractive women waiting anxiously in a hotel conference room. The women were there in response to an ad for stewardesses for a New York-based airline.

Ingrid made a favorable impression on Steedman. She was bright, articulate, and spoke several languages, including German, Swedish, English, and a little French. Steedman's only concern was her age. Ingrid was just eighteen at the time. To make sure he didn't forget the striking young woman, he wrote a note to himself on Ingrid's application. The note, written along the margins, simply read: "exceptional Swedish beauty."[6]

Ingrid accepted a job offer at ONA and moved to New York to begin work as a stewardess. She hadn't been working very long before she was asked if she would be interested in doing some public relations work. Ingrid agreed and was subsequently featured in an ONA print advertisement. The advertisement had Ingrid posing in a bikini. The public relations work put Ingrid in direct contact with Steedman. She accompanied him on a return trip to Sweden to interview additional stewardesses. Steedman met Ingrid's mother on the visit and promised her that he would personally look after Ingrid.

A few months after their return to New York, Steedman learned that Ingrid was involved in a serious relationship with an older man. Steedman, remembering his promise to Ingrid's mother, invited Ingrid to dinner. He admonished Ingrid on the perils of marrying too young and suggested that she not rush into anything. Ingrid took his advice and broke off the relationship. Steedman and Ingrid began seeing each other shortly thereafter.

Steedman soon found himself in the awkward position of having to defend his relationship with Ingrid. More than a few people felt that it was inappropriate for the president of the airline to be involved with a stewardess, especially one who was still two years shy of the legal drinking age. The hushed comments didn't sway Steedman, who was single only because his first marriage had ended in divorce.[7] He was, however, concerned for Ingrid, who was still flying and having to deal with gossipy co-workers. His solution to the growing controversy was to have Ingrid quit her job and move in with him. They were married in Sweden in August 1967. He was sixteen years her senior.

Despite their age difference, Ingrid and Steedman seemed to be the perfect couple. She was an alluring young woman with poise and grace beyond her years. He was a clean-cut executive, trim and fit, and considered good looking by anyone's standards. Yet, no matter how many accolades he might receive from former employees and associates, no matter his accomplishments, Steedman would always be remembered for having married a stewardess.

The same year that Steedman and Ingrid married, ONA went public. The money raised by the stock offering was used to fuel an expansion that included new aircraft and upgraded facilities. Construction was begun on 36,000 square feet of additional office space. To accommodate the airline's training needs, an adjacent building was leased and converted into a training center that rivaled the major airlines. Steedman also invested in new technology, leasing an IBM 360-20 mainframe computer. The bulky computer had a whopping 32kb of memory.

While he spared no expense in his quest to turn ONA into a leader in the industry, Steedman himself had a reputation for frugality. His tiny office, for example, was so spartanly furnished that the only indications one had that it was Steedman's office and not the office of some newly hired vice president were the models of company aircraft that he proudly displayed. If he had to fly on another airline, he flew coach. Steedman's parsimony, however, did not extend to his vacations. In the summers, he and Ingrid sailed on their forty-three-foot Erwin sailboat. In the winter months, they took ski vacations, tackling the slopes of top-rated ski resorts in both Europe and the United States.[8]

Ingrid would often accompany Steedman on his frequent business trips. When Steedman persuaded the board to consider ownership in a cruise ship, he and Ingrid spent several weeks abroad checking out cruise ship manufacturers and operators. Steedman eventually convinced the board to invest in the construction of a seven-hundred-passenger cruise ship, with options for two more identical ships. ONA became the first airline to have ownership in a cruise ship.

One weekend while at home reading the *New York Times*, Steedman saw a story about an old river boat, the *Delta Queen*, which was about to shut down due to a lack of financing. Steedman convinced the board members of ONA to buy the company that owned and managed the boat. The river boat company became a subsidiary of ONA. It was a profitable business that ONA justified by marketing charter flights that included tours on the river boat. A second boat, the *Mississippi Queen*, was added a short time later; Steedman's brother Albert designed the boat.

In addition to the cruise ships and river boats, Steedman partnered with another company to build a four-hundred-room luxury hotel in the Bahamas. Steedman wanted to receive revenue from every aspect of a charter package — the airfare, the hotel, and the cruise. It was a bold plan but ultimately flawed, as other airlines that followed suit would eventually learn. While Steedman sold the plan to the board and to shareholders as diversification within the pleasure travel industry, the businesses were too closely related and vulnerable to a downturn in the economy.

By the end of 1967, ONA employed just over three hundred people.[9] The airline continued to expand in 1968, tripling the number of aircraft and doubling the number of employees. In October, a long-range 250-passenger Super DC-8 was added to the fleet. The plans for 1969 included even more ambitious growth. Steedman wrote the following summary in the 1968 annual report:

> The outlook for 1969 appears to be very promising. We feel that, with the equipment now in service and the six new jets being delivered, we are in an excellent position to expand our commercial business and to maintain and enlarge our position in the military market in areas that we expect will be affected least by the hoped-for cessation of hostilities in Southeast Asia.
>
> Having embarked on two significant diversification programs in the hotel and marine resort areas, we will be actively seeking other opportunities for growth in the pleasure travel field.[10]

While the future looked promising for ONA heading into 1969, the company ultimately lost money. ONA reported a loss of $677,353, despite a 93% increase in gross revenues. The primary reason stated for the poor financial performance was over-capacity in the airline industry combined with declining revenue rates due to competition. Competition from United Airlines on flights to Hawaii forced ONA to completely withdraw from the market. Operating expenses for the airline increased 130% over the prior year. The number of employees swelled to 1,286. In his letter to shareholders, Steedman wrote the following:

Faced with a difficult airline industry overcapacity situation, compounded by destructive attacks on our industry by many of our scheduled carrier competitors, I believe we face at least two more years of rough weather.[11]

Unaffected by the turmoil in the U.S. airline industry was a small Caribbean airline looking to expand its route structure. The airline was Antilliaanse Luchtvaart Maatschappij, better known as ALM. ALM was based in Curaçao, an island located thirty-five miles north of South America and some two thousand miles distant from New York.

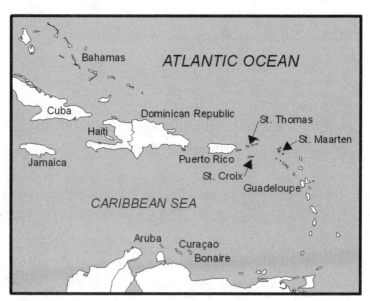

Figure 3. Caribbean.

ALM had its beginnings in August of 1964 as a wholly owned subsidiary of KLM Airlines. KLM had been providing island service in the region since 1935, transporting employees of the Royal Dutch Shell Oil Company. ALM began operations with three Convair 340s and three wet-leased Convair 880s, flying to destinations in the Caribbean, South America, and the east coast of the United States.[12] The airline expanded as more emphasis was placed on tourist traffic. In early 1969, the Dutch Antillean government purchased 96% of the stock of ALM, making it an independent airline.

The president of ALM was Ciro Octavio Irausquin, a soft-spoken man who preferred to be addressed by his nickname, Tawa. Before taking on the role of President of ALM, Octavio had been the Director of Civil Aviation for the Netherlands Antilles.[13] He was the impetus behind the formation of the new airline and led the push for independence from KLM.

On the surface, Octavio looked like someone you wouldn't want to cross. He had thinning hair and a stern glint in his eyes like that of a drill sergeant. Those features, however, belied an amiable man who was held in high regard by his employees and customers alike.

Far from being just a figurehead of a government-owned–and-operated airline, Octavio was a shrewd businessman who knew the Caribbean market better than anyone. He wasted little time moving forward with expansion plans once ALM gained its independence from KLM. One route high on his list was a direct route from St. Maarten to New York.[14]

ALM's fleet in 1969 consisted of two Fokker F-27 turboprops dubbed the Friendship aircraft and three Douglas Aircraft DC-9-15s. Neither aircraft had the range to fly the route Octavio was contemplating. It was not uncommon in those days for one airline to contract with another airline to supply aircraft and crew on routes for which it had authority to fly, but had insufficient aircraft and or crew. ALM already had such an arrangement with KLM. ALM operated a Curaçao–New York route using a KLM DC-8. It was a wet-lease agreement in which KLM provided the aircraft and flight crew while ALM provided the flight attendants. The flight was sold and operated as an ALM flight.

Octavio had first learned of ONA from several letters sent to him by Steedman Hinckley. Steedman had read in a trade publication that ALM had placed orders for several DC-9s. He had written Octavio to inform him of the availability of ONA's new training facilities in New York.[15] Octavio wasn't interested in sending his pilots to New York for training, but from Steedman's letters he knew of ONA's interest in the Caribbean. He decided to draft a letter to Steedman to determine his interest in a wet-lease agreement between the two airlines for a St. Maarten–New York route.

For Steedman, the request could not have come at a better time. Not only would the flights provide some much needed capital, they would also give ONA a presence in the Caribbean. It fit perfectly with his plans. He phoned Octavio and began negotiations for a mid-January startup.

Chapter 3

A S *ALM 980* CONTINUED ITS CLIMB HIGH ABOVE *the Atlantic, the three flight crewmembers unbuck-led their shoulder harnesses and sat back in their seats. It was the autopilot's turn to fly. While not as sophisticated as today's flight management system (FMS) equipped aircraft, the autopilot on the DC-9 could maintain altitude and track to and from a VOR station.* There was little for the crew to do but set the inbound and outbound course and monitor the instruments. Since they were out of radar contact for a good portion of the flight, they were also required to make position reports. These were made through a ground relay station utilizing a high frequency radio. Balsey took the opportunity to show Harry how to tune in the seldom used radio.

In the back of the plane, the three flight attendants met in the forward galley to prepare the lunch service. Lunch included a choice of two hot meals – chicken or beef, or a cold sandwich.

The passengers meanwhile settled in for the long three-and-a-half-hour flight. Some moved to take advantage of the half-empty plane. Out of a total

---

* A VOR is a ground-based navigation aid.

of 105 available seats, only fifty-seven were occupied. The seating config-
uration consisted of twenty-one rows of seats with two seats on the left side
of the aisle and three seats on the right. There was no first class section.

Planning for the New York–St. Maarten flights began in early
October 1969. Problems on the proposed route surfaced almost
immediately. A preliminary review of performance data revealed that
the flight was at the extreme range of the DC-9. Another problem was
the short 5,200-foot runway at St. Maarten. Not only was the runway
short for operating a jet aircraft, but there was a mountain off the east
end of the airport. After poring over the performance charts, it was
determined that the DC-9 could make the trip but with a few restrictions. First, if there were headwinds in either direction the plane
could not make the flight nonstop. Second, there would be takeoff
restrictions when taking off toward the east because of the mountains on that side of the airport. Lastly, the short runway at St.
Maarten was weight restricted. The plane couldn't take off with a full
load of passengers and full fuel. The only way to make the numbers
work was to lower the takeoff weight. A lower takeoff weight meant
faster acceleration and less energy to bring the aircraft to a stop in
an aborted takeoff. The suggested solution was to take on only
enough fuel in St. Maarten to fly to San Juan, where the runways
were longer and the plane could takeoff fully loaded.

Steedman wasn't overly concerned with the findings. He had
already come up with a solution to the fuel problem: Bermuda.
The island of Bermuda lies near the halfway point along the route.
If fuel became an issue, the plane could land in Bermuda. The
only thing wrong with his plan was that he was figuring the lease
based on a nonstop flight. The extra costs associated with landing
and taking off from Bermuda were enough to make the flight lose
money.

There was another solution that everyone agreed on and that was to add an extra fuel tank. The extra fuel tank was an auxiliary tank capable of carrying an extra 780 gallons of fuel or approximately 5200 pounds, allowing nearly an extra hour of flying time. Steedman had already placed orders for two of the tanks. He had made the orders long before the negotiations with ALM had begun. He was certain that they could have the tank installed before the flights were scheduled to begin in mid-January 1970.

With the performance information in hand and two solutions to any possible fuel concerns, Steedman left for Curaçao to discuss the wet-lease agreement face to face with Octavio.

Octavio Irausquin didn't know much about Steedman or ONA prior to their meeting, but he soon learned that the two men and the airlines they operated had much in common. Like Steedman, Octavio was a former pilot, having worked as a first officer for KLM. Both men were indefatigable promoters of their respective airlines. ONA was the larger of the two in terms of aircraft and employees, but most of ONA's size difference had occurred within the past year.

Following a brief tour of ALM's facilities, Steedman and Octavio sat down to work out the details of the agreement. From the start, Octavio expressed concern over whether the DC-9 was the right aircraft for the route. He was concerned about flying the route with a two-engine aircraft. In 1970, a two-engine aircraft was not permitted to make an extended overwater flight unless the aircraft was within one hour of a suitable landing field, on one engine. Octavio preferred the Boeing 727, a three-engine jet. He also expressed concern about the range of the DC-9. Steedman assured Octavio that the flight was within the range of the DC-9, assuming normal winds and weather. The only other aircraft ONA operated that had the range for the route was the DC-8, but the short runway in St.

Maarten precluded the use of that aircraft. Steedman told Octavio about the planned installation of the extra fuel tank. He also told him of his intention to use Bermuda as a backup fuel stop. Octavio seemed satisfied with the answers. He told Steedman that he was confident they could work something out but that he needed more time to look things over.[1]

The next day, after having dinner with Octavio and his wife the previous night, Steedman left Curaçao. Instead of returning directly to New York, he took a DC-9 flight to St. Maarten to get a firsthand look at the airport and surrounding terrain. He rode in the cockpit so he could question the flight crew, who flew in and out of the airport on a regular basis.[2]

What Steedman saw was a short east-west runway on a narrow strip of land with the Caribbean Sea at one end of the runway and a large bay at the other. Off to the east was a modest-sized mountain range that rose to twelve hundred feet above sea level to the south and fourteen hundred feet above sea level to the north. The only instrument approach to the airport was a Non Directional Beacon (NDB) approach to runway nine.[3] While the airport wasn't ideal, the pilots assured him that the DC-9 could handle the short runway, pointing out that there were a number of suitable alternates to choose from should the weather turn sour. Steedman left St. Maarten with renewed confidence that the flights could be operated safely.

A few weeks after returning to New York, Steedman received word that Octavio was willing to proceed with an agreement under the condition that the extra fuel tank be installed. Steedman set to work drafting the agreement. His next two hurdles were with the Federal Aviation Administration (FAA) and the Civil Aeronautics Board (CAB). Both agencies needed to be notified of ONA's plans for the intended route. Steedman also put in a request for a special waiver. Upon closer inspection of the route, it was determined that the flight could not meet the single-engine drift-down requirement. This was the FAA requirement for a two-engine aircraft to be within one hour of a suitable landing field in the event of the loss of one engine. There was a small segment of the flight where the closest suitable landing field was more than one hour away.

As fall passed into winter and the January start date inched closer, additional problems surrounding the flight surfaced. Adam Paul Salkind, the head of the navigators union, had learned of the plans for the St. Maarten route and pointed out to Steedman that according to their contract a navigator was required to be on board. Steedman took the contract to Bob Wagenfeld, ONA's corporate attorney and a former ONA navigator himself, and asked him to take a look. Wagenfeld told Steedman that Salkind was correct. The contract specifically stated that a navigator was required on any flight that was flown over water for more than two hours. Steedman asked Wagenfeld if he thought there was any chance the union would be willing to amend the contract. Wagenfeld told him he didn't think so. There were only twenty-eight navigators employed by ONA, and these twenty-eight had already been notified that their jobs were going to be phased out starting May 1, 1971 due to automation.[4]

Despite Wagenfeld's comments, Steedman asked Salkind if he would consider amending the contract. He began by reminding Salkind that the DC-9 was a two-man cockpit. The only seat available for a navigator was an uncomfortable observer's seat intended for only short-duration flights. He pointed out that there was only a small segment of the route where normal navigation would be unavailable and that he intended to install a Long Range Navigation (LORAN) system in the DC-9 for that portion of the flight. The pilots could be trained to use the LORAN in two or three days. He also mentioned that several airlines were operating a similar route from New York to San Juan and that they were flying the route without navigators. Salkind refused to budge on the contract, stating that he had an obligation to the remaining navigators to keep them flying for as long as possible.

Steedman wasn't one to wage war with the unions. He had maintained a good working relationship with the company's employee groups and wanted to keep it that way. He put the issue aside and shifted his attention to a new problem that developed in early December. Steedman learned that the FAA had turned down ONA's request for a special waiver for the single-engine drift-down procedure, stating that an alternate route was available. The FAA claimed that the route could be flown legally via the Bahamas. But flying over the Bahamas required a large deviation, necessitating a fuel stop or an extra fuel tank. The distance from New York to St. Maarten via Nassau was nineteen hundred nautical miles; the direct distance was fourteen hundred nautical miles. Without a more direct route the flight was economically unfeasible.

A few weeks before the flights were scheduled to begin, Steedman was faced with yet another problem. He was informed by Douglas Aircraft that the earliest date that it could schedule the DC-9 for the installation of the auxiliary fuel tank was March 1970 — two months after the planned start date. Steedman phoned Octavio to discuss the latest setback. He told Octavio that despite the problems he would agree to fly the route even if it meant flying via the Bahamas and making a fuel stop. But there was nothing he could do to get the extra fuel tank installed earlier than March. The two men discussed the pros and cons of delaying the start date. Both agreed that waiting until March or April to begin the flights didn't make good business sense. They would miss the peak travel season. Octavio agreed to amend the wording of the contract, pushing back the requirement for the auxiliary fuel tank. The final lease agreement was signed with the following statement: "Overseas shall arrange and install a center tank to increase the fuel capacity of this aircraft by 780 gallons on or before April 1, 1970."[5]

For reasons that will be explained shortly, as ALM 980 made its way to St. Maarten on May 2, 1970, the auxiliary fuel tank had yet to be installed.

Chapter 4

THE DECISION ON WHETHER IT WOULD BE NECESSARY to stop for fuel was usually made well in advance of Bermuda. The crew needed time to plan their descent and to call ahead for fuel and to make other arrangements. The early indications on this flight were that a fuel stop was not going to be needed. The winds were favorable, the load was light, and the flight was on schedule. This was good news for the flight crew. Landing at Bermuda increased the workload considerably. It also tacked on an additional thirty minutes of flying time.

The passengers, of course, knew nothing of the possibility of having to stop for fuel. They had purchased tickets for a non-stop flight. A landing anywhere other than St. Maarten would have been cause for concern. On those occasions when the plane did have to stop for fuel, the job of placating the passengers was usually left to the flight attendants. Few people argued with the decision, though. One look at the vast expanse of open water beneath them was enough to convince even the most irascible of passengers of the merits of having adequate fuel.

With lunch having been served, the three flight attendants made a pass through the cabin to collect the trash. Once that task was completed,

they had some free time to themselves. They usually found an empty pas-
senger seat to sit in and spent time reading or working on company-
related paperwork.

The passengers took the opportunity to stretch. A few walked to the rear
of the cabin to visit one of the two lavatories on board. Others slept, lulled
to sleep by the quiet hum of the slipstream.

Entertainment choices on the flight were limited. There was no in-flight
movie. While that amenity was available on some of the larger commercial
jets, such as the Boeing 747 first introduced a few months earlier, the DC-9
was not so equipped. There were also none of the electronic accoutrements
that today's airline passengers enjoy. There were no laptop computers,
PDAs, CD players, MP3 players, personal DVD players, in-seat video dis-
plays, etc. The walkman would not be introduced for another nine years.

A few passengers lit up cigarettes to help pass the time. Not only was
smoking permitted, there wasn't even a separated smoking section. Smoking
sections would not appear on commercial airline flights until 1973. The
total banning of smoking on domestic flights and most international
flights would not occur until 1991.

The primary source of entertainment on board was reading. Some of
the bestselling titles out during this time period include *I Know Why
the Caged Bird Sings* by Maya Angelou, *Love Story* by Erich Segal, and
The French Lieutenant's Woman by John Fowles. Other notable titles
that might have been in the hands of passengers include three 1969 best
sellers: *The Godfather* by Mario Puzo, *Deliverance* by James Dickey, and
The Andromeda Strain by first time novelist Michael Crichton.[1]

A few passengers no doubt would have been reading the newspaper.
The *New York Times* for May 2, 1970 offered a perfect snapshot of what
was going on in the world at the beginning of the new decade. The lead
story concerned troops arriving in Cambodia. The story was accompanied by a photograph showing troops jumping out of a helicopter

that had just touched down on Cambodian soil. Two weeks earlier, President Nixon had addressed the nation with news of a planned withdrawal of over 150,000 troops from Vietnam. The Cambodian involvement, which Nixon claimed was necessary to eliminate a major Communist staging and communications area, fueled the fires of war protesters and demonstrators who felt that Nixon had gone back on his word. A few states were forced to call out the National Guard to help control disorderly protestors. A day earlier, the *New York Times* had run a story on the front page concerning students protesting on the campus of Kent State University in Ohio. A photograph showing student demonstrators going head to bayonet with National Guardsmen dressed in full battle gear and wearing gas masks took up most of the front page.

Inside the paper there was a story concerning two of the three Apollo 13 astronauts. Jim Lovell and Jack Swigert, along with several of the Apollo 13 flight controllers, were honored with a parade in downtown Chicago. Fred Haise, the lunar module pilot on Apollo 13, was still recovering from the urinary tract infection he developed on the historic flight the month before.

In the sports section, the big story was the ninety-sixth running of the Kentucky Derby, scheduled for later that afternoon. The favorite to win the race was the horse Terlago. In golf, Arnold Palmer and Jack Nicklaus battled for the top spot at the Byron Nelson Golf Classic in Dallas, Texas. Arnold Palmer had the lead going into Saturday's third round.[*]

Lastly, in the business section there were several stories related to the struggling economy. The country was at the halfway point of a recession that had begun in the third quarter of 1969. The DOW closed at 733.63.[2]

---

[*] The winner of the Kentucky Derby on May 2 was the horse Dust Commander, a 15–1 long shot. Jack Nicklaus edged out Arnold Palmer to win the Byron Nelson Golf Classic.

In early January, a few days before the New York–St. Maarten flights were scheduled to begin, Steedman received word that Douglas Aircraft had come up with a new drift-down procedure for the DC-9. This was the requirement for a two-engine aircraft to be within one hour of a suitable landing field in the case of the loss of one engine. Douglas Aircraft engineers had come up with a procedure that met the FAA requirement. It meant that ONA would not have to fly the longer route via the Bahamas. That same day, Steedman learned that the FAA and the CAB had granted approval for the flights. Steedman, who had given ALM the go ahead to market the flights even though the route had yet to be approved, breathed a sigh of relief.

The New York–St. Maarten flights finally began on January 14, 1970. The plane was N935F, nicknamed the *Carib Queen*. All of ONA's aircraft were given nicknames. The nicknames were painted on the aircraft below the Captain's window. Steedman most likely came up with the name while dabbling with the riverboats the *Delta Queen* and the *Mississippi Queen*. The sleek jet was less than a year old.

Several weeks after the twice-weekly flights to St. Marten began, an FAA examiner threatened to suspend the flights indefinitely. The reason: the FAA examiner wanted to do a line check on one of the flights and was told that he couldn't because the jump seat was occupied. An agreement was worked out very quickly, in writing, that stated the navigator was to occupy the jump seat unless an FAA examiner requested the seat. In this case, the co-pilot was to perform the navigator's duties. The agreement satisfied the FAA examiner, and the flight resumed after a lengthy delay. The examiner occupied the jump seat, and the navigator sat in the cabin.

Another problem that surfaced early on with the first dozen or so flights to St. Maarten was a problem with the fuel totalizer. The aircraft had four analog circular-type fuel gauges for the center tank, the forward auxiliary tank, and the two wing tanks, and a digital fuel totalizer that indicated the total fuel remaining for all four tanks. The readout was in pounds of fuel. The amount shown on the fuel totalizer could change based on the density of the fuel. Fuel density was determined both by the type of fuel being used and the temperature of the fuel (colder fuel is denser and thus weighs more). Douglas Aircraft claimed that the fuel density error should be in the plus or minus 800-pound range for a fully loaded plane. ONA's DC-9s were getting errors plus or minus 2,000 pounds.

The problems with the fuel totalizer seemed to be more pronounced with the aircraft involved on the St. Maarten flights. It was determined that the problem was related to condensation forming on the fuel probes, especially the master probe. The aircraft was flying in very cold temperatures for up to three hours and then descending into a very warm and humid climate. The solution was to coat the probes with a plastic like covering in a procedure called plasticizing. The plasticizing didn't completely solve the problem, but it did reduce the occurrence of highly erroneous readings.[3]

In addition to the problems with the fuel totalizer, pilots were reporting discrepancies between the planned fuel burn and the actual fuel burn. All of ONA's DC-9s were burning more fuel than what the fuel planning charts indicated they should burn. Douglas Aircraft engineers were notified of the problem. Their response was to have ONA keep a fuel log for each of its DC-9s to help it more accurately determine the extent of the error.[4]

Steedman was made aware of the fuel problems during his weekly safety meetings. He wasn't too concerned. Minor problems like these could be expected with new aircraft. The erratic fuel totalizer readings and the higher-than-expected fuel burns did not pose a safety hazard as long as the discrepancies were accounted for in the flight planning. Steedman did, however, call the dispatch office to ask for a summary of the St. Maarten flights that had been flown to date. He wanted to know what the average fuel burn was for each leg, and he wanted to know what the average loads had been. The summary he received showed that on average planes were landing with just under 6,700 pounds of fuel. The highest fuel burns, as expected, were on the return flights to New York. About a third of the return flights had to stop in Bermuda for fuel. The summary also indicated that the average load factor was 67%.[5]

The agreement Steedman had signed with ALM required him to have the extra fuel tank installed by April 1, 1970. Steedman wanted the tank installed as badly as anyone. The St. Maarten flight lost money every time the plane had to land in Bermuda for fuel. But Douglas Aircraft had informed him that it was going to take three to four weeks to install the tank. The same plane flew all of the St. Maarten flights. The only plane Steedman had to replace it with was an older model DC-9 with slightly less range.

Steedman phoned Octavio Irausquin to discuss the situation. He told Octavio that if they pulled N935F off the route to get the tank installed, the replacement aircraft would probably not be able to make the flight non-stop. If, on the other hand, they were to wait until spring or early summer when the loads dropped off, the replacement DC-9 could probably make the flight without having to stop for fuel. Octavio agreed. There were still several weeks left of the peak travel season. He didn't want to inconvenience passengers unnecessarily by adding an extra stop. He told Steedman to disregard the April 1 deadline. It was an oral agreement between the two men. No specific deadline for having the extra fuel tank installed was discussed.*[6]

---

* While having the extra fuel tank more than likely would have prevented the accident, it was not a direct contributing factor. The flight departed with legal fuel reserves. It could be argued that there would have been no legal requirement to add additional fuel even if the tank had been installed. However, Captain DeWitt has stated that had the tank been installed, he would have filled it to its capacity.

As the flights to St. Maarten continued into April, everyone was keeping a close eye on the fuel burns. Fuel logs for three aircraft were sent to Douglas Aircraft for evaluation. The results of the evaluation showed that all three aircraft were burning a few percent more than what the fuel planning charts indicated they should burn, with one of the three burning as much as 10.6% more. N935F, the plane used on the St. Maarten route, burned approximately 4.6% more fuel than charted.[7]

Another alarming trend that caught the attention of management was several St. Maarten flights that had landed with minimum fuel. One flight in particular, on April 15, 1970, landed with just 3,400 pounds of fuel.[8] The captain on the flight was Balsey DeWitt. Also on the flight was Carl Morgan, an FAA examiner. Carl was giving the first officer a line check on the LORAN. The indicator for the LORAN was located on the co-pilot's center instrument panel. This particular flight occurred on the same day that air traffic controllers were on strike. Traffic delays caused by reduced controller staffing resulted in a much higher fuel burn than planned. A favorable weather report in St. Maarten convinced them to continue rather than stop for fuel in Bermuda.

The low fuel landing in St. Maarten alarmed Carl Morgan enough that he felt that ONA needed to set minimum fuel guidelines for the route over and above the FAA minimums. ONA agreed and subsequently issued the following pilot bulletin two weeks later:

> The following minimum fuel requirements will be strictly adhered to:[9]
>
> A. New York — St. Marten direct requires planned EFA of 7,000 pounds.

B.   St. Marten – San Juan segment requires minimum take-off fuel of 10,000 pounds.

C.   San Juan – New York segment requires
planned EFA of 7,000 pounds.

The memo did not define what EFA meant. The intention was to require pilots to have at least 7,000 pounds of fuel on arrival over the airport, with EFA defined as expected fuel on arrival. To account for the higher-than-charted fuel burn, the memo imposed an additional requirement:

> Until revised fuel consumption charts are delivered
> by Douglas Aircraft Company, ONA is imposing
> an additional 10% added to flight fuel burn off to
> all DC-9-33 aircraft.[10]

When Balsey showed up for work Saturday morning, he found the memo in his mailbox. Balsey read the first line under the heading Minimum Fuel Requirements. "The following minimum fuel require-ments will be strictly adhered to: New York – St. Marten direct requires planned EFA of 7,000 pounds." Balsey had no idea what "planned EFA" meant. He assumed it meant expected fuel on arrival. But arrival where? At the airport? Over the airport? Over the beacon? When Balsey read further and noted that an additional 10% fuel burn was being imposed over and above the minimum FAA fuel requirements, he concluded that it could not have meant on arrival at the airport. None of the flights he had flown had landed with that much fuel. He decided that the 7,000 pound figure was a planning figure to be used in determining whether the flight could be flown non-stop.

The navigator normally computed the fuel burn. Hugh Hart, the navigator on this flight, didn't have any flight planning charts for the DC-9. He lamented that he hadn't been given any documents related to the DC-9, nor had he received any training on the aircraft, which was a good indication of how management perceived the navigator's role on the flights. Balsey gave Hugh the cruise charts from his manual. He told Hugh that the DC-9 burned approximately 100 pounds of fuel per minute. It was a useful number to remember because it allowed for quick fuel burn calculations. If you had 6,000 pounds of fuel on board, you had roughly one hour of flying time remaining. The 100 pounds per minute rule was useful for performing quick mental fuel calculations, but long-range flights required more careful planning. After reviewing the fuel planning charts, Hugh and Balsey computed a fuel burn of 19,100 pounds for the three hour and twenty-six minute flight. Adding the 10% additional burn off imposed in the bulletin they computed a total fuel burn of 21,000 pounds (19,100 + 1,900). The minimum fuel required by the FAA was for an additional 6,400 pounds of fuel reserves over and above the planned fuel burn.[11] Since the 6,400 pound figure was less than the 7,000 pounds required by the memo, Balsey used a final fuel figure of 28,000 pounds (21,000 + 7,000). The plane fully loaded held just over 28,500 pounds of fuel, giving them a safety cushion of 500 pounds.[*][12]

---

[*] When ALM 980 departed JFK on May 2, it not only met the legal fuel requirement but exceeded it by nearly 3,000 pounds.

The last item to be completed on the flight plan was the time to fuel exhaustion. Hugh spent a few minutes with the charts and came up with a time of four hours and thirty-six minutes. It was a figure that would later prove to be uncannily accurate.

Chapter 5

A TIME CHECK AT LANDRY INTERSECTION, A POINT approximately six hundred miles southeast of New York, indicated that the flight was on schedule. A few minutes later, ALM 980 passed over Bermuda. It's doubtful that the passengers were even aware they had flown over the tiny island.[1]

Having reached the halfway point in the flight, Balsey slowed from .78 mach (78% the speed of sound) to .76 mach. He had decided early on to fly the first half of the flight at a higher cruise speed and then reduce to a slower long-range cruise speed during the second half of the flight, where he was expecting a slight tail wind. He also elected to remain at 29,000 feet rather than climb to a higher, more fuel-efficient altitude. Jet aircraft burn less fuel the higher they fly. There was nothing preventing him from climbing to a higher cruising altitude. Balsey, however, rarely flew at the maximum operating altitude, an aversion he most likely acquired during training in the Air Force, where high-altitude dangers such as rapid decompression and time of useful consciousness are drilled into the minds of new cadets.[2]

Regardless of the reason for his decision to fly at a lower altitude, the end result was a higher fuel burn. His choice of a high initial cruise speed also contributed to a higher fuel burn. While technically correct – the fuel burn entered on the flight plan was calculated using the lower altitude and the higher cruise speed – both decisions would later come under scrutiny, especially when considering that Balsey had made a low fuel landing in St. Maarten only two weeks earlier.

That Balsey's flight planning acumen would be called into question was no surprise to some. He wasn't the type of pilot to go digging through performance charts looking for ways to save a few hundred pounds of fuel. Fellow pilots described him as a good stick and rudder man. He was known to hand-fly an entire flight just to keep his flying skills sharp. Autopilots can make you lazy, he'd say.

Balsey's father was a gas maker for Central Hudson Gas and Electric. It was a blue-collar job that he hung onto for some thirty years. When he retired, his position was retired along with him. His mother was a homemaker who kept busy taking care of Balsey and his five brothers and sisters.

When he was six years old, Balsey lost a younger brother to leukemia. A year later the family was dealt another blow when Balsey's six-month-old sister Joan died from a blood disorder. Such were the realities of life growing up during the Depression years in rural upstate New York. Balsey himself was born in a house located on his grandfather's farm. The small farm, nestled in the foothills of the Catskill Mountains, was an unlikely place for a young boy to grow up with aspirations of becoming a pilot. But two events in Balsey's childhood led him along that path.

The first of these two pivotal events took place at the county fair in Walton, New York in the summer of 1941. Balsey was a few weeks shy of his ninth birthday. A barnstormer had landed in a grass field adjacent to the fairgrounds and was offering rides for five dollars a person. Balsey spent the day going from relative to relative scrounging up the money he needed for the plane ride, saying instead that he wanted it for games and ride tickets. As soon as he had the five dollars, he made his way to the edge of the fairgrounds where an open cockpit Stearman biplane awaited. It was a two-seater with the passenger seat in front and the pilot's seat in back. To make room for more passengers, the pilot had removed the front seat and had replaced it with two wooden planks. Balsey handed the pilot the five dollars and eagerly took his seat. Minutes later, they were flying above the tents and carnival rides and rows of parked cars, dodging puffy cumulus clouds that sprouted up like popcorn. The ride couldn't have lasted for more than fifteen minutes, but by the time the plane touched back down on the bumpy grass field Balsey was hooked.

A few months after Balsey took his first airplane ride, the Japanese bombed Pearl Harbor. Like other kids his age, Balsey read everything he could get his hands on about the attack and the war that followed. He was especially drawn to stories about American fighter pilots. He and his friends built models of military aircraft like the B-17 and the P-51 Mustang. Balsey had no way to pay for flying lessons, so he read books on the subject and set his sights on joining the Air Force.

Balsey enlisted in the Air Force after completing the equivalent of three years of college credit at New York University, where he was working towards a degree in Aeronautical Engineering. His first assignment was with the 44th Air Transport Group at Grenier Air Force Base in Manchester, New Hampshire. Balsey bought his first car at Grenier. He drove the car directly from the dealer's lot to the driver's license testing center. He was licensed to fly, but at twenty-two he still didn't have a driver's license. Balsey was transferred from

Grenier to McGuire Air Force base in New Jersey in November 1955. His primary mission was to fly troops and their families across the Atlantic. He accumulated a lot of flight time very quickly on those long flights across the Atlantic. A typical route would take him from McGuire to Ernest Harmon Air Force base in Newfoundland to Prestwick, Scotland and from there on to Frankfurt or Paris or other European destinations. It was fifteen or more hours of flying with no backup crew.

Balsey met his wife on one such trip across the Atlantic. He and his crew had gone out for dinner and a few drinks on a stopover in Prestwick. They ended up at a dance hall called *Bobby Jones*. Balsey spotted a pretty, petite young girl with blond hair and a green, sequined dress and spent the rest of the evening trying to get the shy girl out on the dance floor. Edith was a nurse who worked at a nearby hospital. It was the beginning of a long-distance romance. They wrote each other while apart and got together whenever Balsey passed through Scotland, which wasn't frequent enough for either of them. They were married on October 20, 1956. Edith hated the name Balsey and preferred calling him by his middle name, Dean. When their first child arrived twelve months later, they named him Dean. Their daughter Denise was born in August 1959.

It was at McGuire where Balsey first met Steedman Hinckley. Balsey was Steedman's co-pilot on the very first flight Steedman flew as an aircraft commander. In a pilot's career, the first flight as captain ranks nearly on par with that of a first solo. In Steedman's case, the flight was made even more memorable because of what happened. Steedman and Balsey were scheduled to take a C-118 (DC-6) from McGuire Air Force Base to Travis Air Force Base in California with several stops in between. On one stop they picked up Steedman's father, who was serving as a full colonel in the reserves. They also picked up the chief pilot of the C-118 fleet, Major Vere Short. Vere was out doing random check rides. Steedman became so nervous at having his father on board and the chief pilot in the cockpit that he botched an approach. Balsey tried to help, but Vere wouldn't allow it. Steedman subsequently had to get requalified as an aircraft commander.

Balsey and Steedman also flew the Hungarian Airlift together, flying refugees from Munich, Germany to Frankfurt and then on to the United States. On one flight out of Munich, they had an engine fail shortly after takeoff. Steedman was flying at the time and was a bit rattled by the sudden loss of power. Balsey, on the other hand, treated the engine failure more as a nuisance, as if he were upset at the additional paperwork they'd have to fill out. His nonchalant demeanor in handling the emergency made a lasting impression on Steedman.

Steedman left the Air Force in 1957 but maintained a reserve assignment with the squadron at McGuire. Balsey was still active in the squadron and worked as the scheduling officer. On one of Steedman's calls to set up a training flight, Balsey told him about a mutual friend of theirs who had been hired by a non-scheduled airline out of New York. Steedman looked up the friend who later helped Steedman land a job with the airline. The airline was Overseas National Airways. Steedman would later return the favor and help Balsey get on as a captain with ONA. Balsey flew for ONA until the company ceased operations in 1963, at which time he returned to the Air Force. Balsey became an instructor on the new C-130 and spent the next six months training pilots for what was now called Military Airlift Command (MAC).

In late 1965, Balsey was close to finishing out his second military commitment when he received a call from Steedman Hinckley. Steedman, along with several other financial backers, had purchased the ONA operating certificate and was planning to start up the airline again. He asked Balsey to join him. Balsey, however, had already accepted a job with United Airlines as a flight instructor. He told his friend no and left for Denver to train United Airline pilots on the DC-6 and DC-7.

Balsey was just thirty-two when he began working as a flight instructor for United. Most guys his age were out flying the line. He stood just five-foot-seven. He had put on weight since leaving the Air Force. His boyish features were almost lost in his round face. But when pilots heard Balsey's gruff voice, they knew it was time to straighten up. Balsey enjoyed instructing. He was hired as a captain and was considered a part of management. It was the perfect job. So when Steedman Hinckley called a second time asking Balsey to join him in New York, Balsey once again declined.

Balsey was put on the fast track at United. He went from pistons to turboprops and then on to jets. He was working as an instructor on the new Boeing 707-720 when Steedman stopped by on his way to a Colorado ski trip. Steedman wasn't one to give up easily. He treated Balsey to lunch. He told Balsey about his growing operation in New York. The Vietnam War was going full steam and Steedman had more MAC contracts than he could handle. He told Balsey about his plans to acquire more aircraft. He already had one DC-9 and had orders for two more. He was also looking into purchasing a few DC-8s. Steedman wanted Balsey to be the chief pilot of the DC-9 fleet. Once again, Balsey turned him down.

A few months had passed when Balsey got a call at four in the morning. Thinking it was scheduling calling about a training flight, Balsey picked up the phone. "How soon do you need me," he said, half-asleep. Balsey had told the schedulers that they could call any time an aircraft became available unexpectedly. There was dead silence on the other end of the phone. "Are you there?" Balsey mumbled into the receiver. "I can be ready in half an hour." Finally he heard someone on the other end. "Balsey, is that you?" It was Steedman

Hinckley. "I'm making one last phone call. Will you at least come and take a look at my operation before you tell me no?" Balsey had been thinking about Steedman's offer even before the call. He and Edith had talked about it that very evening. Edith had suggested that he should consider taking the job should Steedman call again. Balsey was starting to have second thoughts about United. He loved flying the Boeing 707, but it was an expensive airplane to use for training. Flight simulators were cheaper, safer, and more efficient. It was getting to the point where he was only flying the actual aircraft two or three days a month, and mostly late at night — the only time the plane was available. Balsey seldom flew himself; his time was spent watching his students fly. He hated to admit it, but he was getting bored. "I can probably be there Monday morning," Balsey said finally.

Balsey flew to New York and met with Steedman at ONA's main headquarters. After a brief tour and a few quick introductions, Steedman led Balsey into his office to explain his plans for the future. The current fleet of aircraft consisted of four leased DC-7s, two DC-8s, and one DC-9, with two more DC-9s on the way and options for additional DC-8s. Steedman planned to phase out the four DC-7s and replace them with DC-9 cargo aircraft. ONA would be an all-jet airline by the end of the year.

Steedman painted a rosy picture of ONA, but there were other factors enticing Balsey to leave United. Many of the pilots Balsey knew from the old ONA were working for what was now being touted as the "new" ONA. He would be working for Steedman, whom he respected and considered a friend. And working out of New York would put him closer to his family. Balsey wanted to talk things over with Edith first before making a decision, but he told Steedman that he would seriously consider the offer. He finally accepted the position of DC-9 assistant chief pilot in May 1967. He was promoted to the chief pilot position five months later.

It didn't take long after his arrival for Balsey to discover that not everyone at ONA was as enthusiastic about his hiring as Steedman. There were other pilots at ONA who felt that they should have been asked to run the DC-9 program. One of those pilots was Milt Marshall, the MEC chairman for the local Airline Pilots Association (ALPA). Milt had been the former DC-7 chief pilot. It was Steedman's airline and he could hire whomever he pleased, but that didn't make it right in the eyes of more than a few of ONA's more senior pilots. Steedman had a habit of hiring old Air Force buddies and former Princeton classmates and putting them into managerial positions ahead of other more deserving individuals. That, more than anything else, rankled a lot of pilots.

Balsey was hired at ONA at a time of explosive growth. New aircraft were arriving every couple of months. To keep up with the demands of pilot staffing, Balsey was asked to become a flight examiner. This allowed ONA to give its own checkrides, greatly reducing the amount of time it took to qualify a new pilot. Not everyone was happy with the move. Many of the pilots felt that Balsey was overly tough on checkrides. It didn't help matters when Balsey began referring to himself as the "cherub-faced assassin."[3]

"If Balsey liked you, he was one of the best flight instructors you could have," said one former ONA pilot. "If he didn't like you, you were not going to get through the program. Simple as that."[4]

Despite his feared reputation as a flight examiner, Balsey was well liked by the majority of the line pilots, many of whom had flown with him in the Air Force or at the old ONA. He went out with the crews on layovers and bought his share of rounds, though Balsey himself did not drink. His relationship with ONA management, however, was strained from the beginning.

With Steedman out drumming up business for ONA, the day-to-day operations were left in the hands of William Bailey, another friend of Steedman's. Steedman had first met Bailey while working for the old ONA. Bailey was a sales executive with the former company. When the opportunity arose for Steedman to purchase the old ONA certificate, he asked Bailey, who was in his early forties, if he would be interested in helping him run the company. Bailey accepted and also became an investor. His official title was executive vice president.

Bill Bailey was a former Major in the Air Force and had over 8,000 hours of flying time. He had flown B-17s and B-29s in World War II. Physically, he was an imposing figure, with broad shoulders and a thick neck. He had the rugged features and demeanor of a defensive lineman. His tough exterior made him the perfect choice to play the role of the bad cop to Steedman's good cop persona. Steedman, for example, didn't like to fire people; he preferred less harsh forms of punishment like a demotion or a formal reprimand. If the task was unavoidable, though, Bill Bailey was usually the one to hand out the bad news.

For some, just being in the same room as Bailey made them uncomfortable. One particular habit of his that irked some people involved a hand grip exerciser that he kept in his desk. He would sometimes use the device when he had someone in his office, squeezing it repeatedly with his massive hands as he talked.

While Steedman was the visionary behind ONA, Bill Bailey was the one who kept the airline running smoothly. Steedman often made bids on contracts that were either at cost or sometimes below cost, arguing that he could use the contract to make payments on the aircraft and then make a profit by utilizing the aircraft on other routes. Bailey was left with the task of trying to stay out of the red from the contracts Steedman was signing. He was always trying to cut corners in order to save money. Balsey and Bailey were at odds almost from the start.

One disagreement Balsey had with Bill Bailey concerned the type of tires that ONA was purchasing for the DC-9s. Steedman had signed a contract for the DC-9s to operate out of Hill Air Force Base in Ogden, Utah. The elevation of the airport was over 4,400 feet. The high elevation required special operating procedures for the DC-9s. The FAA gave ONA approval to make zero flaps, slats only takeoffs.[5] The rotation speeds were very close to the maximum tire speed limitations. Balsey wanted better tires to handle the high takeoff speeds. Bailey insisted that the retread tires they were using were adequate. Several aircraft subsequently blew tires taking off from Hill. Bailey's solution was to carry spare tires. He instructed maintenance to load two spare main tires and a spare nose tire in the forward cargo compartments of all the DC-9s. Little did he know then that those same tires would later be used by passengers and crew as flotation devices.

There were other disagreements between Balsey and upper management. One disagreement involved a DC-9 cargo door that had come open on a cargo flight shortly after takeoff. When no one could tell Balsey why the door had come open, Balsey ordered a halt to all DC-9 flying until they could determine exactly what had happened. He didn't want the same thing happening again, especially with passengers on board. Lou Furlong, the Vice President of Operations and a former Douglas Aircraft test pilot, immediately overruled him and told him he was overreacting.

Balsey's decisions were being questioned and challenged at every turn. When Balsey told Lou Furlong that he had a young pilot whom he felt wasn't going to make it through training, Lou Furlong told him to do whatever he had to do to get the kid through, stating that the company had already invested a great deal of money on his training and didn't want to see it go to waste.

Balsey's domineering style and disregard for company politics didn't help his cause. It was only a matter of time before Bill Bailey would find a reason to get rid of the recalcitrant chief pilot. Balsey gave him that reason just four months after having been promoted.

The majority of the flight training in the DC-9s was done at either Columbia, South Carolina or Augusta, Georgia. Both airports had the necessary instrument approaches and were much less congested than the airports in and around New York. The new DC-9 jet drew a lot of attention from the locals. On one training flight in Columbia, South Carolina, several state troopers stopped by to ask a few questions about the plane. The training academy for the state troopers was located on the airfield. Balsey invited the troopers to ride along. He even let them take turns sitting in the jump seat. On another flight, Balsey invited one of the girls from the rental car agency to ride along. It was alleged later, by a pilot who had failed his checkride, that Balsey had allowed the girl to sit in a pilot's seat during a training flight. The pilot claimed that Balsey was doing more showing off than training and that was the reason he had failed his checkride. Word of the incident quickly made its way back to Bill Bailey, who now had the reason he had been looking for to oust Balsey.

Balsey was in Dayton, Ohio when he first got word that his job was in jeopardy. When he returned to New York, he was told that Bill Bailey wanted to see him. What happened next is a matter of some dispute. What is known for certain is that Balsey resigned as chief pilot. He was allowed to stay on as a line captain.[*]

Balsey was replaced in New York by Ed Veronelli.[6] Ed was a personable young man with an easygoing manner that made him a popular choice among the DC-9 crews. He became one of the few in

---

[*] Balsey denies having let anyone other than a qualified pilot sit in a pilot's seat. He says that his only mistake was not clearing the rides with the company first. He also claims that the decision to go back to the line was his. Other pilots whom I've talked to claim that Steedman stepped in and allowed Balsey to remain as a line pilot. In either case, Balsey was out of the chief pilot position just four months after making chief pilot with the Columbia, South Carolina incident as the most likely reason.

management who didn't have some connection with Steedman or the former ONA.

Lou Furlong, one of Balsey's main nemeses, was later replaced as V.P. of Operations by Malcolm Ed Starkloff (Starky), the former chief pilot of the old ONA and Steedman's former boss. Starkloff had been working as the chief pilot for Japan Airlines. Lou Furlong quietly went back to the line, flying as a captain on the DC-9 and later the DC-8.

Less than one year after arriving at ONA, and only four months after becoming chief pilot, Balsey was out of management. The move to line captain suited Balsey just fine. He even picked up a small pay raise, going from $1,700 a month to $1,800 a month. Balsey's problems, however, were far from over. There were more than a few pilots who felt that Balsey should have been fired and would have been if not for Steedman. Other pilots resented the fact that he was given a seniority number based on his date of hire and not on the date he became a line pilot, which was the case with new pilots. All Balsey could do was lie low and hope that things would eventually blow over.

Chapter

As ALM 980 CRUISED ALONG AT 29,000 FEET, A *continuous supply of conditioned air kept the temperature inside the cabin at a comfortable 72 degrees. Outside the story was quite different. Temperatures at that altitude can drop to 50 degrees below zero. Winds can exceed 100 mph. The only thing separating those on board from this inhospitable environment was a thin metal tube and a few inches of insulation. It was a tenuous layer of protection that would soon prove to be no match for the storm-tossed waters of the Caribbean.*

The three cockpit crewmembers aboard ALM 980 had not flown together prior to the May 2 flight. Hugh Hart and Balsey had flown the St. Maarten flight before, but it was the first time for first officer Harry Evans. Harry was also making only his second flight after a three-month absence. The reason for Harry's absence requires some explanation.

Harry was hired by ONA in late 1968. His probationary period began in early January 1969, the day he completed training. Balsey, who was asked to resume his role as a check airman and flight instructor not long after leaving the Chief Pilot's office, was one of Harry's instructors during initial training. Balsey liked Harry but felt he didn't have enough experience to make it through training. Harry had about 3,000 hours of flight time when he was hired, mostly in light single- and multi-engine aircraft. The largest plane he had flown prior to ONA was a DeHavilland Twin Otter, a nineteen-seat turboprop aircraft popular with commuter airlines.[1] Going from a light twin to a medium-sized jet is a big leap for any pilot. To Balsey's credit, he knew that personality conflicts can have a negative impact on a pilot's performance. He was also aware that not all students were receptive to his style of teaching. So whenever he had a student he felt was on the verge of washing out, he would ask another instructor to take the student. If the other instructor concurred with Balsey's assessment, which they usually did, then the pilot would wash out. In Harry's case, he managed to squeak through by sheer determination.

Harry began flying the DC-9 primarily on cargo flights. Since he was new to the aircraft, captains were selective in deciding when they would let him fly. Over the course of his first year at ONA, Harry accumulated close to 600 hours of flight time in the DC-9, with about forty percent of that time as "sole manipulator of the controls," meaning that he was flying under the supervision of the captain.[2]

Harry was in his mid-twenties. He was much younger than the pilots he was flying with. He was married, of average height and weight, and had hair considerably longer than the short military style haircuts favored by the majority of the captains, most of whom were ex-Air Force. The difference in age and background made it difficult for Harry to fit in.[3]

In January 1970, Harry was given a one-year probationary check-ride. He passed the ride, but Malcolm Starkloff, the Vice President of Operations, decided to let him go anyway, stating that he had made the decision after hearing negative comments about Harry from some of the captains.[4]

A pilot dismissed during probation has little recourse. Starkloff, however, had given Harry his termination notice one day after his probation had officially ended. Harry appealed the termination and was reinstated three months later.

Harry was given a new class date in April 1970. Ed Veronelli, who had replaced Balsey in New York, gave him his checkride after the completion of his training. Harry passed the ride, but it was obvious to Ed that Harry still lacked confidence. Harry requested to fly as an observer on a few flights before being assigned a trip. Ed agreed, but every time he tried to set him up to observe a flight someone else had the jump seat. So rather than have Harry sitting idle in New York, he sent him to Norfolk, Virginia to get in some observer time on the DC-9s flying the Quick Transport (QUICKTRANS) cargo flights.[5] Harry received twenty-five hours of observer time. He also flew one trip as a first officer before returning to New York.

On Friday, May 1, Harry learned from dispatcher Tony Delmar that he was scheduled to fly the New York–St. Maarten flight the next day. Harry tried to get out of the trip, stating that he had not received any training on the route. He complained that he didn't have any experience with international procedures, and he hadn't received training on the LORAN. Delmar told him not to worry. He was scheduled to fly with an instructor pilot and would receive whatever training he needed on the flight.[6] Although he never came out and said it, part of Harry's reluctance to take the flight may have had something to do with the knowledge that Balsey DeWitt was going to be the captain. The two had not flown together since Balsey's unfavorable evaluation during Harry's initial training. Had it been any other captain, Harry might not have put up such a fight.

The truth was that there probably could not have been a worse pairing of captain and first officer than Balsey and Harry. The two were at opposite ends of the personality spectrum. Balsey was authoritative and could be intimidating in the cockpit. Harry was passive and lacked confidence. Harry could have elected to fly on the QUICKTRANS cargo flights. That would have given him a chance to learn the aircraft in a freight operation where mistakes are treated less harshly. But Harry wanted to be an airline pilot; he wanted to fly passengers.[7]

Hugh Hart, the navigator on board, didn't care if he was flying passengers or boxes; the pay was the same. Like Harry, Hugh had learned only the day before that he was to fly the May 2 flight. The original navigator had called in sick at the last minute. The fact was that there wasn't a single navigator who enjoyed flying the St. Maarten route. The navigators knew better than anyone that they weren't really needed on the flight. The pilots could just as easily be trained to use the LORAN for the brief period where normal navigation wasn't available.

Hugh Hart was a striking figure at just over six feet tall with reddish brown hair and a full beard. His closely cropped beard, along with his preference for smoking pipes, gave him a distinguished appearance, like that of a college professor or intellectual. When Balsey heard rumors that one of the navigators was working part time as a male model, he assumed (incorrectly) that it was Hugh.

When Hugh got the call about the St. Maarten trip, the dispatcher practically begged him to take the flight, saying that he was the last resort. Hugh had flown the flight twice before. His back ached from a cold even before he got the call. Just the thought of sitting in the uncomfortable jump seat for seven and a half hours caused his back to spasm. Hugh finally agreed to take the trip, thinking it would be a good opportunity to buy some duty free rum.

Hugh had reluctantly become a navigator in the Air Force after failing the vision test for pilot training. He continued to work as a navigator after leaving the Air Force, working for various charter companies in the U.S. and Europe. He earned enough money as a navigator to attend Harvard Business School, where he obtained an MBA. He was working for a packaging company in Atlanta, Georgia when he first learned about a small upstart airline in New York called ONA.

Hugh went to ONA's headquarters in New York and landed an interview with Steedman Hinckley. Steedman was impressed with Hugh's background. He liked that he was a former navigator. Steedman hired Hugh as his direct assistant. All Hugh was told about the position was that he would be working directly under Steedman in the areas of business planning and marketing.

From the start, Hugh was frustrated with his nebulous job duties. Steedman was gone from the office weeks at a time. The few projects that Hugh did work on were not well received. Hugh quickly formed the impression that the only reason he had been hired was so that Steedman could say in some ONA publication that they had an MBA from Harvard working for them. Feeling underutilized and underpaid, Hugh offered to fill in as a navigator. ONA was short of navigators at the time, and Hugh needed the extra income. He told Steedman that flying as a navigator would give him an opportunity to get a better feel for the operation.

Hugh flew as a full-time navigator until October 1966, at which time he resumed his management position, flying occasionally to supplement his income. He had no more success working for Steedman the second time around, and after several months of getting the run around, he made the decision to switch to flying full time while he looked for something else. Hugh became an iconoclast at ONA. He grew a beard. He openly criticized management's decisions. His only reason for staying was that he had heard rumors of a planned crew base in San Francisco. He was hoping to have ONA pay for his move to California so he could look for work there.[8]

Chapter 7

TWO HOURS INTO THE FLIGHT AND A LITTLE OVER nine hundred miles south of New York, ALM 980 approached an area of thunderstorms. Balsey requested and received permission to deviate west around the weather. As the flight proceeded farther south, it encountered some light turbulence. Balsey contemplated going higher to avoid the turbulence, but as he looked out ahead of him he saw some high cirrus clouds that looked as though they were being whipped up by strong upper-level winds. He turned the seatbelt sign on and requested a lower altitude instead.

Shortly after the seatbelt sign was turned on, one of the flight attendants came into the cockpit and asked Balsey if he was going to make an announcement. Balsey replied that he couldn't make any announcements because the PA system wasn't working. The flight attendant laughed and made the comment "that's what they all say" before exiting the cockpit. A few seconds later, the flight attendant made an announcement over the cabin PA telling the passengers to fasten their seatbelts due to expected turbulence. It was the first time since leaving New York that the PA system had been used. Some of the passengers assumed, incorrectly, that the *announcement had come from the cockpit. Both Wilfred and Tobias would later deny having any knowledge that the PA system was inoperative. Harry Evans testified that he was monitoring the instruments at the time and only overheard the conversation and could not identify which flight attendant had entered the cockpit. He did, however, indicate that it was one of the male stewards. He would also say that it was the first indication he had that the PA system wasn't working.*

In the back of the plane, the passengers buckled up for turbulence that never came. Other than a minor bump or two, the ride was smooth and uneventful. Those who did happen to glance out their window saw only a featureless ocean and a dull blue and white sky.

Sitting in seats 8D and 8E on the right side of the aircraft were Gene and Loretta Gremelsbacker.[1] Gene had the window seat. The two spent a good portion of the flight trying to catch up on their sleep. They sat cuddled together with Loretta's head resting on Gene's shoulder. The night before, Gene and Loretta had gone out to a bar to celebrate their planned Caribbean vacation. They were joined by a friend, Rick Arnold, who was also on the flight. A mutual friend of the three, Jean Claude Alexander, a wealthy Frenchman who worked for the World Health Organization, had offered to let the three stay at his villa on St. Maarten. The original offer had been extended to Gene and Loretta, who had married the previous summer but had not yet had a honeymoon. Gene worked as a part-time bartender for a number of downtown eating and drinking establishments. Jean Claude Alexander was a patron at one of the bars Gene worked at called *Pywacket*. Rick Arnold also knew Jean Claude. They were all part of a large group of twentysomethings who hung around together, bar hopping in downtown Manhattan and partying until daybreak. When word got out about the villa in St. Maarten, the list of people wanting to join Gene and Loretta grew. According to Jean Claude, the villa could easily accommodate six or more visitors. The villa even had maid service. Rick Arnold was invited to come along. Gene invited his sister, Ellen. And Loretta invited her sister, Joyce. The latter two were to join the group in St. Maarten in a few days.[2]

Sitting in the aisle seat directly behind Gene and Loretta was twenty-four-year-old Rick Arnold. Like his friend Gene, Rick was sporting a beard. Both he and Gene had served in the military. Growing beards and letting their hair grow out was their way of assimilating back into civilian life. Rick's thick crop of dark, curly hair left no hint that he had once served as an honor guard at Arlington Cemetery.

Rick was just beginning a career in real estate and didn't have a lot of money, but he decided to splurge on this trip, treating himself to some new clothes and a new pair of expensive Italian loafers. After all, it wasn't every day that he got to jet off to the Caribbean to spend a few days in a French villa. When he spotted the attractive stewardess walking his way, he flagged her down and asked for a Bloody Mary. Rick spent his time on the flight sipping Bloody Marys and daydreaming about white sand beaches and bikini-clad women.[3]

Jeannie Larmony, the fifty-six-year-old grandmother who had earlier introduced herself to Walter Hodge, was sitting in 16A. Jeannie was a seasoned traveler and always requested a window seat. She felt safer being able to look outside. She was dressed comfortably in blue slacks and a pink blouse. A lifetime swimmer, Jeannie was in excellent shape for her age. She had five children: four boys and a girl. Three of her sons worked for the airlines. Her son, Charlie

Larmony, worked in the maintenance department at ONA. Charlie had arranged for the non-revenue pass that Jeannie was using on the flight. Earlier in the week, Jeannie had learned that her mother was to be admitted to the hospital. She was flying to St. Maarten at the request of her father.[4]

Sitting in seats 10A and 10B, two rows forward of the aft overwing exits, were Toby and Israel Kruger. They were both in their fifties, and were headed to St. Maarten for a vacation. Both had been to the Caribbean before, but this was their first visit to St. Maarten. They were dressed casually. Israel, who was known to family and friends as Irv or Irving, was wearing a plain shirt and dress slacks and a pair of brown lace-up shoes (the type of shoes that would be difficult to remove in a hurry). Toby was wearing a lightweight dress. She was also wearing a small hairpiece to make her silver hair look fuller. Her evening attire was packed away in the checked luggage. Toby liked to dress up when she went out. She also enjoyed wearing jewelry. The blue suitcase containing her jewelry was in the overhead bin directly above their seats. The suitcase contained over $135,000 worth of Toby's and Israel's jewelry. They weren't about to trust the baggage handlers with such precious cargo.[5]

Sitting two rows in front of Israel and Toby Kruger were Jim and Hedwig (Hedi) Razzi. Jim was thirty-eight and his wife Hedi was twenty-seven. Jim Razzi had arranged for the trip to St. Maarten in an effort to cheer up his wife, who was despondent over the loss of their child the month before. Jim and Hedi's son had been born with spina bifida and encephalitis and died shortly after birth. They also had a daughter, Christina, who was five.

Jim was a graphic artist who had studied at several prestigious art schools including the Academy of Fine Arts in Florence, Italy and the School of Visual Arts in New York. He was currently working for the children's magazine *Humpty Dumpty* by Parents Magazine Press. His work for the magazine led to the development of his first children's activity book. He was already at work on a second.

Hedi was a Swiss citizen born in Zurich, Switzerland. She was a stunningly attractive woman who had first come to the United States six years earlier to work as an au pair. Jim and Hedi had met at a famous dance hall in New York called *Roseland*. They were married three months later.[6]

While there were no celebrities on board, there was one passenger who was fairly well known, especially in the Caribbean where she had lived since 1952. Her name was Christine Cromwell. Christine was the granddaughter of Horace Dodge of Dodge automotive fame. She lived in St. Maarten but also owned a nightclub on the island of St. Thomas. The nightclub, called the *St. Thomas Club*, overlooked the harbor at Charlotte Amalie. Mrs. Cromwell's husband, musician and singer Bob Ellis, performed regularly at the club. The nightclub, which also served meals, had originally been the couple's seven-thousand-square-foot residence.

Emerson Ussery, the last man to board and the cause of the minor commotion just prior to departure, was sitting comfortably in seat 1C, immersed in paperwork. Like several other male passengers on board, Emerson wore a beard. The closely cropped beard and a thin wisp of hair framed the face of a man who had spent a good portion of his life outdoors.

Emerson had the unusual distinction of having been involved in two airplane accidents prior to taking ALM 980, both involving aircraft that had ended up in the water. The first accident involved a small two-seat tail-dragger piloted by Emerson's brother, Clarence. It was the first time Emerson had been in an airplane. After a series of steep turns and stalls, Emerson suggested that they fly over one of his construction projects near the Florida coast. Once they were over the site, they decided to put on a show for the construction crew. Shortly after performing a series of low altitude maneuvers, the engine quit. The plane plummeted into the water some four hundred yards from the beach. Both men escaped uninjured and swam to shore. The second accident involved a takeoff in an overloaded DC-3. The plane ran off the end of the runway in San Juan and ended up in a lagoon.[7]

Chapter 8

SIX MILES ABOVE THE ATLANTIC, TRAVELING AT NEARLY *450 mph, ALM 980 streaked across a pale blue sky, leaving a contrail in its wake. The DC-9, with its swept-back wing and bullet-like nose, was built for speed. The sensation of speed, however, was not apparent to those on board. A lack of surface detail when flying over water makes it difficult to discern movement. Only when in proximity to clouds can passengers appreciate the true speed at which they are traveling.*

For the passengers and crew, the swiftness with which they were slicing through the atmosphere was little consolation. It was still a lengthy flight, especially for an aircraft this size.

The cockpit of the DC-9 was adequately roomy, though more like a sports car than a sedan. Anything over three hours was pushing it. The pilots often complained that while the plane may have cost four million dollars, very little of that money was spent on the design of the pilot seats, which were nothing more than two foam cushions attached to a metal frame. As uncomfortable as the pilot's seats were, the seat that the navigator was forced to sit on was much worse. The seat was situated in such a way that your feet didn't touch the floor. They dangled in mid-air like the legs of a child sitting in an adult's chair. There were foot rests on the sides of the center pedestal, but they snapped back against the pedestal the moment you lifted your foot off of them. Fortunately for Hugh, his legs were long enough that his feet could at least touch the floor.

The cabin, while stout enough to provide stand-up room for most passengers, felt claustrophobic. From the front of the cabin to the back measured just sixty feet across. The twenty-one rows of seats were packed in so tightly there was barely room to cross your legs. The aisle was only nineteen inches wide.

Stewardess Margareth Abraham had no trouble negotiating the narrow aisle. She had learned long ago to ignore the occasional stray elbow or foot that would inevitably prod her in the side. With just over an hour to go before landing, she walked through the cabin and refilled drinks. Rick Arnold took the opportunity to ask for another Bloody Mary. As Margareth leaned over to hand him the drink, Rick noticed her engagement ring and commented on it. Margareth smiled and told Rick about her upcoming wedding, which was just over a month away. This was to be her last trip, she told him. The excitement in her voice was obvious to anyone within earshot.

Margareth had given notice weeks earlier and hadn't expected to still be flying. She had agreed to take the trip at the last minute because she wanted to buy some champagne for her wedding at the duty-free shop in St. Maarten.

Margareth was twenty-four and had been with ALM for three years. Her father was a lab technician and her mother a former nurse. She had a twin brother, Carol, an older sister, and three younger siblings, two boys and a girl. Margareth had applied to ALM at the suggestion of her uncle, who worked for ALM as a purser.

Margareth loved being a stewardess. It was a glamorous job in those days, considered to be nearly on par with that of a model or actress, especially in the eyes of young girls who admired the stylish uniforms. She would often hop on a plane on her days off to explore some of the islands that ALM flew in and out of: Aruba, Bonaire, St. Maarten, Jamaica and Trinidad.

She was an avid swimmer. Long layovers would usually find her out by the pool or strolling along a nearby beach. In her stocking feet she stood just five-foot-five, which was an advantage on the smaller aircraft that ALM flew. She had impish green eyes and long auburn hair that she wore in a French roll under her uniform cap.[1] The rule at ALM was that the hair should not reach the collar. The girls didn't complain. It was a quick and easy hairstyle, which came in handy on those early morning departures. Like most people schooled in Curaçao, she could write and speak in several languages including English, Dutch, Spanish, French, and Papiamento — the local language of the Netherlands Antilles.

Margareth's fiancé, Robby Schouten, was a television producer and on air personality who had his own one-hour television show. The show, which ran two times a month, was a showcase for local musical groups and performers. The TV program aired both in Curaçao and Aruba.

Robby shared Margareth's passion for traveling. They took trips together to Venezuela and Puerto Rico and had romantic getaways on sun-drenched islands like St. Barths. On a whim they would jump on the ALM DC-8 to New York and catch a Broadway show.

When she wasn't flying or out exploring nearby islands, Margareth helped Robby with his television show. She sold advertising time; she helped with the sets; and she took care of the show's guests. As much as Margareth loved her job as a stewardess, she was looking forward to working behind the scenes on Robby's show.[2]

Assisting Margareth on the flight were stewards Tobias Cordeiro, who went by the nickname of Tito; and purser Wilfred Spencer, whom everyone called Boy. Wilfred had been on the very first New York–St. Maarten flight in January along with Margareth.

Wilfred Spencer had decided to become a flight steward in 1964 when KLM first formed ALM. At the time, he was working in the communications department for KLM. His father, who was a police officer and who had died when Wilfred was in the third grade, had once worked for KLM as a security guard. Wilfred was ready for a change of pace, and the steward job paid more.

While male flight attendants were somewhat of an anomaly among domestic carriers, they were not uncommon among foreign carriers. Thirty-percent of the flight attendants at ALM were male. Wilfred had worked his way up to the purser position in just three years. He had also developed an interest in union activities. His interest in labor unions began after forming a friendship with the head of the ALM flight attendants union. Wilfred volunteered his services, helping with union correspondence on layovers and other miscellaneous tasks. The skills he learned working in the communications department were well suited for union work. It was the beginning of a long association with labor unions for Wilfred.

At thirty-one, Wilfred Spencer was enjoying life. He was married and had two children: six-year-old Francis and one-year-old Shahaira. He had a comfortable home with a view of the Caribbean Sea. He was in good physical shape. Had he not been married, he could easily have attracted the attention of one or two of the stewardesses with whom he worked.[3]

Steward Tobias Cordeiro on the other hand had not yet grown into the features that would serve him well in later years. He had turned twenty only the month before and still had the awkwardness of someone unsure of himself. He was pencil thin. With his short hair and unflattering dark-rimmed glasses, he looked young enough to pass for a high school student.

Tobias's parents had divorced when he was just two. He and his brother and three sisters moved to the nearby island of Aruba to live with their mother. They lived close to the airport. Tobias made frequent flights to Curaçao to visit his father. He would often linger at the airport after a visit, watching passengers and crewmembers come and go. He would ride his bike to the airport to watch planes takeoff and land, sometimes positioning himself near the end of the runway where the planes would pass directly over him. A few years after graduating from high school, an acquaintance told him about some openings at ALM for flight stewards. The job sounded appealing to Tito, whose horizons had not expanded much beyond that of Aruba and Curaçao. He applied for the job and started work at ALM in June 1969.[4]

Prior to taking the May 2 flight, all three flight attendants were required to receive differences training, which was intended to cover the differences between ONA's DC-9s and ALM's DC-9s, as well as the differences in emergency procedures between the two airlines. The training was held in Curaçao in January and March 1970. ONA stewardess supervisor Kristina (Chris) Linder conducted the training.

ALM operated three DC-9-15 series aircraft. The planes were smaller than the DC-9-33 series aircraft that ONA was using on the route. ALM's planes carried eighty-five passengers as opposed to the 105 passengers that ONA's DC-9 carried. There were major performance differences between the two aircraft, but Chris was only concerned with the location and type of emergency equipment installed. One major difference she discovered was that the ALM DC-9s did not carry life rafts. ONA's DC-9 had two large bins mounted in the ceiling just aft of the overwing exits. Four 25-man life rafts, weighing 125 pounds each, were stored in the bins. Chris was told that the management at ALM had decided not to carry life rafts aboard their DC-9s. It had been and continued to be a subject of much debate between the flight attendant and pilot unions and management.

The decision to not carry life rafts was purely an economic one. ALM was able to fly without life rafts by claiming that the aircraft was never more than an hour away from a suitable landing field. Life rafts took up space and weight. Besides, management argued, the escape slides could be used in place of life rafts.*

The differences between the two aircraft from a flight attendant's standpoint were minor. Some emergency equipment was stored in different locations. ALM's DC-9s had a rope and cargo tie down in the back of the plane, while the ONA DC-9 did not. Chris talked about the flight attendant call lights, which were located in a small strip in the ceiling just forward of the cockpit door. If a passenger pressed the call button, then the blue light would come on. If the cockpit called, then a red light would flash on. Two bells from the cockpit meant either take your seat for takeoff or come to the cockpit. There was no discussion of what three or more bells from the cockpit indicated.[5]

The two topics that caused the most discussion were life vests and life rafts. All of the life vests on ONA's aircraft were the same size. ALM's aircraft carried two sizes of vests: one for adults and one for children. More than one person taking the class wanted to know what they were supposed to do if there were children on board. Chris pointed out that the vests that ONA carried were approved for use on anyone thirty-five pounds or greater.[6] She had one of ALM's

---

* While the suggestion that escape slides could be used as flotation devices was a good one, the fact was that escape slides had not been approved for that purpose and would not be approved for that purpose for many years to come. Some of the reasons the slides were not approved as replacements for life rafts include lack of hand holds, the slides were too small to support a full load of passengers, and lack of survival equipment.

adult life vests and tried to demonstrate using a doll how the straps were to be tied between the legs of a child, as opposed to around the waist of an adult. Not everyone in the class was convinced that it was a workable solution.

The next discussion concerned the life rafts. Since ALM didn't carry life rafts aboard its DC-9s, several people wanted to know what the procedure was concerning the pre-positioning of life rafts in the event of a ditching. The procedure on the ALM DC-8 was to pre-position the life rafts prior to ditching. In the case where there were no life rafts, as with the DC-9, they were told to remove the escape slides from their containers and pre-position the slides near the exits. Chris informed the class that because ONA did not have a raft tie-down kit, they were not to pre-position any of the life rafts, including the life raft stored in the coat closet.[*7] Furthermore, the escape slides were to be disarmed so as not to interfere with the deployment of the life rafts.

There were a total of twenty-seven flight attendants qualified to fly the New York–St. Maarten route. The flights ran every Wednesday and Saturday. The flight attendants scheduled to work the St. Maarten flight would deadhead (ride as a non-revenue passenger) to New York on the ALM DC-8 on Tuesday. Work the roundtrip to St. Maarten and back on Wednesday. Have Thursday and Friday off in New York. Work the St. Maarten flight again on Saturday. Then deadhead back to Curaçao the next day. It was a grueling schedule, but the flight attendants liked it. The St. Maarten flights were much

---

* The instruction to not pre-position life rafts was later countermanded by ALM in a memo to its flight attendants, instructing them to pre-position the raft located in the coat closet. This was done in order to standardize their training since they were required to pre-position life rafts aboard the DC-8.

easier to work than the long DC-8 flights from Curaçao to New York. They especially liked the two-day layover in New York City. They stayed in downtown Manhattan at the Edison Hotel on 47th Street and Broadway. It was an older hotel, but the staff was friendly and knew the ALM flight attendants on a first-name basis.

Chapter 9

AFTER DEVIATING WEST AROUND WEATHER, BALSEY descended to flight level 270, hoping for a smoother ride. He also slowed to .74 mach. Unable to get below the shelf of cirrus clouds, he once again asked for a lower altitude and was cleared to descend to FL 250. He then slowed to .72 mach. The ride improved, but the tradeoff for the smoother ride was a higher fuel burn.

A time check at Grant intersection showed that they were running a few minutes behind flight plan. The deviations and power reductions were part of the reason, but it was also becoming apparent that the winds had shifted. Hugh theorized that a low-pressure area that they were counting on to provide a slight tail wind had shifted to the west and was instead giving them a slight headwind. A second time check seemed to verify Hugh's theory.

Throughout the flight, Balsey had been taking periodic fuel readings. Douglas Aircraft was still working on the fuel burn discrepancy and wanted ONA to continue to track the fuel burns. Balsey made entries into a fuel log every thirty minutes. As a result, he had been monitoring the fuel situation more closely than usual. Even with the deviations and the *lower altitude, Balsey calculated that they would land with more than the legally required fuel reserve. He pulled out the weather documents and once again reviewed the weather for St. Maarten. The forecast was reported as:*

Scattered clouds at 2500 feet, variable to 1500 feet, variable to broken, 10,000 feet overcast, 6 miles visibility, haze, wind 110 degrees at 10 kts. gusting to 15 kts.[*1]

The forecast also carried a warning for a chance of thunderstorms, with visibilities of 1½ miles and ceilings as low as 500 feet possible. The forecasted weather for St. Thomas, the planned alternate, was similar to that of St. Maarten.

There was nothing in the forecast to warrant concern. There was a mention of thunderstorms, but there were always thunderstorms in the forecast for the Caribbean, especially in the spring as the colder air masses over the Atlantic collided with the warm air masses over the Caribbean. The only thing in the forecast that could have been considered out of the ordinary was the mention of a visibility restriction due to haze. Haze is not normally a factor in the Caribbean, especially the farther away you get from the larger islands. What the weather documents didn't say was that the haze in the forecast was caused by a sand storm that had occurred over Africa a few days earlier. The blue skies over the Caribbean were obscured by millions of minute particles of sand and dust. These minute particles, in turn, acted as condensation nuclei – the seeds of cloud formation. Thunderstorms grew in number and intensity as ALM 980 proceeded along its course.

---

[*] The bases of clouds are reported as height above the ground – 2500 scattered means that there are scattered clouds at 2,500 feet above the ground. Cloud tops are given as height above mean sea level. Wind speed is always given in knots (kts). A conversion table is used to convert from kts to mph.

On the island of St. Croix, one of the U.S. Virgin Islands, the thunderstorms were the source of much frustration for twenty-three-year-old pilot Bill Bohlke. The flight school he operated was unable to launch a single aircraft due to the stormy weather. Thunderstorms and high winds had plagued the island all afternoon. Sitting in the office with Bill were two pilots — George Johnson, a low time flight instructor, and Andy Titus, a student pilot. They were hoping the weather would improve so they could go flying. But just when the weather looked like it might clear up, the winds would start swirling and another band of showers would pass through. So they talked and drank coffee. The only flying this day would be hangar flying.

Bill was a little on edge this day even without the weather. His wife Tuddy (pronounced Toody) was nine months pregnant with their first child. Tuddy worked at the airport with Bill and had gone to work as she had been doing throughout her pregnancy. She had left work a few hours earlier, though, after feeling what she thought were labor pains. She drove to a girlfriend's house to rest.

Bill's dad, Bill Bohlke Sr., started the first commuter airline in the region in 1964. In 1968, Bill's dad sold the commuter airline and formed Caribbean Air Services, which flew cargo over many of the same routes that the commuter airline flew. Bill flew for his dad, building up flight time in light twin aircraft like the Cessna 310 and the Piper Aztec.

Bill Jr. was a garrulous young man who had flown long enough in the Caribbean that he could identify islands solely by their silhouettes. He had a young face and a stocky build. Family and friends still referred to him as Billy, a moniker he didn't encourage. He was also a budding airline pilot. When his dad sold the commuter airline, he took a job as a flight engineer on a Boeing 727 with Trans Caribbean Airways. He had returned to St. Croix a few months earlier after having been furloughed for the second time. Bill had spent some time in the Air National Guard and knew of several guardsmen who had used VA benefits for flight training. He decided to start his own flight school on St. Croix with the hope of drawing students with VA benefits. He had been operating the flight school for several months. There hadn't been too many days when the weather had kept his aircraft on the ground. This day, however, was unusually stormy. In all his time flying in the Caribbean he could remember only one or two times when the thunderstorms were as relentless as they were that afternoon.[2]

One person who did manage to get some work done at the airport that afternoon was George Stoute. George worked as an aircraft mechanic for Bill's dad. George was from the island of Barbados. He was well liked and an excellent mechanic. George Stoute was also a convicted murderer.

George was a heavy drinker. On one particular day in June 1966, George had been drinking when he learned that his girlfriend had been cheating on him. George spotted his girlfriend and her brother sitting in a car. He confronted her. There was a brief exchange and then the car sped off. George jumped into his car and pursued the pair through the narrow streets of St. Croix, eventually ending up at the front steps of the police station in Christianstead. He shot his girlfriend in the head as she sat in the car. Her brother was inside trying to get help. George was immediately arrested and later sentenced to a thirty-five-year prison sentence. He had been working as a mechanic for Bill's dad before the incident. Bill Bohlke Sr. had some influence on the island and worked out an arrangement with prison officials at the Richmond Penitentiary to let George out on a work release program four days a week. In return, George set up a machine shop in the prison and taught other inmates how to work on aircraft engines as well as maintain the prison's fleet of vehicles.[3]

Elsewhere in the Caribbean soon to be rescuers went about their daily routine. One of those rescuers was twenty-one-year-old Corporal John Barber, a short but muscled marine with an angular face. John was on the flight deck of the USS *Guadalcanal*, which was anchored off the southern coast of Vieques Island, located just six miles from Puerto Rico.

The *USS Guadalcanal*, designated LPH-7, was an *Iwo Jima* class amphibious assault ship. The ship resembled an aircraft carrier but was considerably smaller. The flight deck could accommodate only helicopters and V/STOL (vertical/short takeoff and landing) aircraft. The ship's primary mission was to transport Marine assault troops along with their armament, vehicles, equipment, and support personnel. The landing force would arrive on land via helicopter, allowing for a dispersal of troops as well as eliminating the need for a concentrated beach assault. In addition to transporting up to seventeen hundred marines, the ship required another seven hundred men whose primary job was to operate and maintain the ship. Sometimes referred to as helicopter carriers, the ships were also used as the primary recovery vessels during the Apollo space program. The *Guadalcanal* was responsible for two such recoveries: the astronauts from *Gemini X* and the spacecraft and astronauts from *Apollo 9*.

John Barber had joined the Marine Corps in 1967, signing up with three high school classmates under the buddy system, which promised to keep the four together at least through boot camp. He had signed up for a four-year commitment, hoping to get a job working with helicopters. John had been interested in helicopters since the age of seven, after seeing helicopters bringing survivors from the *Andrea Doria* to the Brighton Marine hospital complex located behind the housing projects where he lived. The *Andrea Doria*, an Italian cruise ship, had collided with the Swedish ship *Stockholm*. The helicopters landed in the basketball courts behind Barber's house. The life and death drama played out that day had a huge impact on the young boy from the Dorchester section of Boston. He knew from that point on that he would be involved in some manner with aviation. Following boot camp at Cherry Hill, North Carolina, John was assigned to aviation structural mechanic's school in Memphis, Tennessee. After graduating from mechanic's school at the end of 1967, he was assigned to the Marine Medium Helicopter squadron HMM-261 based at the Marine Corps Air Station, New River, Jacksonville, North Carolina. His job as a metal smith was not a flying position. But he was only nineteen. He figured he had lots of time to get the position he truly wanted, which was a flying position as a crew chief aboard a Marine helicopter.

By late 1969, Barber was certain that his next assignment was going to be Vietnam. He had been hearing stories from other guys in the squadron who had been to Vietnam. He had even volunteered to go. But in early November he was told that he would be going on another Caribbean cruise. It would be his second Caribbean cruise in two years. He was ambivalent about the assignment. On the one hand, he felt an obligation to serve a tour of duty closer to where the action was. On the other hand, there were worse assignments he could have drawn than cruising the Caribbean in the middle of winter in a relatively new, air-conditioned ship. More importantly, this cruise held out the promise of his being crossed-trained as a crew chief. He knew that a number of the crew chiefs going on the cruise were scheduled to complete their military commitments before the end of the cruise. He would be in the perfect position to move into one of the expected vacancies.

There was something else about this cruise that would be different from the previous one. John Barber was engaged. He had met a girl a few months earlier during a trip to Cape Cod. He had asked the girl, Kathy Vitt, to marry him. They hadn't set a date, but at least

John had something to look forward to when he returned. HMM-261 departed Morehead City, North Carolina aboard the *USS Guadalcanal* on January 13, 1970. The squadron consisted of two Bell UH-1E Huey helicopters and sixteen twin-engine Boeing CH-46 Sea Knight helicopters. The helicopters were supported by some three hundred marines including the pilots, mechanics, and miscellaneous support staff.

In March of 1970, three months into his second Caribbean cruise, John Barber was promoted to CH-46 crew chief. His helicopter was EM-13; each crew chief was assigned a specific helicopter.

John took his new position seriously. The crew chief was an integral part of the crew. It was his job to ready the helicopter before each flight. After a quick break on the *Guadalcanal,* John prepared the helicopter for an afternoon of flying. He began with a walk-around inspection of EM-13. He then stepped inside and fired up the auxiliary power plant to check the fuel and hydraulics. He looked out through a thick haze toward Vieques Island. EM-13 and three other CH-46s were scheduled to fly shuttle flights to Vieques, bringing troops back from Camp Garcia to the ship. The *Guadalcanal* was planning to leave for San Juan on Monday. It would take several days of what the pilots referred to as "troop back-loading" to get all the marines back on ship. John called for fuel and waited for pilots Art Nash and Bill Murphy to show up on the flight deck.[4]

Less than thirty miles from where the *USS Guadalcanal* was anchored, Lt. Commander James Rylee was at home at the Naval station at Roosevelt Roads, Puerto Rico, fighting a cold and hoping the phone wouldn't ring. Jim was the Operations Officer of VC-8 Fleet Composite squadron, a combined fixed- and rotor-wing unit. Jim was a quiet, reserved man, who sported a haircut as closely shaved as fine sandpaper. He was forty-two and nearing the end of a twenty-five-year naval career. Some of the younger guys in the squadron referred to him as the "old man."

Jim was a naval aviator with over 5,000 hours of flight time in both rotor wing and fixed wing aircraft. He also served a six-year stint as an airship (blimp) pilot. None of the aircraft he flew were particularly known for their speed. The faster of the two helicopters he flew at Roosevelt Roads had a top speed of just 120 knots. Back in his blimp days he cruised around at the leisurely pace of 35 knots, about 43 mph.

Jim's flying duties at Roosevelt Roads included the transporting of people and supplies and drone recovery. Drone recovery was his primary job. The turbine-powered drones were launched from beneath a P2V-5 Neptune. This unique aircraft had two inboard reciprocal engines and two outboard turbine-powered engines. The P2V was the precursor to the popular P3 Orion. The radio-controlled drones were used as target practice by fighter pilots. Whenever a drone was successfully shot down, the pilot would make the radio call "boola boola." Each time one of the drones was shot down, the squadron responsible for the hit was given a plaque by the Ryan Company, which made the drones known as *Firebees*. The drones were hit about 20% of the time. Those that weren't shot down would continue to fly until their fuel was exhausted. A parachute would deploy and the drone would fall harmlessly into the sea, where it would be recovered by helicopter. The helicopter would hover a few feet above the water while a crewman snagged the drone with a long hook. After attaching a long cable, they would transport the 2,500-pound drone back to the air station, with the drone dangling beneath the helicopter. The red drones were easy to spot, especially if the parachute hadn't deflated. It wasn't the most exciting job in the world, but it did sharpen the hovering skills of the pilots.

Jim lived on base in a hurricane-proof home made of concrete. He was married and had three boys aged fifteen, twelve, and eleven. Jim was a family man who preferred time with his wife Donna and three boys over hobnobbing with the other officers on base. He didn't drink or smoke. His hobby was coin collecting. Jim knew his time in the Navy was coming to an end. Roosy Roads was the ideal place to close out a career. Located on the southeastern coast of Puerto Rico, the picturesque naval base was known by the enlisted men as the "Country Club of the Navy."[5]

On the opposite side of the island of Puerto Rico, at the Isla Grande airport in San Juan, pilots for the Coast Guard Air Detachment unit were several hours into a twenty-four-hour shift. Every four days the pilots were required to be on standby for a twenty-four-hour period. There were always at least five officers on duty: two fixed-wing pilots; two helicopter pilots; and a duty officer, who ran the rescue desk and coordinated the other aircraft. Pilots on twenty-four-hour duty normally remained at the airport for the entire period of their duty.

The primary Coast Guard unit in the Caribbean was Commander Greater Antilles Section (COMGANTS), located in Old San Juan across the harbor from the Isla Grande airport. COMGANTS was the rescue coordination center (RCC) for all rescues conducted in the Caribbean. The Air Detachment unit at Isla Grande consisted of three amphibious HU-16 Albatross fixed-wing aircraft and two HH-52A helicopters.

When the pilots weren't training or out on a mission, they performed other administrative duties known as collateral duty. This could be anything from maintaining training records to setting up work schedules for the enlisted men. The two helicopter pilots on airport standby were aircraft commander Lt. junior grade (j.g.)

William Shields and co-pilot Lt. (j.g.) Carmond "Fitz" Fitzgerald. Both pilots had started their day at 7:00 A.M. Bill Shields, a five-year veteran of the Coast Guard, spent most of his day filling out administrative paperwork.[6]

Carmond Fitzgerald, the on-call co-pilot, spent his day studying his training syllabus. Carmond was working toward first pilot status on the HH-52A, a transition position halfway between aircraft commander and co-pilot.[7]

Both pilots kept a close eye on the weather outside. They knew from experience that their chances of being called out on a rescue increased as the weather deteriorated.

Part Two

LAST FLIGHT OF
THE *CARIB QUEEN*

Chapter 10

A S ALM 980 NEARED GUAVA INTERSECTION, A POINT
some 211 miles north of St. Maarten, a time
check showed that they were a full twenty minutes behind flight plan.
The fuel totalizer indicated 8,600 pounds of fuel remaining. Balsey
estimated that they would land at St. Maarten with approximately
6,000 pounds of fuel — still within legal limits. Balsey tuned in the St.
Maarten tower frequency on the number two radio and called for a
weather update. He was given weather of 1,000 broken, 5,000 overcast, and visibility of 2 to 3 miles in rain showers. He was also told that
the rain showers were moving westward. The weather was marginal
for shooting an NDB approach but well within the legal limits. Balsey
called Wilfred into the cockpit and told him that the new ETA (estimated time of arrival) for St. Maarten was 15:00 (3:00 P.M.). Earlier
in the flight, the passengers had been given an ETA of 14:42. The
ETA had been written on a form along with other information about
the flight, such as the cruising altitude and speed, and then handed
to the passengers to read and pass on. This time Wilfred announced
the new arrival time over the PA system.

Hugh Hart, who no longer had a reason to be in the cockpit now that Balsey and Harry were able to navigate by normal means, decided to step in back to stretch. He poured himself an orange juice then sat down on the aft-facing flight attendant jump seat next to the cockpit door.

The three flight attendants were busy making a final pass through the cabin. Once those tasks were completed, Margareth walked through the cabin and handed out individually wrapped pieces of candy before taking her seat in the aft jump seat. With the flight running late, Margareth glanced at her watch and tried to estimate if she would still have enough time to run to the duty-free store once they landed. She had bought a few items for her wedding in New York, but she was still hoping to get some champagne in St. Maarten. She smiled as she held the watch out in front of her. The watch actually belonged to her fiancé Robby. She had forgotten hers and Robby, who had driven her to the airport, offered her his watch, which had been a birthday gift from Margareth only a week earlier. Her thoughts undoubtedly turned to her upcoming wedding and the myriad tasks still before her.[1]

After securing the forward galley, Wilfred and Tobias took their seats. Wilfred sat down next to Hugh in the jump seat closest to the main cabin door. Tobias sat in a passenger seat next to the forward right overwing exit.

A few minutes passed when Hugh felt the aircraft bank to the right. The turn was unexpected, so Hugh stuck his head into the cockpit to find out what was going on. Balsey told him that they were diverting to San Juan because the weather at St. Maarten had deteriorated and was now below landing minimums. Hugh stepped inside the cockpit and closed the door behind him. He started to fill out some preliminary paperwork for the return trip to New York. He knew that the diversion to San Juan would put them behind schedule. There wouldn't be much time on the ground at St. Maarten once they got there. He remained standing and used the folded jump seat as a makeshift table to write on. The new clearance was direct to San Juan, maintain FL 210 (21,000 feet).

Two minutes later at 14:47, the San Juan Air Route Traffic Control Center (ARTCC), which had radar control of the aircraft, advised ALM 980 that the St. Maarten control tower operator wanted to speak to them on the tower frequency. The following is the recorded transcript of that radio call (Balsey is the one making the call):[2]

18:48 LM980:   Juliana tower, nine eight zero over.

Juliana tower: LM980, Juliana tower go ahead.

LM980:   Well, I just got a message you were below minimums from San Juan ... ah, so I've already started my diversion for San Juan. Where did the message come you were below minimums?

Juliana Tower: Roger, that is what we passed to the center, but at the present time there is a slight improvement. It calls for estimated ceiling 1,000 broken, 5,000 overcast, visibility 4 to 5 nautical miles in continuous rain.[3]

18:49 LM980:   What is your visibility please?

Juliana tower: Four to 5 nautical miles in continuous rain and intermittent rain showers.

LM980:   Standby one.

18:50 LM980:   Juliana, nine eight zero...it's almost impossi-
               ble to work you this frequency...you are being
               blocked completely... ah, would you give me
               your visibility again at the present time?

Juliana tower: Roger, I'll say again, 4 to 5 nautical miles in
                 continuous rain and rain showers.

LM980:   Uh, Roger, and do you have these continuous
             rain showers coming over at the present time?

Juliana tower: Negative sir, not at the present time. They
                 have moved westward.

LM980:   Uh, Roger, what's your ceiling right now?

Juliana tower: Estimated ceiling 1,000 broken, 5,000
                 overcast.

LM980:   Okay...standby one...I'll go back to San Juan.

Balsey was now faced with a difficult decision. A little over five minutes had elapsed since he had first begun his diversion to San Juan. In that time, they had not only burned additional fuel, they had also increased the distance between themselves and St. Maarten. Every minute they proceeded toward San Juan the farther away from St. Maarten they traveled. The NDB approach to runway 9 required a ceiling of 600 feet and a visibility of 2 nm (visibility is the only required approach criterion). The weather provided by the Juliana tower operator of ceilings of 1,000 broken, 5000 overcast, visibility 4 to 5 nautical miles, was well above minimums. But the tower operator's comments about continuous rain showers were reason for concern, especially since minutes earlier the airport had been reported to be below minimums. (Wind direction and speed were not given or requested in this initial radio call. The winds, however, would play an important role in what was to take place later.)

An NDB approach is a non-precision approach, meaning no vertical guidance is provided. All the pilot has to guide him to the runway is a needle that always points to the station, which may or may not be located on the airport. The St. Maarten NDB was located south of the runway. The approach was a full fifteen degrees offset from the runway centerline. Airline pilots rarely fly NDB approaches, except in training. Some airlines today don't even allow their pilots to accept NDB approaches because of their lack of precision. Balsey, however, was a flight instructor. He had spent most of the previous summer in Augusta, Georgia training pilots and had seen more NDB approaches in one month than most pilots see in their entire career. Shooting an NDB approach in marginal weather was not a major concern for him.

There were, however, other factors to consider. Diverting to San Juan would mean an extra hour of flying time on a route that was already pushing eight hours. The crew's duty time would also be increased by several hours as they waited for the weather to clear. Then there is the hassle factor involved with any diversion: dispatch has to be called; the plane has to be refueled; a decision has to be made as to whether to leave the passengers on the plane or let them deplane, in which case the passengers have to be rounded up again when it's time to depart. Landing in St. Maarten was definitely the better of the two choices from an operational standpoint.

To what extent Balsey included Harry and Hugh in on his decision is unclear. In May 1970, the concept of Crew Resource

Management or CRM had not yet been developed.[4] Certainly Hugh and Harry would have had opinions on the matter. In fairness to them, though, neither crewmember was likely to disagree with Balsey. Hugh was not a pilot and was unfamiliar with the performance capabilities of the DC-9. Harry had flown only once in the previous three months, and he was flying with an FAA designated flight examiner, who also happened to be the former chief pilot. It would have been difficult for any pilot in Harry's position to challenge the captain on what amounted to a judgment call.

Forty-five seconds after talking with the Juliana control tower, Balsey asked the San Juan Center for a direct heading to St. Maarten. The fuel totalizer indicated 5,800 pounds of fuel. Balsey estimated that they would land at St. Maarten at 15:05 with 4,400 pounds of fuel remaining. The legal minimum was 4,300 pounds (2,100 pounds of fuel to the alternate plus 2,200 pounds of hold fuel). It was enough fuel in Balsey's mind to at least go down and take a look. If the weather turned sour on the approach, he would proceed to his alternate of St. Thomas.

Chapter 11

AFTER CHECKING BACK ON THE FREQUENCY, ALM 980 was re-cleared direct to the St. Maarten radio beacon (identifier PJM) and given a clearance to descend to 10,000 feet. The weather north of San Juan was hazy but clear with just a few cumulus clouds. The weather toward St. Maarten, however, looked more ominous with towering cumulus visible in the distance. Balsey turned the radar on to get a better look. Precipitation returns filled the screen. He tilted the radar antenna down toward the water in hope of picking up St. Maarten. The Juliana airport didn't have distance measuring equipment. One way to determine the distance from the airport was to point the radar antenna toward the water. Depending on the scale the radar was set to, it was easy to determine distance. If the radar was set to the eighty-mile scale and a shoreline was visible halfway down the scope, then the island was forty miles away. This time, however, they couldn't pick out the shoreline. There was too much precipitation.*

---

* The weather radar on the DC-9 used a monochrome display, making it even more difficult to discern ground returns from precipitation.

Shortly after reaching 10,000 feet, San Juan Center issued a vector of 090 degrees due to conflicting traffic with another inbound aircraft to St. Maarten.[1] The DC-9 was the faster of the two aircraft and would be cleared for the approach once the other aircraft was out of the way. The second aircraft was told to hold over the beacon at 5,000 feet. ALM 980 was then cleared to descend to 6,000 feet. The short vector would not normally have been a concern, but the turn took them away from the airport and cost them additional fuel.

With the conflicting traffic out of the way, ALM 980 was re-cleared direct to the PJM radio beacon and cleared for the NDB approach to runway nine. Descending through 5,000 feet, they were told to contact the Juliana control tower. On their initial contact with the tower, they were given a visibility of 2 to 3 nautical miles. The tower operator also reported that it was raining at the airport.

The runway at St. Maarten was 5,249 feet long. It was a short runway for a jet aircraft. When the runway is wet, landing distance is increased significantly.[2] While Balsey didn't pull out any landing charts to check to see what effect the wet runway would have on their landing distance, he knew it was going to take every square-inch of runway to stop the plane.

The NDB approach began at the PJM radio beacon, which was located on the airfield. As they neared the NDB, the tower operator reported the winds as 090 at 8 to 10 knots.[3] The ceiling was reported as 800 scattered, 1,000 broken, 5,000 overcast. Visibility was given as 2 to 3 nautical miles. What the crew was seeing outside their windows, however, did not correspond with the weather that was being reported. They were level at 2,500 feet and almost directly over the airport, but their forward visibility was practically zero due to heavy rain showers. Concerned about the poor visibility, Harry asked for another visibility report as they passed over the beacon and proceeded outbound on the approach. Once again the tower operator reported a visibility of 2 to 3 nautical miles.

The weather reports given by the tower operator were estimates based on visual observations and pilot reports. Visibility was determined by reference points located on the mountains to the east. There were no visual references looking west toward the water where the approach was to be conducted. As the crew would soon discover, the visibility west and northwest of the airport was significantly less than 2 to 3 nautical miles.

The first part of the NDB approach involves a maneuver known as the procedure turn. The purpose of the procedure is to turn the aircraft around so it is aligned with the inbound course. During this portion of the approach, the tower operator, apparently concerned about the weather, advised ALM 980 that it was free to make any turns as necessary in the event of a missed approach.

After completing the procedure turn, Balsey called for gear down and flaps to twenty-five degrees. He slowed to 140 knots then started his descent to 600 feet, which was the lowest altitude he could descend to on the approach. He elected to leave the flaps at twenty-five degrees. A higher flap setting would have required a much higher power setting. Flying the approach in that configuration was standard operating procedure for ONA at the time. Balsey told Hugh and Harry to keep an eye out for the runway. Harry reported to the tower that they had completed the procedure turn. The tower operator acknowledged the transmission and gave an updated wind report of 060 at 15 knots gusting to 20 knots. The winds had shifted to the northeast and had increased by 10 knots.

Hugh Hart elected to remain standing rather than strap himself into the jump seat. He wedged himself in behind Balsey's seat in order to get a better look outside. He saw occasional vertical glimpses of the water, but forward visibility was still poor.

Hugh and Harry kept their attention focused outside as the rain continued to pound against the windscreen. It was coming down so hard in some places it was like flying through a car wash. The ride was fairly smooth — just an occasional bump in the heavier areas of precipitation. Reaching 600 feet, they were in and out of the clouds. It was obvious to each of them that this was going to be a tight approach. Spotting the runway in time to set up for a landing was going to be difficult. As they neared the airport, the rain lightened and the visibility improved. Hugh was first to spot the runway. He saw the bright Visual Approach Slope Indicator (VASI) lights on the left side of the runway.[4] Balsey and Harry spotted the VASI lights shortly after Hugh pointed them out, but the runway was well left of their position. They were too close and too high to get properly aligned for landing.

The weather directly over the airport and to the north appeared somewhat better. Balsey had good visual contact with the runway and decided to circle the airport to the north to make a visual landing. The controller had already approved him to make whatever turns he needed. Balsey stayed at 600 feet and began his circle to the left, telling Harry to keep an eye out for the hills east of the airport. He left the gear down and the flaps at 25 degrees. Doing so allowed him to make a tighter turn, but the added drag from the gear and flaps required additional power to maintain altitude.

The ceiling was ragged, and precipitation northwest of the airport made it difficult for Balsey to keep the runway in sight. Poor visibility forced him to stay in tighter to the runway than he would have liked. As he turned from base leg to final, he overshot the runway and flew through the final. He was well south of the runway centerline. Unable to realign the aircraft in time, Balsey was once again forced to go around.

The winds at the airport had shifted from the east at the start of the first approach to the northwest at some point during the second landing attempt. It's unclear from the record whether the crew was given this information. Balsey did, however, call for full flaps on the next landing attempt in an effort to keep from overshooting the run-way. Flying at 128 knots as opposed to 140 knots, Balsey was able to align the aircraft as he made the turn from base to final. But as he pulled the power back, he realized that he was too high. He shoved the yoke forward, but the sink rate increased to over 1,500 feet a minute. Rather than force the aircraft onto a wet runway in an unsta-bilized approach with both engines unspooled, Balsey was forced to once again pull up. Had he continued, the aircraft would have more than likely run off the end of the runway and into the bay at St. Maarten. The DC-9 passed over the end of the runway at 200 feet. Balsey called for flaps to 25 degrees. He left the gear down because he wanted to stay close to the airport. He was afraid of losing visual contact with the mountains to the east.[5]

Balsey had already made the decision that if he was unsuccessful on the third landing attempt he was going to proceed to his alternate of St. Thomas. He was too busy flying the airplane to look at his fuel. The last time he remembered looking at it was on the downwind leg of the third landing attempt. At that time, he noted that he had 3,800 pounds of fuel.[*] He needed 2,100 pounds of fuel to reach St. Thomas. Surely he hadn't burned up that much fuel in the last landing attempt. He climbed back up to 600 feet and made a wide circle to the north. The plane veered far enough to the north that some residents on the French side of the island heard the plane flying overhead. Balsey continued turning until the aircraft passed almost directly over the tower cab. He called for the gear and flaps and told Harry to tell the tower that they were going to their alternate. Harry raised the gear

---

[*] Balsey testified that he had noted the 3,800 pound figure on the downwind leg of the second circling approach. A fuel study conducted by the Douglas Aircraft Company (DACO) and the Safety Board concluded that the 3,800 pound figure could only have been taken sometime between the time of completion of the NDB approach and the start of the first left-hand circling approach and not later. (Official NTSB report NTSB-AAR-71-8.)

and flaps and made the call to the tower. When the tower operator didn't respond, Balsey got on the radio: "Juliana, nine eighty. We would like to have an immediate and direct route to St. Thomas." He said it in an authoritative voice that left no doubt in the controller's mind that there was no time to waste. The controller acknowledged the request and cleared them to 4,000 feet. Two minutes later at 19:31 GMT (3:31 P.M.), the Juliana tower operator told ALM 980 to contact San Juan center. Shortly after they left the frequency, the tower operator closed the airport due to low ceilings and visibility.

The passengers were fully aware that there was some difficulty in landing at St. Maarten. Many of them had had their eyes glued to the windows as the plane banked repeatedly. Emerson Ussery had flown into St. Maarten hundreds of times and knew the layout of the airport and surrounding terrain. Emerson had lost an eye in a bow and arrow accident when he was ten, but even with only one good eye he could tell that they were circling dangerously low to the ground. He continued to monitor the approaches by looking out the windows over the shoulders of other passengers. He couldn't help noticing that the woman sitting next to him in seat 1E appeared nervous throughout the multiple landing attempts.

"What's going to happen?" the woman asked after the second failed landing attempt.

"Don't worry," Emerson said in an attempt to reassure the woman. "He'll make it." But Emerson had his doubts. He was well aware of the mountains on the east end of the runway. He was secretly hoping that they would abandon the approach and head for their alternate.

Jeannie Larmony, sitting in 16A, kept her eyes peeled to the window. She caught brief glimpses of the water and land, but the clouds and rain obscured her view most of the time. On the last circle, however, she was able to see the ground for an extended period of time.

The plane was flying so low that she became concerned that they might hit a tree or the roof of a house.

Rick Arnold, sitting behind Gene and Loretta Gremelsbacker, wasn't overly concerned. He was well aware of the fact that the aircraft was making multiple approaches and that there seemed to be a lot of banking going on, but the ride itself wasn't particularly rough or uncomfortable. Had he been able to see outside, he might have had a better sense of the struggle going on inside the cockpit. The only clues he had that the pilots were having trouble were the sound of the engines and the sound of the hydraulic pumps, which came on every time the flaps and slats were raised or extended. When the banking stopped and the landing gear was raised, his thoughts turned to guessing which island they were going to next.

Sitting directly behind the cockpit and facing rearward, Wilfred Spencer was wondering the same thing. His view outside the aircraft was restricted. He had only the small windows in the main cabin door and galley door to peer through. He had been a flight steward long enough to recognize that they were probably headed for somewhere other than St. Maarten. He also knew not to bother the flight crew in this situation. It was best to wait until he was given further instructions. He glanced back toward the cabin and noticed a few quizzical stares directed his way. He sat back against his seat and hoped that the pilots would make some announcement. Wilfred didn't know that the PA system wasn't working.

Chapter 12

PASSING OVER THE ST. MAARTEN RADIO BEACON, Balsey took up a westerly heading for St. Thomas. Hugh, who was still standing in the cockpit, glanced down at the fuel totalizer. The digits on the totalizer were spinning erratically.

"Balsey," Hugh said, pointing to the totalizer, "this sonofabitch is spinning like hell."

"It should stop spinning when we level out," Balsey said. The plane was in a nose-high attitude and rocking from side to side in moderate turbulence.

Leveling at 4,000 feet, Hugh once again glanced down at the fuel totalizer. "You're kidding," Hugh said incredulously. The totalizer was indicating just 850 pounds. Balsey again assured Hugh that the bad readings were due to their low fuel status and the turbulence. "When we get into some smooth air, she'll stable out," Balsey said. "There's no way we can have less than 2,000 pounds of fuel on board this aircraft." Seconds later, the totalizer started spinning again. It was spinning like a slot machine whose lever had just been pulled. It went from 800 pounds to 2,000 pounds and then back down again.

The one reading they noted that registered the longest was 1,400 pounds. Harry pointed out that the fuel-used counter for the right engine was showing 13,156 pounds. This was an indication of how much fuel the engine had burned. The second engine had a similar reading. Harry doubled the figure for a total fuel burn of just over 26,300 pounds. Since they had started with 28,900 pounds of fuel, there should have been 2,600 pounds remaining in the tanks.* They only needed 2,100 pounds to make it to St. Thomas.

Harry called San Juan Center. The following is the recorded transcript of the communication between ALM 980 and San Juan Center. (Note: Both Balsey and Harry were talking on the radio. There is no way to determine who was talking at any given time. However, it would be safe to assume that whenever a transmission was made in the first person that it was likely being made by Balsey. Some of the communications have been edited out due to redundancy. Times are based on UTC — Coordinated Universal Time — 1900 = 3:00 P.M. Atlantic Time. The flight was operating in the Atlantic time zone, which is equivalent to Eastern time when the U.S. is on Daylight Savings time.)

1931:15   ALM 980:   San Juan, nine eighty.

1931:20   SJU ARTCC: Antillean nine eighty, San Juan
                         Center...er...squawk...ah...two one
                         zero and ident. Verify maintaining
                         four thousand.

---

* Fuel burned by the APU is not recorded on the engine fuel-used counters. If you subtract the 250 pounds of fuel estimated to have been burned by the APU prior to takeoff, that still would have left approximately 2,350 pounds of fuel in the tanks (2,600 - 250 = 2,350). That figure is very close to what the DACO fuel study indicated the aircraft should have had at that point in the flight. (Note: The official NTSB report has a math error of 100 pounds in reference to these numbers.)

1931:22   ALM 980:   Four thousand (unintelligible).

1931:24   SJU ARTCC: Antillean nine eighty, roger, standby for higher.

1931:25   SJU ARTCC: Antillean nine eighty ident again, please.

1932:40   SJU ARTCC: Antillean nine eighty radar contact, uh...one two miles northwest of (unintelligible), traffic...eh...(unintelligible) twelve o'clock ten miles landing... ah...St. Maarten. [This is the aircraft holding at the beacon at 5,000 feet and the reason why the controller couldn't give him higher.]

1933:25   ALM 980:   San Juan, Antillean nine eighty.

1933:35   SJU ARTCC: Antillean...ah...nine eight zero request your...ah...altitude you're requesting.

1933:45   ALM 980:   Anything you've got higher. I'm a little short on fuel and I gotta get up.

1933:45   SJU ARTCC: Nine eighty, roger, standby...ah...I'll have higher for you shortly.

By now the low-fuel status was on the minds of everyone in the cockpit. All eyes were glued to the spinning fuel totalizer. Balsey knew that he was burning through his precious fuel at an alarming rate. Each thousand feet higher he could get meant a little less fuel burn. Also in the back of his mind was the idea of getting to an altitude that even if he did flame out he could possibly still make it to the airport. He turned to Hugh and asked him to get the charts out to see if there was anything closer than St. Thomas. Hugh glanced at the chart and said that it looked like St. Croix was closer.

1934:30	SJU ARTCC:	Antillean nine eighty climb and maintain flight level one two zero. [12,000 feet]
1934:35	ALM980:	Roger, up to one two zero out of four.
1934:50	ALM 980:	Antillean nine eighty, do you have radar contact with us?
1934:55	SJU ARTCC:	Antillean nine eighty that is affirmative. You're on radar.
1934:58	ALM 980:	How far from St. Thomas are we?
1935:00	SJU ARTCC:	Roger, from St. Thomas you're nine two miles southeast.
1935:05	ALM 980:	Say again that distance please for nine eighty.
1935:10	SJU ARTCC:	Nine two miles southeast.
1936:10	ALM 980:	San Juan, Antillean nine eight zero.

1936:12   SJU ARTCC: Nine eight zero, San Juan Center.

1936:15   ALM 980:   How far am I from St. Croix?

1936:17   SJU ARTCC: Nine eighty, you're from St. Croix...
you're seventy miles northeast, seven
zero miles.

1936:20   ALM 980:   Okay, how's the weather at St. Croix?

1936:25   SJU ARTCC: The St. Croix weather is...ah...two
thousand scattered (unintelligible)
thousand overcast, visibility one five.

1936:30   ALM 980:   Okay, I'd like to divert to St. Croix.

1936:35   SJU ARTCC: Nine eighty cleared present position
direct St. Croix maintain one two
thousand.

1936:37   ALM 980:   Roger nine eight zero.

Balsey turned to Harry and asked him to get the approach charts
out for St. Croix. Harry fumbled with the chart books trying to find
the correct one. "They're in the Caribbean Jep book!" Balsey
snapped. Harry grabbed the Caribbean chart book and quickly
thumbed through to where the St. Croix charts were supposed to be.
The St. Croix approach charts weren't there. Harry held the book
up for Balsey to see that the charts weren't where they were supposed to be. The charts were most likely in the book but misfiled.

Balsey didn't have time to look through the chart book himself. He'd have to get the information from the controller later.

At some point after getting the clearance to St. Croix, Wilfred Spencer opened the cockpit door and asked if anyone had called him. The red flight attendant call light had come on, indicating a call from the cockpit. Someone in the cockpit said that they hadn't called him, and Wilfred closed the door and returned to his seat. Later during questioning, neither of the three cockpit crewmembers could remember this incident. While the three men in the cockpit were busy with multiple tasks, Wilfred was not so preoccupied. He is certain that the call light came on and that he was turned away from the cockpit. The incident is important in the final outcome because precious seconds would pass before Wilfred would once again be called to the cockpit — seconds lost that could have been used in preparing the cabin.[*]

As they approached 7,000 feet, the ride improved and the fuel totalizer indicated a steady 550 pounds. A few seconds later a yellow caution light on the annunciator panel blinked on momentarily. It was on just long enough for Balsey to see that it was the right fuel inlet pressure light. Balsey reached up and turned on all the boost pumps, then opened the fuel crossfeed, which allowed all four fuel tanks to feed fuel to the engines. He wanted to squeeze every drop of fuel out of the tanks. If Balsey had any doubts about the accuracy of his fuel readings before the light came on, he didn't have any now. For the first time since departing St. Maarten, Balsey seriously considered the possibility that he might have to ditch the aircraft. He turned to Hugh and told him that he'd better get the purser up to the cockpit. One of the three men

---

[*] When Wilfred testified in San Juan, he recounted this incident. When I interviewed him, he informed me that he had actually been called and turned away from the cockpit twice before he was finally told to prepare the cabin. Both Balsey and Hugh have no recollection of this happening. Harry Evans has elected to not be interviewed. I have chosen to go with the official record of him being turned away just once.

pressed the flight attendant call button. Hugh, who had already come to the same conclusion as Balsey about the seriousness of the situation, grabbed the spare life vest from under the jump seat and was in the process of ripping open the plastic packaging when Wilfred opened the cockpit door. Hugh looked at the startled Wilfred. "Problems," Hugh said, shaking his head, "we're running out of gas." Wilfred stepped into the cockpit and closed the door behind him. "We're running out of fuel," Balsey said. "We might have to ditch the aircraft."

Wilfred could tell by the look on Hugh and Harry's faces that the situation was serious. Several seconds went by without anyone making a comment. When nothing else was said, Wilfred asked, "Shall I inform the passengers?" Once again the cockpit fell silent. Up until this point, everything that had transpired could be chalked up to bad luck. If they were to make it to St. Croix, it would probably be the last any of them would hear about the whole incident. But telling the purser to prepare the cabin for an emergency landing was a different matter altogether. Regardless of the outcome, there would be some explaining to do.

Finally, Harry Evans turned toward Balsey. "Captain, I think we have to inform [them] now."[*]

"Go ahead, Spence," Balsey said. "Inform the passengers."

Pilots in emergency situations often draw on past experiences to help them deal with their current crisis. An engine failure, for example, might be considered a minor problem to a pilot who has had prior engine failures. Balsey was a flight examiner. He was a former Air Force pilot with over 12,000 hours of flight time. He had experienced

---

[*] Wilfred testified that Harry had said, "Captain, I think we have to inform *him* now," the implication being that Harry was referring to Balsey informing the purser and not so much the passengers. One possible scenario is that Harry and Balsey had argued about the need to notify the flight attendants of the possibility of having to ditch. This would explain Wilfred having been called to the cockpit and then turned away.

numerous emergencies in his career. One emergency in particular flashed through his mind. He was flying a DC-6 on a MATS flight from Europe across the Atlantic. An hour or two into the flight, Balsey noticed a decrease in airspeed. The aircraft felt unstable. Balsey turned his wing lights on and discovered that they were loaded with ice. He was having trouble maintaining his altitude. The anti-icing equipment was already turned on, but the ice was accumulating faster than the de-icing equipment could discard it. The aircraft began vibrating so severely from the ice on the wings and tail that Balsey felt that he might have to ditch the aircraft. He called the flight attendant forward and told her to prepare the cabin for ditching. Upon hearing this unfortunate news, the flight attendant promptly fainted. Balsey asked the navigator to assist the flight attendant; he then sent the navigator in back to help get the cabin ready for the possible ditching. Balsey finally got the aircraft stabilized at around 10,000 feet. He was able to maintain that altitude until reaching Harmon Air Force Base, where he landed safely. If there was any reluctance on Balsey's part to inform the purser of the possibility of having to ditch, this prior incident was most likely a factor in his hesitation.

As soon as Wilfred left the cockpit, Balsey picked up the mike and radioed San Juan Center.

1938:10	ALM 980:	San Juan, Antillean nine eight zero.
1938:12	SJU ARTCC:	Nine eighty go ahead.
1938:15	ALM 980:	Roger, I'm running pretty low on fuel. How far am I from St. Croix now?
1938:20	SJU ARTCC:	Okay, standby one.

1938:25   ALM 980:   ...and you might...ah...send (unintelligible) need some help.

1938:26   SJU ARTCC: Say again.

Balsey knew that he was in serious trouble. He had maybe five to seven minutes of fuel on board if he was to believe the 550-pound figure. At 250 knots, he was traveling at just over four miles a minute, not accounting for winds. That gave him about twenty to thirty miles of flying before the engines quit. He had been seventy miles away from St. Croix the last time he had talked to San Juan. The numbers weren't adding up, and he knew it.

He looked outside and saw only clouds and rain. He was passing through 7,000 feet in the climb to 12,000. He had no idea what the bases of the clouds were, but he knew that he didn't want to make a power-off descent in instrument conditions and then try to ditch the aircraft. He turned to Harry and Hugh. "You know, we don't stand a chance if we flame out at altitude. We're going to have to get this thing down."[1]

1938:30   SJU ARTCC: Antillean nine eighty, say again.

1938:35   ALM 980:   I'd like to descend now.

1938:38   SJU ARTCC: Okay, descend and maintain five thousand.

1938:40   ALM 980:   Okay, I'm leaving seven for five.

1938:42   SJU ARTCC: Roger.

Balsey had the second radio tuned to St. Maarten's tower frequency. He decided to give the tower operator another call, thinking he might be better off going back to St. Maarten. The St. Maarten tower operator reported the weather as 800 scattered, 1,000 broken to overcast, visibility 2 nautical miles. He then added, "it looks as if it is deteriorating."

St. Maarten was definitely out, Balsey concluded. It was going to be St. Croix or the water.

1938:55	ALM 980:	San Juan, nine eight zero.
1938:57	SJU ARTCC:	Nine eight zero, go ahead.
1939:05	ALM 980:	How far am I from...ah...St. Croix now?
1939:05	SJU ARTCC:	Nine eighty, you're...ah...fifty seven miles.
1939:20	ALM 980:	San Juan, nine eight zero.
1939:22	SJU ARTCC:	Antillean nine eighty, go ahead.
1939:25	ALM 980:	Okay, there's a possibility I may have to ditch this aircraft. I am now descending to the water.

When the controller heard this transmission, he immediately notified his supervisor who in turn called the Coast Guard to alert them of the possible ditching.

Balsey began the process of mentally preparing himself for putting the plane in the water. Normally, if a ditching is imminent, it is preferable to be at a higher altitude to allow for a better approach to the water. The DC-9, however, is not the best glider. A higher altitude would require a pronounced nose-down attitude in order to maintain enough airspeed to prevent the aircraft from stalling, not the best attitude for ditching. More importantly, however, they were in instrument conditions and unable to see the water.

Balsey also had to decide whether to go in with the gear up or down. The recommended procedure is to ditch with the gear in the up position. There are, however, proponents who say that ditching with the gear down is preferred because it prevents the aircraft from skipping over the water, which leads to secondary impacts.

Sea conditions were another important consideration. In calm winds, it is preferable to land parallel to the swells. In stronger winds, it is best to crab slightly into the wind while still trying to land parallel to the swells. Say, for example, the winds are out of the west and the swell movement is west to east; the aircraft should be headed north or south with an appropriate crab for the wind. In addition, the goal is to land on the crest or back side of the swell. The worst way to ditch an aircraft is to land in the face of a swell.[2]

All of these things were running through Balsey's mind while at the same time he was still hand-flying the aircraft, navigating to St. Croix, and talking on the radio. He was doing exactly what every pilot is taught to do in an emergency: aviate, navigate, and communicate. It could also be argued, though, that he was doing too much and that he should have delegated more of the workload to the other two crewmembers.

Passing through four thousand feet, they were still in the clouds and on instruments. Balsey started to slow his descent. He didn't want to be in a steep descent when he broke out of the overcast.

"I'm going to fly this until we get the first dry tank indication," Balsey announced. While he still had hopes of making it to St. Croix, there were some advantages to ditching with power. It would give him a little maneuvering flexibility. But if he ditched the aircraft with the engines still running, how would he explain that to investigators?

Hugh reached over the center console to tilt the radar down, hoping to pick out St. Croix. There was still too much precipitation to see much of anything.

"You better get back to the cabin and see if you can help out," Balsey told Hugh.

Hugh reached for the cockpit door but hesitated. He was considering whether or not to don his life vest. He didn't want to alarm the passengers, but at the same time, he didn't want to get caught without a life vest should they actually have to ditch. He put the vest over his head and secured the straps around his waist. When he opened the cockpit door, he saw Tobias standing in the aisle giving the life vest demonstration. He couldn't see into the cabin past Tobias, so he went to the galley to make sure everything was secure and that there weren't any loose items lying around. He returned briefly to the cockpit and removed Balsey's flight bag and his own briefcase from behind Balsey's seat, placing them in a coat closet. He noticed Balsey was having some difficulty with his shoulder harness, so he extended it for him and placed it on his lap. He turned around to check on the progress in the cabin and spotted Wilfred walking up the aisle. "Are they ready?" Hugh asked Wilfred. When Wilfred indicated that they were, Hugh passed it on to Balsey that the cabin was ready.[*]

---

[*] Wilfred testified that he did not tell the navigator that the cabin was ready. When Hugh asked him if they were ready, Wilfred was referring to the fact that he had completed the life vest demonstrations and that, as far as he knew, all of the passengers had their vests on.

Chapter 13

A S WILFRED WAS LEAVING THE COCKPIT TO PREPARE the cabin for the possible ditching, Hugh Hart asked him if it was okay to use the life vest that he was holding in his hands. The oddly-colored pink life vest had the note "Do Not Remove" imprinted on the plastic covering. Wilfred assured him that it was okay to use the vest. He left the cockpit and walked down the aisle toward the rear of the aircraft. He called to Tobias as he passed the overwing exit where Tobias was sitting. "*Tito, nos tin ku duna demonstrashon di life vest awor unbes,*" he said in Papiamento. Papiamento was the language the flight attendants most often used when conversing with each other. The English translation of what he said was: "Tito, we have to give the life vest demonstration right away." A passenger sitting nearby would later testify that Wilfred had said something to the effect of, "Come with me, something's cooking."

When Wilfred was told to prepare for a possible ditching, he had several important decisions to make. Since the captain hadn't given him a specific timeframe, he had to determine which tasks to perform first. Preparing the cabin for an emergency landing involves many steps: informing the remaining flight attendants of the emergency; informing the passengers; going through the cabin to make sure there are no loose items; making sure everyone has their seat belts secured; making sure that all the window shades are opened (this allows crew members and passengers to see outside as well as allow emergency crews to see inside). Time permitting, the flight attendants must also demonstrate and explain the brace position; have the passengers remove sharp objects such as pens, tie clasps, hair pins, as well as remove ties, high heeled shoes and eyeglasses; secure the galleys; and reposition passengers who can help with the opening of emergency exits. This particular emergency had the added necessity of getting the passengers into their life vests. Since some of the items related to preparing the cabin had already been accomplished prior to the planned landing in St. Maarten, Wilfred decided that the first task to be accomplished was to get everyone into their life vests. The other tasks could be accomplished as time permitted.

Wilfred gathered Tobias and Margareth in the back of the cabin and gave them a quick run-down of the situation as he understood it, telling them that they were running low on fuel and that they were to prepare the cabin for a possible ditching. He told them to use their own life vests and not to use the demonstration life vests, which had no compressed air. Margareth and Tobias already knew this, but it was Wilfred's job to remind them.[1]

When Tobias first heard that they were running low on fuel, he thought about a remark that he had heard from another flight attendant concerning the New York–St. Maarten flights. Tobias had worked several ONA flights prior to this one. It wasn't his job to know how much fuel the plane carried. But the flight attendants who worked the ONA trips knew that it was a fuel-critical flight. For one thing, they all knew of the possibility of having to stop in Bermuda for fuel. They had also heard rumors about an extra fuel tank that was supposed to have been installed. More alarming, though, were the remarks made by some of the ALM pilots who quietly referred to the ONA flights as "suicide missions." The ALM pilots felt that there was a good possibility that the plane would run out of fuel. They felt if it were going to happen, it would most likely happen on the return flight to New York, where traffic congestion might delay the arrival.

Tobias was concerned but not frightened. Even though he had been a flight steward for less than a year, he had already experienced several non-routine flights. He was on one flight in which the pilots had an indication that the landing gear wasn't down. He and the other flight attendants had to prepare for a possible emergency landing. It turned out to be a faulty indication. He was on another flight in which the plane was set to land during a heavy snowstorm in New York but had to go around at the last minute due to poor visibility. In every case the plane had always landed safely without incident. It was the nature of the business to be cautious. This confidence that things would work out allowed the three flight attendants to do their jobs calmly and professionally. The passengers likewise took their cues from the flight attendants. There was no panic in the cabin.

Tobias and Margareth grabbed their life vests from under the flight attendant jump seats and took their positions in the cabin — Margareth in front and Tobias in the middle. Wilfred used the PA system in the rear of the cabin. Wilfred had had his share of non-routine flights himself. This one, however, he sensed was different. He had seen the navigator holding his life vest. He heard the tension in the voices of the crew members. Still, there was no indication that a ditching was imminent. He proceeded under the assumption that there would at least be a warning should the aircraft actually be forced to ditch.* He told the passengers that the plane was running low on fuel and that the captain had requested that they prepare for a possible ditching as a "precautionary measure." He gave the instructions in English and from memory. He instructed them to not inflate their life vests until they were in the water. There are several reasons for this: An inflated life vest is constraining and could interfere with the person's ability to exit the aircraft. An inflated life vest is also vulnerable to puncture inside the aircraft. The most valid reason for not inflating the life vest inside the aircraft is that if the cabin were to rapidly fill up with water, the wearer might be unable to reach the exit.[†2] The passengers were also told to tighten the straps around their waists, but not too tightly. The rationale behind this policy was to prevent a feeling of constraint. But many passengers were rightfully confused by this instruction. How tight is too tight? Why wouldn't you want the straps as tight as possible?

Nothing was said about life rafts. Wilfred also failed to mention where the life vests were located. Most passengers knew to look under their seats either from the previous briefing or from the emergency briefing cards. Those who didn't know where to find their vests quickly observed the other passengers or were assisted by the flight attendants. There was also no attempt made to enlist the help of passengers by placing them in seats where they could help with

---

* ALM's ditching procedures called for the captain to first announce "emergency stations," which was the crew's signal to proceed to their assigned evacuation station. Prior to impact, the captain was to announce "safety positions," which was the crew's signal to have the passengers assume the brace position. Wilfred was not aware that the PA system was out.
† There are also proponents who claim that it is better to inflate the life vest inside rather than waiting until you exit the aircraft. Some of the reasons for this include: If the plane were to break apart, you would be better off having the vest inflated; if you were injured or left unconscious after impact, you might be unable to pull the tabs; lastly, once a person is in the water, the inflation tabs are beneath the surface and may be more difficult to locate. The recommended procedure, though, is still to wait until exiting the aircraft.

the launching of life rafts. In Wilfred's defense, after he made the announcement about the life vests, he was immediately preoccupied with helping passengers. He also had other duties to perform — such as positioning the forward life raft and removing the slide bars from the two front doors. He did what he thought was the most prudent thing to do with the information he had at the time, and that was to get the passengers into their vests as soon as possible.

The life vests were located in a pouch beneath each passenger seat. The pouch had a strap-and-snap fastener holding the life vest in place. The pouch and strap were designed so that passengers could easily remove the vests while seated without having to remove their seatbelts. Although a few passengers were able to accomplish this task, most had difficulty. Some had to undo their seatbelts in order to reach far enough beneath them to reach the pouch. Some couldn't undo the snap. One passenger actually ripped the snap off in an attempt to free his life vest. More than a few people were forced to get out of their seats and onto their knees. Even then some had difficulty undoing the snaps, which had to be pulled down to open. At least one passenger testified that there was no vest in the pouch beneath his seat and that he was forced to remove one from an adjacent seat.

The life vests were sealed inside a protective plastic cover. Many passengers had difficulty with the pull tabs on the covers. Some were easier to open than others. One passenger used a pocket knife to free his vest.

Donning the life vest presented additional problems for the passengers, despite their having had two prior demonstrations. Part of the difficulty was due to the fact that there were two different types of vests on board, each with different methods of donning and securing. One type of vest required the wearer to connect the waist straps to a D-ring located in the front of the vest. The second type of vest had permanent attachments to the waist straps. Many passengers put their vests on correctly and secured the waist straps but neglected to tighten the straps around their waist.[3]

One passenger, after successfully donning and securing his life vest, asked Margareth if it would be better to not fasten his seatbelt, arguing that he would be able to get out faster if the seatbelt wasn't fastened. Margareth assured him that it was best to fasten his seatbelt.*

Wilfred walked from the rear of the plane toward the front, helping passengers as he made his way up the aisle. One man had his vest on backwards. Another man asked Wilfred for help with his two little girls. The life vests were obviously too big, and the waist straps hung below the girls' knees. Wilfred tightened the straps between their legs as he had been instructed and then inflated both vests. This was the proper procedure for children who were too young to inflate the vests on their own.

When he reached the front of the cabin, he was met by Hugh, who wanted to know where the life rafts were located. Hugh hadn't had any formal emergency training on the DC-9; his natural instinct was to revert to his training on the DC-8. Hugh had been shown the raft locations on one of his two prior flights in the DC-9 but didn't want to rely on his memory now. When Wilfred told Hugh about the raft in the coat closet, Hugh asked Wilfred if it was the raft that needed to be repositioned. Wilfred told him yes, and together they went to the coat closet to remove the raft. There were a few loose items resting on top of the raft: some coats, newspapers, and one

---

* This conversation was overheard by passenger Martha Kellner, who was sitting directly behind the passenger who made the comment to Margareth. In an ironic twist of fate, the man who had made the argument for not securing his seatbelt did not survive. His seat was ripped from the floor and collapsed. Had he not been wearing his seatbelt there is some chance that he might have been thrown free and survived the ditching.

or two small bags. Hugh shoved those items to the back then grabbed the raft package and started to pull on it. The raft barely budged. The raft had flattened over time and was wedged in tightly. Hugh abandoned the task and returned to the cockpit. A passenger, Emerson Ussery, saw Wilfred struggling with the raft and got out of his seat to assist. Together they were able to pull the raft from the closet.[4]

Jeannie Larmony didn't have a problem locating her vest and removing it from the plastic pouch; she did have to unbuckle her seatbelt in order to reach under the seat. She put the vest on over her head while still seated. She was confused about what to do with the straps on the bottom of the vest. She looked up to see if she could find someone to assist her and was surprised to see two men standing in the aisle taking pictures. She watched incredulously as the two men worked their way up the aisle, stopping to take pictures of the two little girls, who were smiling and laughing and acting as if they were about to go swimming.

The two men taking pictures were not wearing life vests.* It's quite possible that their motivation for taking such a risk had something to do with another picture taken aboard a plane. The picture in question had been taken aboard a hijacked plane. The photograph had been published in *Life* magazine a few months earlier. The amount of money paid to the amateur photographer who took the fuzzy photo received more publicity than the hijacking.

Rick Arnold had to get out of his seat to get his life jacket. Once he retrieved it, he had no problem removing the vest from the plastic cover and putting it on. About this time, Loretta turned to Rick

---

* There is conflicting testimony whether one or both men were without their life vests. It's possible that one or both of them could have put their vests on at a later time.

and asked him if he wanted to sit with her and Gene. Rick took the aisle seat next to Loretta. Loretta was sitting in the middle seat and Gene had the window seat. Rick fastened his seatbelt. He looked around the cabin at the other passengers. He saw the female flight attendant walking down the aisle with one of the little girls. He didn't see anyone taking pictures, but he did catch a glimpse of the cockpit through the opened cockpit door. What he saw alarmed him — flashing warning lights. It was then he realized the seriousness of the situation. He turned to his friend Gene. Gene hadn't seen the warning lights, but there was no concealing the concern on his face as he told Loretta that he loved her.

Emerson Ussery reached under his seat to extract the life vest from the pouch. He found the pouch but couldn't undo the strap. He got out of his seat and onto his knees but still couldn't unfasten the strap. Frustrated, he finally gave up and removed the vest from beneath the unoccupied seat next to him. After putting on his life vest, Emerson helped the woman sitting next to him and then assisted an elderly man and woman across the aisle in seats 2A and 2B. He was so busy helping other passengers with their life vests that he didn't check to see if he had his on properly. He more or less just put it on around his head and neglected to secure the straps around his waist. Not once did he think about the briefcase with the $350,000 in cash, which was still sitting under his seat. At this moment, the $20 life vest was more important.

When Emerson noticed the purser having trouble pulling the life raft from the closet, he offered to help, and the two of them managed to get the raft out of the closet and into the aisle. Emerson returned to his seat and fastened his seatbelt.[5]

Once they had the raft out of the closet, Hugh, Wilfred, and Tobias dragged the raft to the forward galley. Hugh examined the raft package but couldn't find the inflation lanyard. He found the opening where the lanyard was supposed to be, but there was no handle. The raft had been packed incorrectly; the inflation lanyard was inside the protective bag that encased the raft and not accessible as it should have been. Hugh unfastened a few snaps from the raft case and found the lanyard. The lanyard was attached to a bundle of strings that had become entangled.

While Hugh worked on freeing the inflation lanyard, Tobias and Wilfred removed the girt bars from the cabin door and the galley door. The girt bar was a small metal bar that slid into two brackets attached to the floor. In the locked position, the girt bar provides automatic deployment of the emergency escape slide when the door is opened. Once the slide falls from the container, a crew member must then pull an inflation pin to inflate the slide.[*] The procedure in a ditching was to remove the girt bar. The escape slides on the DC-9 had no quick disconnect. If a slide was deployed in a water landing, there was no quick means of detaching it from the aircraft. There was also the problem of having the slide getting in the way of deploying the life raft.

The life raft weighed 125 pounds and required two people to lift it. The plan was to toss the raft out the main cabin door. There was no raft tie-down. They would have to hold on to the mooring line or try to find something to tie it to once it was launched. Otherwise, the raft would float away from the aircraft and be of no use to anyone. All three men were preoccupied with the life raft. Margareth was standing near the front of the cabin assisting two elderly people with their life vests.

---

[*] Newer escape slides found on most aircraft flying today will automatically inflate upon deployment.

With the flight attendants preoccupied in the front of the cabin, there was little supervision in the back of the plane. A few passengers in back elected to not put on their life vests, apparently feeling that the whole exercise was an unnecessary inconvenience. They would soon realize their mistake.

Chapter 14

TWENTY SECONDS AFTER BALSEY ANNOUNCED THAT there was a possibility he might have to ditch, the San Juan controller suggested that he return to St. Maarten, stating that St. Maarten was closer. Balsey was understandably confused by the controller's suggestion. What Balsey didn't know was that he was talking to a new controller, one that had just started his shift and didn't know anything about the multiple landing attempts at St. Maarten. Balsey asked for the weather at St. Maarten, thinking that perhaps there had been a sudden improvement. After a brief delay the controller replied that the weather was not VFR (visual flight rules).

By this time, Balsey had completely taken over operation of the radio. He didn't want to waste time relaying information through Harry. There were other aircraft on the frequency, and Balsey suggested to the controller that they both switch to 121.5, the civilian emergency frequency. When Balsey was unable to raise the controller on 121.5, he returned to 125.0 and requested that the frequency be cleared of all other traffic. He also asked to have any vessels in the area notified of the possible ditching.

Balsey still wasn't ready to give up on trying to reach St. Croix. He asked the controller what runway they were using. The controller indicated that they were using runway nine, which was opposite of Balsey's inbound heading to the airport. After receiving a wind report of 070 at 10 knots, Balsey requested a straight in landing to runway 27. He still didn't have the approach charts for St. Croix. He had to ask the controller for the runway length and the VOR radial to the field.

While Balsey was getting the St. Croix approach information from the controller, Hugh Hart entered the cockpit and said there was some confusion in back about whose procedure they were supposed to use regarding the repositioning of the life raft. "Go with their procedures," Balsey told Hugh. "I don't have time to teach school right now." Hugh had apparently remembered something having been said about not repositioning the life rafts on the DC-9 due to a lack of a raft tie down. The ALM flight attendants, in fact, had been told by Chris Linder to not reposition the life rafts. The management of ALM, however, had countermanded that instruction because they didn't want to confuse their flight attendants, who were trained to reposition the life rafts on the ALM DC-8. Hugh returned to the cabin but left the cockpit door partially open so he could communicate with Balsey and Harry.

Balsey turned to Harry and told him that he intended to stay clean all the way to the airport, adding that he wasn't going to call for the gear until they were over the runway.[1] He was going to keep flying until the plane fell out of the sky.

Passing through 1,200 feet, Balsey started to catch glimpses of the water. The more he saw, the more concerned he became. Huge swells rose and fell in all directions. It was the worst possible condition for ditching an aircraft. When Balsey looked over at Harry, he could tell that Harry was equally alarmed. Harry was staring straight ahead, transfixed by the swirling sea. Balsey felt that Harry was having a bad case of tunnel vision. He had seen it before with students in training. When a pilot is given more information than he can process, his mind will focus on only one or two tasks while discarding all other input. A pilot who has an engine failure on takeoff, for example, may be so focused on the fact that he has just lost an engine that he'll forget to bring the gear up. Tunnel vision, or cognitive narrowing as it is also called, is a factor in many aviation accidents. Balsey could sense that he was quickly closing in on the same state. As he looked out at the white caps, he felt as if the weight of the aircraft and all of its passengers was resting on his shoulders. He had reached a point where one more piece of information, one more sensory input, one more decision, would have been enough to send his brain into information overload. He resigned himself to the fact that he was going to have to ditch the aircraft, and he immediately calmed down. He discarded all input that didn't have to do with flying the airplane. He slowed his thinking processes down until everything from that point on seemed to proceed in slow motion.

Still in and out of the clouds, Balsey had a flashback of a discussion he had had with an old Air Force buddy concerning ditchings. The man's name was Charles Harpool. Balsey remembered Harpool talking about problems the Air Force was having with aircraft that were forced to ditch. The planes almost always became submerged when they hit the water, Harpool had told him. He told Balsey that if he ever had to ditch an airplane to make sure he took a gyro with him, referring to the attitude indicator.* That would at least provide an attitude reference that could help in preventing the plane from rolling over on its back.

---

* While it may seem improbable that Balsey had time to think about this prior conversation concerning ditchings, he mentioned it during questioning in St. Croix and in his testimony in San Juan.

At 500 feet they finally broke out below the overcast. The aircraft was still clean and flying at 160 knots. Balsey was thinking clearly now and he tried to determine the direction of the swell movement. He descended at hundred foot increments to improve his depth perception, all the while searching for any sign of land.

Hugh stuck his head into the cockpit. "What's our altitude?"

"Two hundred!" Harry yelled back.

"I'll give you a yell at the last second," Balsey told Hugh. He turned to Harry and told him to run the ditching checklist. Harry looked for the emergency checklist but couldn't find it. The emergency checklist was a red-bordered, laminated, eight by ten checklist, normally carried in a holder near the first officer's left knee.[2] Harry searched the holder but found only the normal checklist. As an instructor, Balsey made it a point to know every emergency checklist by memory. It was something he also required of his student captains. Balsey didn't have time to look for the checklist. He knew that he had to depressurize the aircraft and close the outflow valve. The outflow valve was a large circular valve on the aft fuselage that controlled the outflow of conditioned air. Pressurization of an aircraft works by pumping conditioned air into the cabin and controlling the rate at which the air is allowed to escape. If the outflow valve was left open when the plane hit the water, the water would quickly rush in through the open valve and hasten the sinking of the plane. Balsey asked Harry to depressurize the aircraft and close the outflow valve. When he saw that Harry was slow to respond, Balsey pointed to the correct switches. Harry reached up and shut off the two air conditioning packs. He then closed the outflow valve. There wouldn't be time to do anything else.*

---

* The subject of who did what concerning the running of the checklist would come up again during the public hearings in San Juan. Harry claims to have run the checklist from memory. It's unlikely that Harry had enough experience to run the checklist on his own from memory as he claimed in both his written statement and in his testimony in San Juan. Harry Evans did not want to be interviewed for this book.

At 1947:35, the San Juan controller told ALM 980 that they were thirty-six miles from St. Croix. The last transmission from ALM 980 was at 1947:40: "Nine eighty, roger...ah...we're ditching." Other aircraft listening in on the communications would later comment on the calm in the voice of the pilot making the call.

Now that he was committed to ditching, Balsey lowered the flaps to fifteen degrees and slowed to 145 knots. At a hundred feet the low pressure lights came on again; this time they stayed on. Balsey immediately called for full flaps. Fifty degrees of flaps was like having two barn doors attached to the backs of the wings. The airspeed dropped off quickly from 140 knots to just over 90 knots. Any slower and the plane would have fallen out of the sky. But even at 90 knots it meant that the plane would strike the water at nearly 100 mph. Balsey reached up and turned the emergency power switch on. Now he had his gyro (the captain's attitude indicator was powered by the emergency bus). He reached up and flicked the seatbelt sign off and on three times to alert the cabin crew.* Balsey would later say that he wouldn't have had time to make a PA announcement even if it had been working. Ten or fifteen seconds went by before the first engine flamed out. The second engine followed very shortly thereafter. Balsey picked out the back of a swell and angled toward it. He wanted to keep the aircraft flying as long as possible in an effort to slow the aircraft down before it entered the water.

Seconds before the aircraft struck the water, Balsey turned toward the cockpit door and shouted, "It's now, Hugh!" He grabbed the wheel with both hands and told Harry to "hold on tight."

---

* The exact sequence in which Balsey switched to emergency power and flicked the seatbelt sign off and on three times is not known. What is known is that no one heard the bells, although Hugh would later testify that he had heard them. But Hugh's testimony is suspect because he claims that he didn't remember having heard the bells until two days before testifying. If Balsey switched to emergency power and then flicked the seatbelt sign off and on three times, the bells would not have sounded because the bells are not on the emergency bus. It's also possible that he flicked the switch too rapidly for the circuit to trigger the bells. It's unlikely that the bells went off but no one heard them.

At 1948:40 (3:48 P.M.), radar contact with ALM 980 was lost.[3]

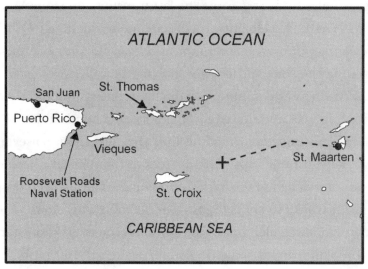

Figure 4. Ditching location.

The flaps were the first part of the aircraft to come in contact with the water. The left flap caught a swell and the plane yawed slightly to the left. To Balsey the sensation was similar to how it feels to push away from shore in a canoe, only in reverse. Next, the fuselage slammed down hard against the water. The sudden deceleration threw Balsey forward in his seat. Fortunately, the inertial reel of his shoulder harness worked as designed and prevented him from flying face first into the yoke or the glare shield. Behind him, Balsey could hear galley equipment crashing to the floor and one or two thumps against the cockpit door. The plane shook violently for several seconds. The instrument panel vibrated so badly that he couldn't read a single instrument. Then it got quiet. Eerily quiet. The vibration stopped and the plane seemed to be gliding through space. Balsey heard the distinct sound of bubbles above him. He looked out the cockpit window and saw only water. They were completely submerged. Balsey glanced down at his attitude indicator and saw that they were in a 45-degree bank to the left, and the bank was increasing. Instinctively, he turned the yoke to the right, and to his surprise and relief, the plane responded. The wings leveled, and they popped back up to the surface like a cork.

Water began entering the cockpit almost immediately. It dripped from the windows. It came in from the floor panels. It wasn't pouring in, but it was coming in fast enough to make its presence known. Balsey looked over at Harry Evans and found him frozen in his seat. He didn't appear to be injured. Balsey released Harry's shoulder harness and seatbelt and physically lifted him out of his seat. He removed Harry's life vest from behind the seat and put the vest over Harry's head. He then told Harry to go in back and help with the evacuation. Harry headed for the door but retreated when he discovered that the partially opened door was jammed. Balsey misinterpreted his actions. Frustrated, he turned Harry around and pushed him through the small opening.* Balsey planned to follow him into the cabin but decided to grab his life vest first. When he turned and stepped toward the door, he heard the loud sound of compressed air escaping. Something had gone terribly wrong. A life raft was inflating inside the aircraft. Balsey looked for something to use to puncture the raft but found nothing. With the door now blocked by the expanding life raft, the only way out of the aircraft was through the side window.

Before opening the side window, Balsey put on his life vest and secured the straps around his waist. He removed his shoes, then grabbed the release bar and slid the side window open. Rain-cooled air filled the cockpit. The opening was two or three feet above the water line. He climbed onto his seat and stepped through the opening and

---

* Harry Evans did not want to be interviewed for this book. The version of events described here is solely the recollection of Captain Balsey DeWitt. Harry's testimony in San Juan confirms that the captain "helped push" him through the jammed cockpit door. His testimony does not mention the captain putting a life vest over his head and, in fact, Harry did not have a life vest on when he later entered the water.

into the water. As he slid down the side of the fuselage, his left hand was cut by the stall vane transducer, a small metal device that protrudes from both sides of the nose.[4] He immediately felt pain in the palm of his hand as salt water came in contact with his wound. He reached over with his good hand and yanked the inflation tab on his life vest.

When Hugh stuck his head into the cockpit to ask what altitude they were at, all he heard was "two" something. He assumed that they were at 2,000 feet. They were actually at 200 feet. Hugh returned to the galley to continue to work on freeing the inflation lanyard on the life raft. Wilfred was standing behind Hugh, and Tobias was standing near the raft.

Hugh was trying to untangle the strings connected to the inflation lanyard when something caught his attention. It might have been the decrease in cabin noise when the engines flamed out. It could have been Balsey yelling from the cockpit just prior to impact, though Hugh claims to not have heard the warning from Balsey. In any case, Hugh sensed that something had changed. He glanced out the small circular window in the galley door and saw that they were only a few feet above the water. "Sit down! Sit down!" he yelled to Tobias and Wilfred. Tobias had no place to sit. He sat on the life raft with his back against the forward bulkhead. Wilfred immediately sat down on the aft facing jump seat adjacent to the cabin door. Hugh sat down in the jump seat closest to the cockpit door. Neither Wilfred nor Hugh had time to buckle their seatbelts before the plane hit the water.

Within seconds of the plane striking the water, Hugh was hit by a stream of water that was coming in from a tiny opening in the main cabin door. The impact had caused a slight buckling in the front part of the door. Water rushed in through this small opening and was redirected by the bulkhead, hitting Hugh squarely in the chest. It hit him with such force that he had trouble breathing. It was like having a fire hose directed on him. In addition to the water that was pouring in on him, he was being bombarded with galley supplies and equipment. He felt a sharp pain in his right knee after being hit by something hard and solid. He couldn't see anything because water was splashing on his face and in his eyes. He was certain the plane was breaking apart. Finally the vibration stopped. Hugh rubbed the salt water from his eyes. He felt a heavy weight press up against him. A passenger had either come forward or had been thrown forward and was now lying across his lap. As Hugh stood up, the passenger was thrown to the floor. Hugh tried to help the passenger, but the man was flailing his arms and legs as if he were trying to swim. Hugh stepped over the man and proceeded to the main cabin door.*

Wilfred, who was sitting just inches away from Hugh, had barely gotten wet. He stood up and immediately went to open the main cabin door. The handle was stuck and would only move a few inches. Several passengers crowded into the galley area looking for a way out. They pressed forward, wedging Wilfred up against the door.

"Everyone move back!" Wilfred shouted.

"Let's get out of here!" a passenger standing in the galley yelled. "We gotta get out of here!"

"Calm down," Wilfred said as he tried once again to turn the handle. Hugh gave the handle a try but couldn't get it to budge either.

While Wilfred and Hugh worked to open the main cabin door, Tobias was busy trying to open the galley door. He rotated the handle halfway, and then it stuck. There were people standing behind him waiting to get out. Tobias didn't look down, but he could feel water lapping against his ankles. He backed away from the door

---

* Hugh Hart later identified the passenger as Emerson Ussery. Emerson's testimony, however, conflicts with Hugh's.

and kicked the handle with his left foot. The handle moved far enough that he was able to get the door open. Two passengers immediately jumped into the water through the opening.

As soon as Hugh and Wilfred realized that Tobias had opened the galley door, they abandoned the main cabin door and went to launch the raft out that door. The galley was littered with galley debris and equipment. All three men started tossing loose items out the door. When they had cleared enough room to move freely, Wilfred positioned himself with his back to the open door. He began pulling on the life raft while Tobias and Hugh pushed. The raft barely budged. Eventually, they managed to move the raft close enough to the door that Wilfred was nearly in the water. Water was washing into the cabin through the open service door. The bottom of the door was nearly level with the water line.

"We're going to get it out," Tobias shouted to Wilfred. "Leave the aircraft!"

With that, Wilfred took one step back and inflated his life vest.

A few seconds later, Harry Evans entered the cabin from the cockpit. Hugh asked him to lend a hand with the life raft. Harry positioned himself near the galley door with his back to the galley. Harry, Hugh, and Tobias lifted the raft by the straps and were getting ready to toss the raft out of the open galley door when a passenger lying on the floor wrapped his arm around the raft package. Seconds later, there was a loud sound of rushing air. Despite their precautions, the life raft was suddenly and unexpectedly inflating inside the aircraft. Hugh's first thought was to puncture the raft to deflate it, because not only was the raft blocking the forward exit but at least two people were now pinned by the inflating life raft: Harry's left foot was pinned, and a passenger was pinned up against the side wall just prior to the main cabin door. Hugh tried to puncture the raft with his pocket knife, but the dull blade was ineffective. Hugh always carried a knife with him. He used the knife to cut up his navigation charts at the end of a flight to make them easier to file. He normally carried a knife given to him by his father. That knife had broken only days before. He was forced to use a replacement knife on this trip. It was the first time in ten years of flying that he didn't have his regular knife with him.

Hugh spotted several plastic knives lying on the floor and reached down to grab one. The small plastic knife broke in two as soon as he thrust it into the hard, rubbery surface. Tobias also tried to puncture the raft using a plastic fork, but it was equally ineffective. Water was coming into the aircraft through the open galley door in large waves that would fill the galley and then wash back out of the aircraft. The inflated raft completely blocked off access to the main cabin. Hugh backpedaled to get out of the way of the expanding raft. The twenty-five man life raft was four or five times larger than the area in which it was inflating. Hugh took one step backwards, and the next thing he knew he was under water. He frantically tried to inflate his life vest but couldn't find the pull tabs. He kept pulling on the fastening straps instead. Hugh began to panic as he continued to sink; he hadn't had an opportunity to take a breath before entering the water. He felt around for the CO_2 cartridges. Finally, he felt the CO_2 cylinder. He followed the strings down to the pull tabs and yanked them both. He popped up to the surface seconds later as the vest inflated.

Tobias worked his way around the raft and to the open galley door. Just as he was about to jump into the water he saw that the raft was deflating — something had punctured it. There were no more passengers waiting to get out through the door, so Tobias exited the aircraft.

Harry Evans got out of the aircraft shortly after the life raft deflated. He would testify later that he couldn't remember exactly how he had gotten out. One thing is known for certain, though. When Harry entered the water, he was not wearing a life vest.

Chapter 15

THE PASSENGERS WERE IN VARIOUS STATES OF READI-
ness when the plane struck the water. Some
were standing in the aisle. Some were standing in front of their seats.
At least five passengers were sitting but had failed to fasten their seatbelts. A few passengers had their seatbelts fastened but had difficulty
tightening them around their waists. The seatbelts were of a metal-to-
fabric design. A serrated cam on the metal side was used to lock and
tighten the belt. Even though the plane was less than a year old, some
of the seatbelts showed signs of wear on the serrated cam. The cam
failed to grab the seatbelt snugly, greatly reducing its effectiveness.

Sitting in the aft exit row on the right side of the cabin were Arthur
and Sybil Johnson, a married couple from New York. Their original
seat assignments had been in the rear of the plane. As they were
boarding, Arthur saw that no one was sitting in the exit row, so he
and his wife moved to be closer to the exit. Arthur was a private pilot
and preferred sitting near the emergency exit whenever possible. His

wife took the aisle seat. Arthur sat next to the exit door. Realizing that he might have to open the door if they did happen to ditch, he reviewed the exit door instructions, which were on a placard next to the door. He looked outside and saw how close they were to the water. He knew that they were too low to be landing. He looked around the cabin and realized that most of the passengers had no idea that they were only seconds away from impact. He removed his shoes and placed them under his seat.[1]

Other passengers took similar precautions. Some grabbed pillows from the overhead bins. A few practiced getting into the brace position, even though the flight attendants hadn't had time to demonstrate it.[*]

In the seats directly opposite of Arthur and Sybil Johnson were Jacinth Bryanth and Walter Hodge. Jacinth Bryanth, who owned a hotel on St. Maarten along with her husband, had been sitting in the forward exit row seat. When she stood up to put on her life vest, Walter Hodge, the New York City bus driver, recognized her and called out to her. Walter was sitting near the aft left wing exit directly behind her. Jacinth decided to join her friend and took the aisle seat next to him.[2]

Jeannie Larmony sat alone in 16A. She glanced out her window and was frightened by the sight of the white caps and the dark

---

[*] While the passengers were not shown how to get into the brace position by the flight attendants, the emergency briefing cards in the seat pockets did graphically demonstrate two different brace positions. The first position required the passengers to lean forward and grab their ankles. For those passengers who didn't have the flexibility to get into that position, a compromise position was shown where the passengers lean forward and protect their heads by grabbing onto the seatback in front of them. In both positions, the primary goal is to prevent the head from flying forward as well as to protect the head from flying objects.

clouds billowing overhead. She whispered a prayer: "Jesus, Mary, and Joseph, I give you my heart and my soul this afternoon. Saint Anthony and Saint Jude, protect me now." Her hands trembled as she reached down and felt around for her seatbelt straps.

Sitting in the first row, Emerson Ussery noticed a change in the sound level inside the cabin. It was a subtle change easily missed in all the commotion. But Emerson was certain that the engines had stopped running. He also heard the navigator telling the two stewards to sit down. He turned around and saw people standing. He noticed the stewardess in the aisle helping two elderly people with their life vests. Emerson looked out the right side window and saw how close they were to the water. "Get in your seats!" he yelled. "The engines are out! We're going in!"

Margareth Abraham heard Emerson Ussery shouting. She saw the cabin lights flick off and the emergency lights flick on. She looked out a passenger window and saw the water rushing up to meet the plane. She instinctively and selflessly started pushing people into their seats, working her way rearward. She was of slight physical stature, but she had no trouble forcing men twice her weight into their seats. She didn't get past row four before the plane hit the water.[3]

What happened next depended a great deal on where in the aircraft a passenger happened to be sitting. Those sitting forward of the aircraft's center of gravity experienced a forward and downward body acceleration with a slight lateral vector to the left. Those sitting aft of the aircraft's center of gravity had a forward and upward body acceleration. The worst place to be sitting was on the left side of the aircraft in the first six rows.[4]

Passengers reported the plane skipping at least once on the water before the main impact. More than likely they were referring to the point at which the left flap first contacted the water. The deceleration was rapid and severe. Anything not secured inside the aircraft was immediately sent airborne, including passengers. It has been estimated that passengers experienced between eight to twelve g's of deceleration force over a time period of .5 to 1.0 second. The seats were rated for nine g's of forward deceleration. It has also been esti-mated that the plane came to a stop within fifty to eighty feet once the fuselage came in contact with the water, which is less than the overall length of the aircraft.[5] Passengers in the forward part of the cabin were struck by flying debris and other passengers. Because most of the passengers were not in a brace position at impact, their heads hit the seatbacks in front of them as they were thrown violently forward; their chests then slammed against their thighs and knees, causing additional injuries to the neck and spinal column. At least seven passengers were thrown from their seats even though their seatbelts were fastened. There were also a number of seat failures in which the entire seat was ripped from the floor.[6]

Arthur Johnson was sitting next to the exit door. He had prepared himself to open the door in the event they actually had to ditch. But when the plane hit the water, his head was thrown forward and struck the seatback in front of him. He was dazed by the impact and has no recollection of what happened next. He testified that he isn't sure if he opened the door.

Someone, however, opened the emergency exit door, at least par-tially. Israel Kruger, the retired electrical engineer, claims to have pushed the door open. Since the door opens inward the only possi-ble explanation is that the door was opened by another passenger reaching over Arthur Johnson. That passenger would have been in an awkward position to lift the heavy door and move it completely out of the way. He or she either abandoned the attempt and left the door blocking the exit, or exited through the partially opened door. In that scenario, it would have been possible for Israel to push on the door until it was completely out of the aircraft.

Once the door was opened, passengers streamed out of the plane through the narrow exit. When Arthur Johnson stepped out onto the wing, the waves were just starting to lap over the upper surface of the wing. He turned around expecting to see his wife right behind him but instead saw her sitting in her seat. She was looking for her purse. "Honey, forget that," Arthur yelled to his wife. "Let's get out of here." Sybil followed her husband onto the right wing. Arthur slid off the back of the wing and into the water along with another passenger. His wife was reluctant to enter the water. She walked the entire length of the wing before gaining the courage to jump in.

Israel Kruger had been standing in the aisle when the plane hit the water. He thought it would be easier to put his life vest on if he were standing, so he stood up from his seat to don his life vest. He then helped his wife with her life vest. He didn't secure the straps around his waist. Israel glanced out the window across the aisle and saw the water. At first he thought they were getting ready to land. But he couldn't remember any landing where the plane had been so close to the water. He instinctively grabbed the seatbacks with both hands. When the plane hit, the deceleration was too great for him to hang on. He was thrown forward down the aisle, eventually ending up with a group of people near the front of the cabin.

When he regained his senses a minute or two later, his first thought was to get back to his wife. He picked himself up off the pile of people and headed down the aisle to where Toby was sitting. He had to force his way around a few dazed passengers who were blocking the aisle. He found Toby in a state of shock. She was unable to speak or respond in any way. Israel opened the overhead bin and grabbed the blue suitcase containing their jewelry. He reached over and unfastened his wife's seatbelt then physically removed her from the seat, still holding on to the suitcase. Together they headed for the emergency exit across the aisle. Israel claims that when he got to the exit he had to push the door open. He inflated Toby's life preserver then pushed her through the opening. He followed right behind her. As he reached the exit, he came to the realization that there was no way that he would be able to swim and help his wife and still hold on to the heavy suitcase. He tossed the suitcase out the emergency exit then stepped onto the wing. The suitcase slid off the wing and disappeared beneath the waves.

Rick Arnold was thrown forward against the seatback in front of him. When he put his hands up to brace himself, the middle finger of his right hand scraped against something sharp. He didn't realize it then, but he had cut his finger to the bone. Rick blacked out momentarily when his head hit the seatback. When he came to, he noticed water was already entering the cabin. He glanced to his right and saw Loretta sitting motionless in her seat. He looked to see how Gene was doing, but all he saw was an empty spot where Gene had been sitting; the entire seat was missing. Rick unbuckled his seatbelt and stood up. Water was slowly filling the cabin. "Loretta!" Rick yelled. "We have to get out of here!"

Loretta didn't respond. Rick reached over and unbuckled her seatbelt. He grabbed her and helped her out of her seat. He could tell that Loretta couldn't support herself, so he wrapped his arms around her and helped her to the exit. The water level inside the aircraft was rising, and people were bumping into each other as they pushed and shoved their way down the aisle.

As Rick and Loretta neared the emergency exit, they became separated. Rick suddenly found himself outside the aircraft and on the wing. He immediately started to search for Loretta. When he didn't see her, he jumped into the water. He pulled both inflation tabs on his life vest but the vest wouldn't inflate. Rick spotted a suitcase floating nearby. He grabbed the suitcase with one hand and continued tugging on the inflation tabs with the other. The vest still wouldn't inflate. He took a minute to catch his breath. He had the presence of mind to reach behind him and button his pants pocket so he wouldn't lose his wallet. The suitcase was keeping him afloat, but he had the strange sensation of being weighed down. As he kicked his legs, he realized that he was still wearing his shoes — the expensive Italian loafers that he had just purchased. He hesitated for a fraction of a second before kicking them off. He then yanked hard on the two inflation tabs once more and finally heard the sound of compressed air rushing into the two chambers of the life vest.

Emerson Ussery was thrown out of his seat and against the bulkhead directly in front of him, despite having his seatbelt on and secured. His forward momentum flung him past that bulkhead and into the cockpit door. He hit the cockpit door square to his back. He then slid down the door until coming to rest on his back. Emerson watched incredulously as an avalanche of debris and people came flying toward him. When the plane finally came to a stop, he was buried beneath bodies and debris. Emerson could feel water coming into the aircraft all around him. Despite the mound of people on top of him, his hands and arms were free. He felt certain that the floor had given way and that water was rushing in through a hole in the floor. He could feel water pushing up against him. He started to panic when he realized that the water was about to cover his mouth. Reaching up through the pile of bodies, Emerson grabbed onto something to help pull himself free.

"You're choking me, you're choking me," a man yelled.

Emerson had hold of a man's tie. The man pulled away but Emerson held on. He continued to hold on until he had enough leverage to move. Finally, he worked himself free. He saw the purser and navigator struggling with the main cabin door. When they left, Emerson took over the task of trying to open the door. He was so focused on getting the door opened that he was completely unaware of the life raft inflating behind him. The water was waist high when he turned around and saw that the entire galley area was empty, except for a few people floating face down. Emerson spotted the open galley door opposite him. He took one last look back through the cabin and observed a heavyset woman a few rows back. She appeared uninjured but stunned. "Come on!" Emerson yelled. "We gotta get out of here." He turned and exited the galley door, assuming the woman was right behind him. He never saw the woman again.[*7]

Jim Razzi didn't fasten his seatbelt prior to the ditching. His wife Hedi did have her seatbelt on. When the plane hit the water, Jim was thrown from his seat and knocked unconscious. When he regained

---

[*] Emerson's recollection of what took place in the galley conflicts with the recollections of Wilfred and Hugh. Hugh testified that Emerson was the passenger on the floor waving his arms in an exaggerated swimming motion. He also claims that it was Emerson who inflated the life raft. While it seems highly improbable that Emerson was not aware that the life raft was inflating directly behind him, it isn't impossible assuming a panicked state and a tunnel-vision like focus on the door handle. Emerson also testified about bodies on the floor in the galley. Both Hugh and Wilfred testified that there were no bodies on the floor, just the one passenger flailing his arms and legs. Emerson also claims that there was a hole in the floor. This aircraft did have an access panel on the floor which covered the hydraulic controls for the cargo door, but it was too small to have been the hole described by Emerson.

consciousness, he looked but could not find his wife. He had been thrown forward in the cabin almost to the forward bulkhead. As his head cleared, Jim noticed that a number of seats had been pulled up out of the floor and were flattened on top of one another. Instinctively, he turned and headed toward the back of the plane. He had to step over at least one body as he made his way back. He glanced to his right toward the left forward overwing exit and it appeared to be blocked. He could see someone through the window trying to open the overwing exit from the outside.[*8] Just then he heard a loud noise. He turned around just in time to see a torrent of water rushing down the aisle toward him. The water seemed to originate from the cockpit. The water level rose up to his chest. Jim saw the opened right aft wing exit. It was partially under water. He also noticed a woman standing by the exit too afraid to move. Jim pushed the woman through the exit and then followed her out, having to go underwater as he made his way out of the aircraft.[9]

Jeannie Larmony didn't have time to fasten her seatbelt before the plane hit the water. She was thrown out of her seat and up against the bottom of the overhead bins. Her head and back scraped against the air vents and the reading lights as she continued forward above the heads of passengers. She was knocked unconscious. When she came to, she found the aircraft completely empty. The plane was dark and rapidly filling with water. As she looked around to get her bearings, she noticed that she was now in row six. She had been thrown forward ten rows. One peculiar sight that caught her attention was what at first looked like heads floating in the water. Upon closer inspection, she realized that they were wigs. There were at

---

[*] The person he saw trying to open the emergency exit from the outside was Balsey.

least five or six of them. She saw a shaft of light in the rear of the plane. Sensing that the plane was only seconds away from sinking, Jeannie crawled over the seatbacks and swam toward the dwindling light. When she reached the exit, there were only six or seven inches of the exit still above water. She worked her way to the opening but a wave forced her backwards. On her next attempt, she clung to the sides of the exit with both hands and waited for the wave to subside. She climbed out of the aircraft and into the water. Jeannie Larmony was most likely the last person out of the plane.

Chapter 16

SHORTLY AFTER BALSEY INFLATED HIS LIFE VEST, A wave swept him forward of the aircraft. He looked back and thought he saw damage to the underside of the plane. He turned his focus to reentering the aircraft. He had no idea how many passengers were still inside. He swam around to the main cabin door. The aircraft was bobbing up and down in the water, making the handle difficult to reach. He looked through the small window in the cabin door and noticed someone trying to turn the handle from the inside. But as he examined the door, he noticed that it had buckled. He abandoned the main cabin door and swam toward the overwing exits. The emergency exits could be opened from either the inside or the outside. He first tried to open the forward overwing exit but couldn't pull the handle all the way. He peered through the window and noticed a seatback blocking the exit. He then proceeded to the aft overwing exit and opened it without difficulty.

It was dark and misty inside as Balsey stepped into the cabin. The water was waist-high. He looked across the aisle and saw that the aft overwing exit on the opposite side of the aircraft had been opened. One row up from the exit row, he noticed a man sitting in his seat. The man appeared to be in shock. Balsey tried to get his attention but got no response. Balsey waded over to the man and grabbed him by the arm. He then assisted him to the overwing exit. Balsey tried to move the seat that was blocking the forward overwing exit, but it barely budged. There wasn't time to fool with it, he decided. The water level was increasing too fast. He turned around and noticed a woman crouching in the aisle calling out a name. "My husband, my husband," the woman repeated frantically. "I'll get your husband," Balsey assured the woman. He led her to the left overwing exit and helped her onto the wing.*

Balsey stepped back into the cabin and scanned the interior of the plane. He didn't see anyone. He concluded that the man that he had helped out earlier must have been the woman's husband. The aircraft was now listing to the right. Balsey sensed that the plane was about to sink. He took one last look through the cabin. He was surprised by the damage. Seatbacks were flattened. Overhead bins were opened and their contents were now floating in the aisle and between the seats. At least one seat, the one closest to the overwing exit that Balsey had opened, was missing. It had been ripped from the floor. Balsey didn't think that the landing had been that severe. His only injury was to his hand, and that had come after the ditching. "Anybody here," he yelled, his voice deadened by the rising water. There was a noise behind him. He turned to see that the male passenger he had helped out of the aircraft minutes earlier was now

---

* The official record is that after helping the male passenger from the plane, Balsey opened the forward left overwing exit. Balsey's recollection now is that he did not open the exit. Balsey also claims that he helped the female passenger out before the male passenger. I chose to go with the official record and Balsey's own statement written days after the accident concerning the sequence of the two passengers he assisted.

trying to reenter the plane. Balsey blocked his path and stepped through the exit and onto the wing. He grabbed the man and woman and started swimming away from the sinking plane.[*]

They weren't much farther than the end of the left wingtip when Balsey turned and saw the left wing rise out of the water. Seconds later the nose dipped below the surface and the plane began a shallow descent. Soon only the V-shaped horizontal stabilizer was all that remained above water, looking like the tail of a whale that had just breached the surface. Balsey spotted Harry Evans swimming over the submerged fuselage and then resting briefly on the elevator before swimming off. There were two loud popping sounds, and the plane disappeared beneath the water.

Wilfred Spenser swam toward the open galley door to see if he could release the escape slide from its container, but the slide wasn't there; it had already broken free. He searched the water around him but saw no sign of the slide. He started swimming toward the right overwing exits in hope of reentering the aircraft. As he swam closer, he looked inside the plane and noticed people still sitting in their seats. Wilfred struggled to climb aboard the partially submerged wing. As he neared the exit, a wave swept him off the wing and back into the sea. He was about to make another attempt when he heard someone yelling from behind, "Help me! I don't have a life vest!" Wilfred turned to see that it was Harry Evans. "Can I hang onto you?" Harry pleaded. Wilfred swam toward him. Harry wrapped his arms around Wilfred's neck, momentarily pushing him beneath the water. He didn't loosen his

---

[*] Some of the survivors reported seeing one person approach the overwing exit then turn around and take a seat, presumably refusing to leave their loved one behind. That person was assumed to have gone down with the plane. More than likely, this was one of the passengers that Balsey helped out of the aircraft before it sank.

grip until Wilfred complained. Harry stayed just long enough to catch his breath, then swam off.

Wilfred turned to make another attempt at getting to the overwing exits but determined that it was too dangerous. It appeared to him that the plane was about to sink. The right wing was fully submerged and the left wingtip was rising out of the water.

The swells were ten to fifteen feet high. One minute Wilfred would be facing a mountain of water. The next he was riding atop a swell searching for other survivors. It was at the top of one these mammoth swells that Wilfred spotted Tobias off in the distance. He yelled to him. "*Tito, bo a mira Margareth?*" he said in Papiamento. Tobias shook his head. He hadn't seen Margareth.[1]

A lifeless body floated by. "Sir," Wilfred called out. "Are you all right?" The man was wearing an inflated life vest, but his eyes were closed and his head was barely out of the water. Wilfred watched helplessly as the man floated away.

Wilfred became increasingly concerned that the weather was going to hamper any rescue attempts. He was also concerned about it getting dark before they could be rescued; it was already hard to see beneath the overcast skies. He thought of his wife and children as he considered the possibility of not being found in time.

Hugh Hart wasn't in the water long when he spotted Harry Evans swimming toward him. "I don't have a life vest," Harry said. "Can you help me?"

"I'll see if I can find you one, Harry," Hugh said, thinking that he might find a life vest floating in the water or inside the aircraft. He started to swim toward the right side overwing exits when he felt something brush up against his leg. He hadn't thought about the possibility of sharks, but now the thought flashed through his brain.

He looked down and was relieved to see not a dorsal fin but a rigid plastic package. When he pushed the package away, he got a better look and realized that it was the escape chute. He found the inflation lanyard but was unable to gain any leverage to pull it. He enlisted the help of a female passenger. He had her hold on to the package while he swam away from her. Hugh yanked on the lanyard, and the bright yellow slide inflated. The slide immediately became a focal point for anyone near enough to reach it. Hugh began gathering people and helping them toward the slide. There were only a few hand-holds to hang onto. Hugh took off his belt and had a few of the other passengers do the same. He looped his belt through one of the hand-holds, creating a makeshift tether line to which other survivors could cling.

Hugh was helping passengers get to the slide when he saw the passenger he had last seen lying on the galley floor. He had assumed that the man had been pinned by the raft and was startled to see him. The man was clinging to an aircraft tire along with a woman. "Are you all right?" Hugh asked as he swam toward them. When there was no answer, Hugh repeated the question. The woman finally spoke up. "He's all right. He's just a little dazed."

Tobias was floating alone in the water. At first he didn't see any passengers. Soon he started to see other survivors scattered around him. He said a brief prayer. When he rose to the top of one swell, he spotted people off in the distance gathering around what at first looked like a life raft.* He swam toward the group of passengers, at one point grabbing onto an aircraft tire to use for additional support.

---

* Rescuers and survivors alike mistakenly identified the escape slide as a life raft. In all instances where there is a reference to "a large group of people in or around a life raft," it is the escape slide that is being referenced.

He assumed that the tire had broken free from the plane. It looked to him like a nose tire. Two passengers swam toward him and also held on to the small tire. Together they made their way to the large group of survivors.

Harry Evans was understandably panicked at being in the water without a life vest. He spotted Hugh and asked for his help. He then swam over to Wilfred and clung on to him long enough to catch his breath. The aircraft was still visible, though only the tail remained above water. Harry left Wilfred and swam over the submerged fuselage toward the tail, thinking that he could hang on to the tail for support while he looked for something else to cling to, such as a suitcase or a seat cushion. The plane was in a slight bank to the right. When he reached the tail, he draped himself across the left elevator. The elevator was flapping up and down in the heavy seas, making it difficult to hold onto. Harry looked over his left shoulder and noticed a woman ten to twenty feet away. He left the tail and swam toward the woman. He didn't get very far before he felt something pulling him from below. It was the undertow from the sinking plane. Fortunately, Harry spotted something floating in the water and grabbed onto it. He then swam over to the woman. When he turned to look back at the aircraft, he spotted what appeared to be a life raft. He was about to head toward the raft when he saw Balsey swimming toward him. He waited for Balsey to reach him, and then the three of them made their way to the escape slide.[2]

Once they reached the main group of survivors, Balsey helped Harry onto the slide. He then climbed onto the slide himself in order to help an injured passenger. The passenger was an elderly woman who was bleeding from cuts on her forehead. The escape slide was upside down in the water. It could accommodate only two or three people and only if they were sitting. Balsey and several passengers helped to get the woman onto the slide. Balsey then slipped back into the water.

Rick Arnold wasn't a religious person. He considered himself an agnostic. But there was a brief moment in the water when he seriously considered the prospect that he might not survive. He thought briefly about praying but decided that if he was going to make it out alive, it was going to be fate and not divine intervention that would save him. He surveyed his surroundings. There were people and debris bobbing up and down all around him. He felt as if he were watching a movie — one that he was in. He called out for Loretta. When he didn't get a response, he pushed aside the suitcase that he had been clinging to and started swimming toward a large group of people. He found Loretta holding on to what Rick believed was a life raft. As he neared the slide, Rick saw one of the crew members kneeling atop it, instructing people to stay off the slide for fear of it overturning. Rick felt it was a selfless act. He didn't notice how little room there actually was on the slide, or that the crewmember wasn't wearing a life vest.

"I can't find Gene," Loretta said as Rick neared.

"Don't worry," Rick said. "I'm sure he's around here somewhere." Rick surveyed the faces of the people in the water around him. There was no sign of Gene.

"He's gone," Loretta said fatalistically. She told Rick that she couldn't feel her legs. Rick swam over to her. Some of the other passengers were removing their belts and ties and attaching them to the escape slide, so Rick took off his belt. He found a tie that was already attached to the escape slide and looped the tie around his belt buckle. It was then that Rick noticed the deep gash in his hand. He was surprised that he didn't feel any pain, even with the salt water washing away the blood.

A young black girl with braided hair swam over and grabbed onto Rick's belt. The waves were thrashing people about and Rick kept hitting his mouth on the back of the woman's head. He continued to hold onto the belt with one hand and Loretta with the other. It wasn't an easy task in the sea conditions. Letting go would have meant certain separation from the main group. Adding to his difficulty was his life vest, which was pinching his neck. Like a lot of other passengers, Rick was having difficulty with his life vest. It tended to float away from his body.

At one point Rick looked at his watch and noticed that it had stopped at twelve minutes to four. Radio transcripts would later confirm that radar contact was lost at exactly twelve minutes to four.

As soon as Emerson Ussery hit the water, he pulled the two inflation tabs on his life vest. The vest inflated immediately but failed to offer much support. He had neglected to secure the waist straps; the vest simply floated away from his body. It barely kept his head out of the water. He had to arch his back in an awkward manner in order to keep the life vest from coming off. Emerson struggled with the vest a while before giving up on it. He decided to search for the life raft. He assumed that there had been plenty of time to launch the raft that had been sitting in the galley. He was stunned when he didn't see it floating nearby. He spotted the woman who had been sitting next to him and started to swim toward her. "Where's the life raft?" he asked.

"They put it in the water and it sank," the woman said. She apparently had seen galley equipment being tossed out and assumed it was the life raft.[*]

---

[*] Life raft packages are designed to float in the event they are put into the water without being inflated. Had the crew thrown the life raft into the water as the passenger claimed, it would have resurfaced seconds later.

The woman who reported having seen the crewmembers toss the life raft into the water was Vivian Rosotto. She had been sitting in seat 1E next to Emerson. Vivian had been in a brace position when the plane hit the water and as a result was not injured. She escaped through the open galley door. As Emerson approached her, she noticed an aircraft tire floating in the water. She pointed it out to Emerson who swam over and grabbed it. They both assumed that the tire had been ripped from the aircraft. They didn't know that the tire was actually a spare that had come from the cargo compartment. Minutes later, two people, a man and a woman, swam over to Emerson and Vivian. "Do you mind if we join you?" the man asked rather nonchalantly. "Certainly," Emerson replied. "Grab a wheel." The man and woman were Arthur and Sybil Johnson.

The four paddled their way toward a large group of survivors. When they were close enough that they could grab onto a belt or tie, they pushed the tire away. It was too difficult to hold onto in the rough seas. Emerson saw a woman who appeared to be drifting away from the main group. He swam toward her to see if he could help. When he reached her, the woman flung herself on him, forcing him underwater. Emerson felt a sharp pain in his back as he managed to free himself from the woman's death-grip. He left her and swam back to the main group. When he turned to look back, the woman had drifted a considerable distance from the main group. He lost sight of her soon after.

Israel Kruger inflated his vest and swam over to help his wife. She was still dazed and taking in big gulps of water. "Toby, spit the water out," he shouted to her. He continued swimming with one arm wrapped around her. "Spit the water out," he repeated over and over. Eventually, his wife responded by spitting out a mouthful of salt water. Israel spotted a group of people around a yellow flotation device and swam toward them, towing his wife along with him. Israel had been a lifeguard in his younger days and knew how to assist someone in the water. Three people were on what Israel believed was a life raft — two crewmen and one woman. Israel yelled at the man he believed to be the captain, telling him to get off the raft so other people could get in. He didn't know that the captain was assisting an injured passenger.

Israel felt pain around his ankle. He tried kicking off his shoes, but they wouldn't come off. He reached down and could tell that his right ankle was swollen. He unlaced both shoes. The shoe on his left foot came right off. He was still having trouble removing the shoe from the foot with the swollen ankle. He swore at that moment he would never again wear laced shoes.[*] He loosened the laces on the remaining shoe and eventually managed to get the shoe off. Israel then helped Toby remove her shoes. He clung to both the slide and Toby. He was exhausted but relieved to have made it out of the plane safely. He scanned the horizon looking for a rescue ship but saw only an angry sea.

Jeannie Larmony started swimming away from the aircraft the moment she entered the water. She didn't want to be near it when it sank. She kicked off her shoes as she furiously pedaled away from the sinking plane. Jeannie had spent most of her life around water. She was an excellent swimmer. She was so determined to get away from the sinking plane that she never took the time to inflate her life vest. When she turned around to look back at the plane, it was gone. In that instant, Jeannie thought about her children, wondering what they would think when they found out what had happened to her.

---

[*] Israel kept his vow and never again wore shoes with laces, at least not on an airplane.

Jeannie fought to keep her head above the water. She still didn't think to inflate her life vest. She saw a group of passengers around what she believed was a raft and swam in that direction. When she reached the other survivors, she vomited and complained that her back and neck hurt. Her forehead was bloodied. One of the passengers, Christine Cromwell, insisted that Jeannie be put up on the slide. Two male passengers and the captain helped pull her onto the slide.

The reactions of the passengers around the slide were mixed. Some responded as if the whole incident was just a minor inconvenience. Some stared off into space, never uttering a word. A few passengers complained of their injuries, but no one complained loud enough to bring attention to themselves. The air temperature was about 76 degrees. The water temperature was in the upper sixties. It wasn't cold enough for hypothermia to be an immediate threat, but it was cold enough to cause several passengers to shiver. Adding to their discomfort were several rain showers that passed overhead.

"Are they going to find us?" a passenger asked.

Hugh assured the passenger that help was on its way, though as he scanned the horizon and saw the stormy weather he had his doubts.

Figure 5. Captain Balsey DeWitt shown here in a picture taken a few months before the accident.

Figure 6. Stewardess Margareth Abraham, Pursor Wilfred Spencer, Steward Tobias (Tito) Cordeiro.

Figure 7. Navigator Hugh Hart and his daughter Jennifer in a picture taken a short time before the accident.

Figure 8. Passenger Hedwig
(Hedi) Razzi.

Figure 9. Passenger Emerson
Ussery.

Figure 10. Passengers Toby and Israel Kruger.

Figure 11. Passenger Jeannie Larmony.

Figure 12. Passenger Rick Arnold.

Figure 13. Passenger Gene Gremelsbacker.

Figure 14. An ONA DC-9 similar to the one that ditched.

Figure 15. A Coast Guard HU-16 similar to this one, commanded by Lt. Tom Blank, flew a circular orbit over the passengers until the last passenger was rescued. Lt. Blank became the On Scene Commander of the rescue effort.

Figure 16. The *Point Whitehorn* was the first ship to arrive on the scene. The crew was involved in the night search of survivors.

Figure 17. LPH-7 *USS Guadalcanal*, home to the HMM-261 Marine helicopter squadron. Six helicopters were launched from the ship and were involved in the search and rescue of passengers. The ship, which had been anchored off the coast of Vieques Island, reached the scene shortly after sunset.

Figure 18. This is the
actual SH-3A Sea King
helicopter used in the
rescue of 26 survivors.

Figure 19. This is one
of six CH-46 U.S. Marine
helicopters used in the
search and rescue of
passengers.

Figure 20. This is one of two HH-52A Coast
Guard helicopters used in the search and
rescue of passengers.

Figure 21. From left to right in flight suits: Lt. Commander James E. Rylee, Lt. (j.g.) Donald G. Hartman, Chief Aviation Machinist's Mate William A. Brazzell, and Aviation Machinist's Mate C.V. Lindley. The four are being congratulated by Vice Admiral Robert E. Townsend. The helicopter used in the rescue is in the background.

Figure 22. Corporal John Barber was the crew chief aboard CH-46 EM-13.

Figure 23. Coast Guard pilot
Lt. Tom Blank.

**Figure 24. Coast Guard pilot Lt.
(j.g.) William Shields. He and
his crew rescued four survivors.
Bill did not have a beard at the
time of the accident.**

Figure 25. Coast Guard pilot Lt. (j.g.)
Carmond (Fitz) Fitzgerald.

Figure 26. ONA CEO and President G. F. Steedman Hinckley.

Figure 27. ALM President Ciro Octavio (Tawa) Irausquin.

Figure 28. Dick Baker, NTSB Investigator In Charge of ALM 980.

Figure 29. ONA Executive Vice President and General Manager Bill Bailey.

Figure 30. ONA Assistant Chief Pilot Ed Veronelli.

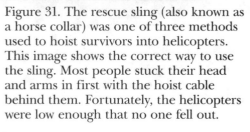

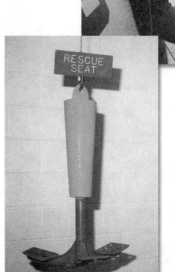

Figure 31. The rescue sling (also known as a horse collar) was one of three methods used to hoist survivors into helicopters. This image shows the correct way to use the sling. Most people stuck their head and arms in first with the hoist cable behind them. Fortunately, the helicopters were low enough that no one fell out.

Figure 32. The first rescue was made using a rescue seat similar to the one pictured here.

Figure 33. A Coast Guard rescue basket like this one was the primary method used in the rescue of passengers.

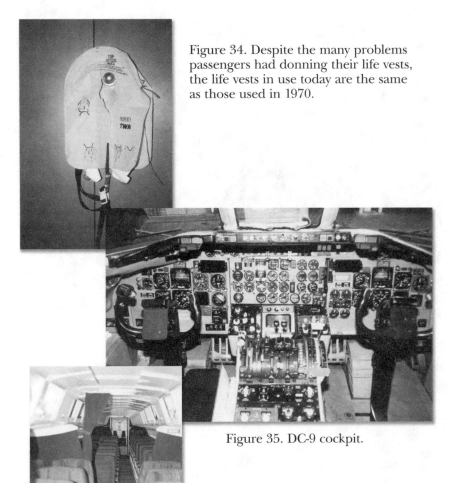

Figure 34. Despite the many problems passengers had donning their life vests, the life vests in use today are the same as those used in 1970.

Figure 35. DC-9 cockpit.

Figure 36. This picture gives a good representation of the interior size of the DC-9. This DC-9 was configured with sixteen first-class seats and eighty-four coach seats. The ONA DC-9 had 105 seats and no first-class section.

Figure 37. From left, Wilfred Spencer, Octavio (Tawa) Irausquin, and Tobias (Tito) Cordeiro at a press conference held in Curacao on their arrival back on the island.

Figure 38. This is a picture of the actual aircraft that ditched. It was taken in St. Maarten on the inaugural flight in January 1970, just three months before the accident. The steward at the top of the stairs assisting a passenger is Wilfred Spencer.

Figure 39. Margareth Abraham and Robby Schouten.

Figure 40. Bill Bohlke Jr. was a civilian pilot who, along with four others, aided in the rescue by dropping two life rafts and also acted as a communications relay for the Coast Guard.

Figure 41. Tito Cordeiro and Balsey DeWitt. This
picture was taken at the ALM exhibition in Curacao
on August 1, 2005. It was the first time the two men
had met since the accident.

Chapter 17

IN A DARKENED ROOM NEAR THE SAN JUAN INTERNA-
tional Airport, controller Charles Silvia marked
an X on his radar scope at the point where the tiny blip represent-
ing ALM 980 and its sixty-three passengers and crew disappeared.
He called out to the watch supervisor that Antillean 980 had just
ditched. The supervisor, who had already been alerted to the possible disaster, notified the Coast Guard station in San Juan, setting in
motion one of the largest rescue operations in the history of the
Caribbean.

The closest aircraft to the X on Silvia's scope was a Pan American
727 Clipper flying from Point A Pietra Guadeloupe to San Juan.
The aircraft was at 24,000 feet. The crew consisted of Captain
William Pash, First Officer William M. Hall, and Flight Engineer
James L. Phillips, who went by his middle name, Larry.[1]

Charles Silvia radioed Pan Am 454 and asked for their assistance.
The first officer on the 727 made a brief announcement to the
twenty passengers on board explaining the emergency taking place
in the waters below. The captain then pulled the power back and

began a rapid descent in an effort to not over-fly the scene. Their eyes were glued to the radar altimeter as they descended through the thick overcast. At around 800 feet, they started to break out below a ragged ceiling. They were on a north heading as they passed over the spot where Silvia had marked an X on his scope. There was no sign of the aircraft or any survivors. It wasn't what the crew was hoping to find. Captain Pash took up a southerly heading and descended to 500 feet to get below the clouds. He called for flaps and slowed to 140 knots. He then began flying a boxed search pattern.

Looking out the first officer's side window, flight engineer Larry Phillips spotted an oil slick about three hundred meters long. He followed the thin dark line until he saw what looked like oranges floating in the water. He pointed out the spot to the other two crewmembers. As they approached the scene, details began to emerge and they saw what they believed was an inflated life raft with two or three people inside and twenty or more people in the water around it. Other passengers were scattered around an area about the size of a football field. There was debris floating in the water but no sign of the aircraft. Having arrived over the accident scene within minutes of the ditching, the Pan Am crew assumed the plane had broken apart on impact, and the detritus below them was all that remained.[2]

Captain Pash made a low pass over the survivors to let them know that they had been spotted and that help was on the way. He banked the plane around and told the controller to "mark" as he passed over the scene a second time. Silvia placed another X on his scope a few centimeters from the first.

As news of the ditching spread at the San Juan Air Route Traffic Control Center (ARTCC), off-duty controllers began gathering around controller Charles Silvia. He had started his shift at 3:30 P.M., about the time Antillean 980 had begun its diversion to St. Thomas. The controller he was to replace, Alexander Sambolin, had been too busy with other aircraft to give him a briefing. So Silvia had plugged in his headset next to Sambolin in order to get up to speed on the traffic in the sector. He was listening in when ALM 980 first reported that it was "a little short on fuel." He took over the radar from Sambolin at 3:37 P.M.[3] Two and half minutes later, ALM 980 reported that there was a possibility that they might have to ditch.

Sitting to Silvia's right was controller Charles Saunders. He was working the D3 sector. Saunders was also supposed to have been relieved at 3:30 P.M. He continued to work his sector because he didn't have time to give his replacement a proper briefing. There was too much going on between the weather, traffic, and Antillean 980. The D3 sector was not a radar control position. The D3 controller's primary job was to issue clearances to traffic outbound from San Juan to points east including St. Thomas, St. Croix, St. Maarten, and other points to the southeast and Europe. Directly in front of Saunders was a speaker and two rows of toggle switches that allowed him to communicate directly with the tower controllers at St. Thomas, St. Croix, and St. Maarten. The following transcript is the inter-facility communications related to ALM 980 from the start of the approaches at St. Maarten to the ditching.[4] Once again the times are UTC.

1924:07   SJU ARTCC D3:   Juliana Tower, San Juan Center.

1924:11   Juliana Tower: (Unintelligible). [The Juliana control tower operator was Robert Seijkens]

1924:15	SJU ARTCC D3:	Okay, is Antillean nine eight zero on the ground?

1924:20   Juliana Tower: He's shooting approaches...he's shooting approaches (unintelligible) I'll keep you advised.

1924:25   SJU ARTCC D3:   I cannot understand you, Juliana. One more time. He is not on the ground — right?

1924:25   Juliana Tower: Negative...negative. I'll keep you advised. I'll keep you advised.

1924:30   SJU ARTCC D3:   Okay and uh...we'll send eight one Whiskey over to you also to hold at six thousand.

1928:30   SJU ARTCC D3:   Go ahead, Juliana. [Robert Seijkens, the Juliana tower operator, is now calling San Juan to report that ALM 980 is diverting to its alternate.]

1928:40   Juliana Tower: Roger, Antillean nine eight zero to ah...St. Maarten...to St. Thomas and he's wanting flight level one zero zero. The aircraft is diverting. (unintelligible)

1928:45   SJU ARTCC D3:   ATC clears Antillean nine eight zero to the...ah...you want to go to St. Croix, he said.

1928:55   Juliana Tower: St. Thomas...St. Thomas.

           SJU ARTCC D3:   Okay to St. Thomas VOR via direct maintain four thousand and have him come over to us and we'll get him up.

1929:01   Juliana Tower: Roger, squawk one one zero zero.

1929:05   SJU ARTCC D3:   Affirmative.

1929:32   Juliana Tower: (Unintelligible) [Communication between the D3 controller and the Juliana control tower was hindered by poor radio reception and trouble understanding the heavily accented English of the Juliana control tower operator.]

1929:35   SJU ARTCC D3:   Juliana Tower, go ahead.

1929:37   Juliana Tower: (Unintelligible) five thousand. [He is referring to another aircraft holding at the NDB at five thousand.]

1929:45   SJU ARTCC D3:   Roger, have him maintain five
                            thousand until further notice.
                            Until I get the Antillean nine
                            eight zero out of the way.

1929:50   Juliana Tower: (Unintelligible). Nine eight zero,
                             proceed west-bound at this time
                             (unintelligible).

1936:15   SJU ARTCC D3:   St. Thomas Approach, San Juan
                            Center two inbounds. [The D3
                            controller must now coordinate
                            with the St. Thomas tower opera-
                            tor informing him of the inbound
                            traffic.] [St. Thomas Approach and
                            St. Thomas Tower are the same.]

1936:20 St. Thomas Tower: St. Thomas Approach.

1936:21   SJU ARTCC D3:   Okay, it's Antillean nine eight zero
                            DC-9 estimating St. Thomas one
                            nine four seven at three thousand,
                            coming St. Maarten direct, be your
                            control one nine four three.

1936:35   St. Croix Tower: San Juan Center — St. Croix.

1936:40 St. Thomas Tower: Okay, Antillean nine eight zero
                            four thousand.

1937:00   SJU ARTCC D3:   St. Thomas Approach, San Juan.

1937:03 St. Thomas Tower: St. Thomas.

1937:05   SJU ARTCC D3:   Yes I did. Antillean nine eight zero
                              changed his mind for the fifteenth
                              time. He wants to go to St. Croix
                              now. [The D3 controller can't hear
                              the communication between the
                              R3 radar controller and ALM 980,
                              nor can he speak directly to the
                              aircraft. He gets his information
                              either verbally or by a strip of
                              paper from the R3 controller.]

1937:10 St. Thomas Tower: (Unitelligible) Okay, we'll chalk
                              him up.

1937:15   SJU ARTCC D3:   Okay, C.S. [C.S. is the controller's
                              initials — Charles Saunders]

1937:50   SJU ARTCC D3:   Antillean nine eight zero DC-9 esti-
                              mating St. Croix at one nine four
                              seven and he'll be at five thousand,
                              coming from St. Maarten direct,
                              your control one nine four three.

              St. Croix Tower: Roger...D.J. [Donald J. Bishop]

1941:00 St. Thomas Tower: Center, St. Thomas. St. Thomas
                              Tower — Center. St. Thomas
                              Antillean nine eighty is hearing you
                              loud and clear. [The St. Thomas

tower operator is referring to ALM
980 trying to reach San Juan on
121.5, the emergency frequency.
He is indicating that ALM 980 can
hear San Juan Center but San Juan
apparently cannot hear ALM 980.]

1941:00 SJU ARTCC D3: Okay, thank you.

1944:00 Juliana Tower: Roger, are you still working the
Antillean nine eighty? [Robert
Seijkens, the St. Maarten Control
Tower operator, has also heard
ALM 980 trying to reach San Juan
on 121.5 and is growing increas-
ingly concerned over the fate of
the aircraft.]

1944:05 SJU ARTCC D3: Yes, sir. We're having trouble with
him...uh...we got him though.

1944:10 Juliana Tower: Is he going to make it to St. Croix?

SJU ARTCC D3: We don't know yet. Sir...uh...I'll
keep you advised.

1944:15 Juliana Tower: Roger, what is the distance you're
showing?

1944:17 SJU ARTCC D3: Right now he is fifty-five miles
east and we don't know if he's
going to make it in or not.

1944:20	Juliana Tower:	Okay, roger. Turn around! Turn around! (unintelligible)

1944:25	SJU ARTCC D3:	No. He cannot come back to you. He's going to try to make it St. Croix. He's running low on fuel.

1944:35	Juliana Tower:	Affirmative, I understand. I say again...requesting, requesting November one nine eight one Whiskey return, return St. Croix (unintelligible). [Here the controller mistakenly refers to another aircraft. It is assumed he was still trying to get ALM 980 to return to St. Maarten.]

1945:50	SJU ARTCC D3:	St. Croix, San Juan. Do you have any helicopters or anything that would help us if the ALM doesn't make it in?

1945:55	St. Croix Tower:	Negative.

1946:00	SJU ARTCC D3:	Stand by just a second.

1946:05	St. Croix Tower:	Hey, can I offer a couple of Antilles Airboats?

1946:10	SJU ARTCC D3:	Okay, yeah. You may have him stand by if you can; he might not make it here.

1946:15	St. Croix Tower:	Alright, I'll check with Antilles Airboats and see if they'd be willing to do the thing...uh... (unintelligible) St. Croix Airboats (unintelligible).
	SJU ARTCC D3:	Okay.
1946:25	SJU ARTCC D3:	St. Thomas and St. Croix when you send 'em over to us now put him on one two five point eight please. [On Balsey's request the San Juan radar controller had all other aircraft on the frequency move to 125.8 to clear up 125.0.]
1946:35	SJU ARTCC D3:	Okay, thank you.
1946:37	St. Croix Tower:	Okay, will do.
1946:40	St. Thomas Tower:	One two five point eight for all traffic?
1947:45	SJU ARTCC D3:	St. Croix Approach Control, San Juan Center.
1947:50	SJU ARTCC D3:	Okay, the Antillean nine eight zero is going to ditch.
1947:53	St. Croix Tower:	St. Croix.

1947:55   SJU ARTCC D3:   He is about forty miles to the east of your place and is Antillean Airboats going to be able to go out there?

1948:00   St. Croix Tower: (Unintelligible) Uh...there's nothing on the ground at St. Croix, but I told 'er I'd contact St. Thomas.

1948:07 St. Thomas Tower: St. Thomas Airboats has advised they'll go out. How many people on board the airplane?

1948:10   SJU ARTCC D3:   Standby. I'll get all the information for you. [The controller never did get that crucial bit of information.]

1948:20   SJU ARTCC D3:   Okay, St. Thomas. If you would please, have 'em start out now. He's on the zero eight zero radial of St. Croix at about forty-five [to] thirty-five miles. We'll get all the information and he is going down, so...so get him out there, please.

          St. Thomas Tower: Okay.

          St. Croix Tower: Thirty-five miles what radial?

1948:30   SJU ARTCC D3:   Zero eight zero and he is down now.

St. Croix Tower:　Zero eight zero.

1948:35　SJU ARTCC D3:　Yes.

St. Croix Tower:　...and he's down, D.J.

As soon as Silvia had a good fix on the site of the ditching, he passed on the information to Saunders, adding that the Pan Am captain had indicated that the seas were extremely rough. Saunders then passed on this information to the St. Thomas Tower controller.

1951:20　SJU ARTCC:　Okay, you might advise the Antilles Airboats there's heavy seas out where the aircraft ditched and see if they still want to go. [Antilles Airboats was a commuter airline that utilized an amphibious Grumman Goose, also known as the flying boat.]

1951:30　St. Thomas Tower:　Okay, I'm waiting for a call back from them. I've also notified the Coast Guard station here at St. Thomas. They've got an eighty-five-footer but Goddamn forty miles it'll take 'em...uh...just about three hours to get there.

1951:40　SJU ARTCC D3:　Okay, thank you.

St. Croix Tower:　Center, St. Croix.

1951:45   SJU ARTCC D3:   Go ahead, St. Croix.

1951:45   St. Croix Tower: We got an Airboat leaving St. Croix in the next couple of minutes going out there.

1951:50   SJU ARTCC D3:   Okay. He's on the zero eight zero at three five and you might advise your airboat that we've got a Clipper seven zero seven out there at five hundred feet circling the...ah...the...ah...scene. [The transcripts refer to Pan Am 454 as a Boeing 707. It was actually a Boeing 727.]

1951:55   St. Croix Tower: Okay. We'll do.

The Antilles Airboat departed St. Croix shortly after this last radio call. The pilot elected to fly below the overcast. He tuned in the St. Croix VOR and flew the 080-degree radial outbound toward the site of the ditching. Silvia provided radar separation between the Airboat and the Pan Am 727, which was still circling the scene.

Chapter 18

THE SEARCH AND RESCUE (SAR) ALARM SOUNDED at the Coast Guard Air Detachment unit at the Isla Grande airport at 3:55 P.M., along with the announcement: "Man the ready helo, DC-9 ditching." The alarm made a loud ahhooga, ahhooga sound and could be heard by anyone within several hundred yards of the hangar. Bill Shields, Carmond Fitzgerald, and the ready crewman dropped what they were doing and immediately headed for the ramp. They were already wearing their orange NOMEX flight suits.

The crews were trained to be in the air within five minutes of hearing the alarm. Shields wasted little time getting airborne, launching with only a minimal briefing about the ditching. He knew there would be plenty of time to get briefed en route. They had 1,200 pounds of fuel, enough for about three hours of flying. With a top speed of just over 100 knots, they were an hour and a half away from the accident scene.

The next Coast Guard crew to be notified of the ditching was an HU-16 crew that had departed Isla Grande earlier in the day. They were some seventy-five miles north of San Juan on an intercept mission to escort a C-130 to Ramey Air Force Base. The crew of the C-130 had shut down one of its four engines and had requested a Coast Guard intercept to monitor their flight to Ramey in case the aircraft developed another problem and the crew was forced to ditch. After a brief conversation with the C-130 pilot, the HU-16 turned and headed for St. Croix. Lt. Tom Blank was at the controls.

Coordination of the search and rescue operation was the job of the Rescue Coordination Center (RCC) in San Juan. After notifying the Air Detachment unit at Isla Grande, the duty officer at the RCC then tried to locate additional helicopters and ships that could aid in the rescue. One of the primary tools for locating ships is the Automated Merchant Vessel Reporting system (AMVER). AMVER is a tracking system set up to track ship movements worldwide. Merchant ships voluntarily report their position and expected tracks, which are then added to the AMVER database.[1]

Once the coordinates of a vessel in distress are known, the Coast Guard can check the database to see if there are any ships nearby that can be redirected to aid in a rescue. A quick check of the AMVER system didn't show any ships in the immediate vicinity of the ditching. It did, however, show a Navy LPH-7 anchored off the Coast of Vieques Island.[2] A call was placed to the *USS Guadalcanal* to request its assistance.

When the call came in to the *Guadalcanal*, four CH-46 helicopters were in the pattern, shooting touch and goes. They had spent the day shuttling crews from Camp Garcia back to the ship. Once that task had been completed, the crews decided to get in a few extra landings before calling it a day. Art Nash and Bill Murphy were the two pilots on John Barber's helo. Both were captains. There was a shortage of co-pilots, so Bill Murphy had volunteered to fill in as Art's co-pilot. All four helicopters were notified by the ship's control tower that a commercial jet had just ditched. The four helicopters landed on the *Guadalcanal* and were hot fueled, meaning they were fueled while the engines were still running and the blades were still turning. Art and Bill received a briefing about the ditching while still seated. As the helicopters were being refueled, additional crewmen hopped aboard, hoping to lend a hand. Randy Logan, a Huey pilot, and Vince Perron, another CH-46 crew chief, hopped on Barber's helicopter. At 4:15 P.M., the four helicopters departed off the *Guadalcanal*. They flew in a right echelon formation, with each helicopter staggered to the right and behind the helicopter immediately in front. The helicopters always flew in pairs. Twenty minutes later, at 4:35 P.M., two additional helicopters were launched off the *Guadalcanal*. The *Guadalcanal* then raised anchor and left Vieques to aid in the rescue.

On the island of St. Thomas the crew of the Coast Guard Cutter *Point Whitehorn* was notified of the ditching. The boat was docked at the CG Pier near King's Wharf, St. Thomas Harbor, Charlotte Amalie. The crew of the eighty-two-foot patrol boat had spent the early part of the day repairing a navigation buoy and later did some routine training. They had arrived back at the dock at noon. It was just before 4.00 P.M. when Commander Billy Cobb got word that a commercial jet had ditched off the coast of St. Croix. Most of the crew was just returning from liberty. The boat was still hooked up to water, power, and telephone service via shore tie. It took nearly thirty minutes to ready the boat. At 4:30 P.M., the *Point Whitehorn* was finally underway for position 17:53 N, 64:14 W.

In a straight line, they were about sixty miles away from the site of the ditching. But they first had to negotiate their way out of St.

Thomas harbor, which was always crowded with an assortment of yachts, sailboats, and cruise ships. The *Point Whitehorn* had a top speed of 23 knots. Rough seas, however, would prevent them from attaining anywhere close to that speed. With the sun setting in less than three hours, Billy Cobb knew it would be dark before they would reach the survivors.[3]

Lt. (j.g.) Donald G. Hartman got the call about the ditching just after 4:00 P.M. He had been hanging out in his room with his girlfriend at the Bachelor's Officer Quarters (BOQ) at the Roosevelt Roads Naval Station. He was on call to fly the H-34, a small helicopter powered by a single-rotary piston engine. When he heard that the plane that had ditched was a commercial jet, he knew the H-34 wasn't the right helicopter for the mission. He was going to need the SH-3A Sea King, a much larger helicopter known for its lifting capacity. The SH-3A, powered by twin-turbine engines, was new to the VC-8 squadron, having been acquired at the beginning of the year as a replacement for the H-34s. There weren't that many pilots and crewmen qualified to fly the new helicopter, including Hartman. He called the Operations Officer, Lt. Commander James Rylee, to report the ditching and to discuss with him the possibility of using the SH-3A.

Jim Rylee hadn't planned on doing any flying this day. He wasn't feeling all that well, thanks to a nagging cold. But he agreed with Hartman that they should use the SH-3A. He told Hartman to call the hangar and have them ready the helicopter. He also told him to make sure they had two qualified crewmen in back to work the hoist. Jim told his wife about the ditching as he was running out the door. He was in a hurry and had to swerve around traffic as he pulled out onto the main road leading to the airport. His erratic driving caught the attention of an MP, who hadn't failed to notice the tiny Renault

Dauphine speeding in the speed restricted housing area. Jim thought about pulling over but decided he didn't have time. At one point, he looked in his rearview mirror and noticed that the MP, who was driving a jeep, had drawn his gun. There was a brief second or two when Jim thought he might not make it to the airport. Fortunately, the MP decided that the tiny car wasn't much of a threat.

Pulling up to the hangar, Jim was met by the duty officer who informed him that the helicopter was ready and that the rest of the crew was waiting for him inside. Jim left the duty officer to explain things to the MP as he ran into the hangar to put on his flight suit.

Rylee met with the other three crewmen in the maintenance office. Donald Hartman, the on duty pilot, was going to be Jim's co-pilot. Bill Brazzell and Calvin V. Lindley were going to work the rescue from the back of the helicopter. Brazzell was a supervisor of maintenance and quality assurance. Lindley, who went by C.V., was the senior crewman in the squadron and the most experienced hoist operator on the SH-3A. Both men had been at separate barbeques when they first got word of the accident.

There were few details about the ditching other than it was a DC-9. Rylee figured that a DC-9 might hold up to 100 passengers. He had no idea how many people he could carry in the SH-3A. The normal passenger configuration was for fifteen passengers. Fortunately, the helicopter they were planning to use had no passenger seats. It was empty in back except for the two crew seats and a small canvas troop seat. The fact that there were no seats in back was an advantage. They could squeeze in more people. They departed Roosevelt Roads at 4:40 P.M.

Bill Bohlke learned of the ditching from an excited airport employee who had burst into his office with the news. Bill ran up to the tower to get more information from the tower operator, Don Bishop. Don confirmed that an aircraft had just ditched and mistakenly said that it was a CaribAir DC-9. CaribAir, short for Caribbean Atlantic Airlines, was the only airline in the area that operated the DC-9 on a regular basis. Bill raced back downstairs to the flight school and started to formulate a plan for dropping life rafts to the survivors. The best aircraft for the task was the Skyvan, a boxy aircraft with a clamshell-type cargo door that could be opened in flight. Unfortunately, the Skyvan was loaded with four thousand pounds of dirty laundry. Bill's father had a contract with the Cadillac Uniform Company to fly twice a week to San Juan. They would fly the dirty uniforms to San Juan and then pick up clean uniforms to return to St. Croix. The next run to San Juan was scheduled for Monday morning. Bill ran to the hangar and told George Stoute about the ditching and his plan to drop life rafts. George headed for a storage room to grab an old war surplus twenty-man life raft. The Skyvan already carried a small four-man life raft. George Johnson and Andy Titus, the two pilots who had been grounded by the weather, eagerly offered their assistance. Another pilot, Paul Wikander, who had stopped by the airport to ready an aircraft for an early morning flight the next day, also agreed to go along. Bill called to have the aircraft fueled, then he and the others grabbed a few cargo carts and started throwing dirty laundry into the carts.

As soon as the laundry from the Skyvan was unloaded, the overflowing cargo carts were pushed aside and Bill fired up the Skyvan's two engines. He called the tower from the aircraft to get an update. By this time Don Bishop, the controller who had confirmed the ditching, had been relieved and a new controller, Jimmy Gingrich, was on duty. Bill was told the general location of the ditching and was also told that it was an ALM and not a CaribAir DC-9. There were no seats in the back of the Skyvan. George Stoute, Paul Wikander and Andy Titus sat on the floor; George Johnson sat in the right seat.

Rather than fly under the ragged ceiling, Bill requested an IFR clearance to the accident scene. The small plane was soon swallowed up by the thick, dark clouds. The plane was still in the clouds at 1,800 feet when it reached the point where the Antilles Airboat was still circling. Bill coordinated his descent through the overcast with Center to make sure the two aircraft had adequate separation. The Pan Am 727 had already left the scene.

The Skyvan broke out of the overcast at around 500 feet. Bill didn't see anything except for the rough sea. He started flying a boxed search pattern, searching for both the survivors and the Antilles Air Boat. "Look to your left," someone in back shouted excitedly. Bill looked out his window and spotted people in the water gathered around what looked like a life raft. He swung the aircraft around in a tight turn but lost sight of the people as soon as he took his eyes off them. He had to fly another circle before reestablishing visual contact. This time he told the guys in back to keep their eyes on the people in the water and to not let them out of their sight. The VORs on the islands didn't have distance measuring equipment (DME), so Bill did a cross reference of two VORs to help pinpoint the site. This way he could find the scene again if he were to lose visual contact.

Not long after spotting the escape slide, Bill spotted the Antilles Airboat flying a few hundred feet below him. Bill established radio contact with the pilot of the Grumman Goose and asked him what his intentions were. The pilot radioed back that he had thought about landing but decided that the seas were too rough. When Bill told the pilot he wanted to drop some life rafts, the pilot of the Airboat agreed to depart the scene.

Bill flew a racetrack pattern around the slide, flying counter-clockwise so as to keep the slide in sight off to his left. He told the three men in back to drop the four-man life raft first so he could get a good read on the drift.

The laundry that had been in the aircraft had been secured by long straps called Aeroquip straps that stretched from the front of the cabin to a tie down in the rear. George Stoute and Paul Wikander each took one of the Aeroquip straps and wrapped one end around their waists. The visibility was so poor they couldn't see anything out the side windows. So they opened the rear door and shimmied on their stomachs until they were able to look straight down at the water.

Of the three men in back, one of them, Paul Wikander, had some actual SAR experience. Paul had spent four years in the Coast Guard as a crew chief on an HU-16. He knew that the proper way to drop a life raft was to have the raft inflate prior to entering the water. This prevents the raft from becoming damaged during the drop and assures that the raft is inflated for immediate use. Inflating a life raft in the water is difficult at best. Paul used one of the Aeroquip straps and attached it to the inflation lanyard on the four-man life raft. He and George Stoute then shimmied their way back to the open door.

Bill brought the Skyvan down to as low as thirty feet above the water and slowed to sixty knots. As he neared the main group, he yelled back for them to get ready. He was flying into the wind. The plan was to drop the raft immediately after passing over the main group. This way the raft would drift back toward the survivors. Andy Titus pushed the four-man raft toward the open door. As soon as Bill passed over the main group of survivors, he gave the signal and George Stoute and Paul Wikander shoved the raft out the back of the Skyvan. The raft hit the water seconds later and only partially inflated. "We need to be higher," Paul Wikander shouted toward the cockpit. He wanted the raft to have more time to inflate.

They used the same procedure for dropping the twenty-man life raft. Bill brought the plane overhead and slowed to sixty knots. He was slightly higher this time and when the raft was pushed out, it inflated fully before hitting the water. Unfortunately, the large raft was caught by the strong winds and was blown downwind thirty yards from the closest survivor.

After dropping both life rafts, the three men in back looked for anything else they might be able to toss out that could be of some help. They found six life vests and tossed those out on the next pass.

While Bill Bohlke was dropping his life rafts from the Skyvan, Tom Blank arrived overhead in the Coast Guard HU-16. He had been listening in to the conversation between the Antilles Airboat and the Skyvan. Once the Antilles left, Tom asked for a descent through the overcast. San Juan Center maintained separation between the two planes. Tom spotted what looked like yellow or orange objects floating in the water. He assumed the objects were life vests but couldn't make out any details. He lost sight of them as he passed overhead. Once he regained visual contact, he flew a counterclockwise racetrack pattern to keep the survivors in view.

The HU-16 Tom was flying had a crew of five: Tom and his co-pilot, Richard Evans, plus a radio operator, a mechanic, and a drop master. The radio operator sat in the cockpit in a seat directly behind the co-pilot; his radio console was located on the overhead panel. The aircraft could carry up to twelve passengers and could stay aloft for up to ten hours — hence the name Albatross. Although the HU-16 was an amphibious aircraft, the Coast Guard did not allow its pilots to land the aircraft in open water without special permission. The restriction came as a result of several accidents involving HU-16s trying to land and takeoff in rough seas. The Coast Guard didn't even practice making takeoffs and landings in open water. Neither Tom Blank nor Richard Evans had ever made a takeoff and landing in anything close to the sea conditions that existed at the time they arrived on the scene. More importantly, though, they didn't need to. They knew that helicopters were on the way.

One of Tom's first tasks was to determine wind direction. This was usually done by dropping a smoke flare. The winds were strong this day, and Tom could easily determine the wind direction just by looking at the water. High winds create visible wind streaks in the water that indicate the direction the wind is blowing. What he could use, though, was a marker beacon. The aircraft carried a portable radio beacon that he and other properly equipped aircraft could home in on. The beacon was cylindrical, about two feet long and six inches in diameter. It had an antenna that protruded out the top. The batteries in the beacon were saltwater activated and capable of transmitting a continuous signal for up to twelve hours. It had a range of up to twenty miles. If he lost the scene, he could find it again by homing in on the marker beacon.

The marker beacon was capable of transmitting on two frequencies. The recognized military emergency frequency was 243.0, also referred to as the guard frequency.[4] Once activated, the marker beacon also transmits a continuous Morse code identification. The Morse code can interfere with radio communications, so a second frequency is provided to free up the emergency frequency for voice communications. The drop master, however, failed to switch to the secondary frequency and dropped the beacon with it set to 243.0. The incessant beeping became so annoying that Tom had to switch off the guard frequency.

Next, Tom told the drop master to prepare for a raft drop. He wanted to drop two of the three life rafts that he had aboard.

Before tossing out the life raft, the drop master attached a two-hundred-foot bayonet line, called a trail line. The trail line could be used by someone in the water to grab onto and pull the raft toward them should the raft drift away or be blown away, which was a good possibility in the prevalent conditions. The floatable trail line was colored a bright orange. After attaching the bayonet line, the drop master attached a twenty-foot line to the inflation lanyard. In a perfect raft drop, the raft would become fully inflated fifty to one hundred feet above the water.

Once the raft was prepared for the drop, the drop master attached a safety harness around his waist and opened both halves of the entrance door. On Tom's command he shoved the raft out the door. Tom knew that the wind was strong and had tried to time the drop so the raft would have the best opportunity to reach the survivors. The first raft, however, was caught by the strong winds and cartwheeled past the survivors. On the second raft drop Tom made an adjustment, but the raft failed to inflate. It too landed out of reach of the survivors. It was the first time Tom Blank had ever had a raft not inflate during a raft drop.

Bill Bohlke saw the HU-16 drop the marker beacon and then the two life rafts. He was monitoring the frequency and heard the HU-16 pilot trying to reach San Juan Center. Bill could hear the Center controller responding, but the Coast Guard plane apparently could not hear San Juan Center.

The HU-16 was designed to be a flying command center. It was decked out with enough radio gear that it could communicate on virtually any frequency. Unfortunately, the radios, like the aircraft, were old and not in the best of shape. Once the plane descended to a lower altitude, the crew could no longer receive San Juan Center.

Bill Bohlke got on the radio. "Coast Guard 7245 this is Skyvan 33BB (three three bravo bravo). I'm reading San Juan Center loud and clear. I can relay for you if you'd like."

"Roger," came the reply from the HU-16. A minute or two later, the Coast Guard pilot came back on the radio. "Skyvan 33BB, how much fuel do you have?"

Bill informed the pilot that he had plenty of fuel and would be happy to fly the Coast Guard's wing and act as a relay to San Juan Center.

"Roger, that's great. We'll do that."

Bill notified San Juan Center that he would be acting as a communication relay for Coast Guard 7245. Bill maneuvered the Skyvan slightly behind and to the right of the HU-16, pushing the throttles up slightly to keep him in sight. He would remain in that position, passing on communications between San Juan Center and the Coast Guard HU-16, for the remainder of the rescue.

The Coast Guard HU-16 had direct contact with the RCC in San Juan. Tom Blank and his HU-16 became the On Scene Commander (OSC) for the rescue.

Chapter 19

WHILE EVERYONE IN THE WATER WAS CERTAIN THAT help was on the way, the ominous-looking sky led some to ponder the possibility that the deteriorating weather might hamper any rescue attempts. Thick, dark clouds with ragged tendrils of virga drifted menacingly overhead. When the Pan Am 727 appeared from seemingly out of nowhere, it buoyed everyone's spirits. Several passengers waved at the jet as it thundered by. The second plane to appear overhead was also greeted enthusiastically, even though its attempt to land was thwarted by rough seas.

Now a third aircraft appeared beneath the ragged ceiling. The boxy aircraft was flying so low and slow that it looked like it was standing still. The plane made a tight circle to the left and then dropped a life raft about thirty yards upwind from the main group. Balsey knew the value of a raft in this situation. It would be dark soon. If they weren't rescued before sunset, hypothermia would become a factor, despite the warm water temperature. Hypothermia is defined as a core body temperature of ninety-five degrees or less. A person immersed in water will cool twenty-five to thirty times faster than in air.* One of the first signs of hypothermia is shivering, a condition that several passengers were already exhibiting. While the water temperature was sufficiently warm enough that those in the water could expect to survive for up to forty hours or more, many would lose consciousness long before that. Getting people out of the water and into a life raft would increase the chances of survival considerably. Balsey made the decision to go after the raft, despite the risk of becoming separated from the main group. Before heading for the raft, he told Harry Evans, who was still on the slide, that he was leaving him in command in his absence. Whether it was Balsey's show of confidence, or whether it was the fact that Harry was no longer facing the fear of being in the water without a life vest, Harry rose to the occasion and became a visible authority figure to those around the escape slide. He repeated Hugh's suggestion for the men to use their belts and ties as extra hand-holds. He calmed the people and assured them that rescuers were on the way. Satisfied that Harry had things under control, Balsey started to swim toward the raft. He was joined by Hugh Hart.

Balsey and Hugh were about fifteen yards away from the raft when the civilian aircraft made another pass and dropped a second life raft. This raft inflated on the way down and was blown downwind a good fifty yards. Balsey told Hugh to continue after the first raft and that he would go for the second one.

"Balsey, are you crazy?" Hugh said. "You'll never get that sonofabitch. The way it's blowin' it's going to end up in Africa or someplace."

"Hugh," Balsey said, "I'm still in command. Do what I tell you. We need a raft. If I don't come back, I don't come back. At least we'll

---

* Other factors affecting the rate of cooling include: activity — an active person will expel more heat than a person who remains stationary in the water; body weight — a heavier person will cool at a slower rate than a thin person.

have a better chance of getting a raft than if we both go after the same one."

Balsey swam as hard as he could but quickly tired. His progress was impeded by the waves and his life vest, which made swimming an arduous task. His left hand, which had been cut when he exited the aircraft, was stinging from the salt water. He opened and closed his fist to help ward off the pain. He swam using a modified breaststroke, keeping his head as high above the water as he could. The raft would come in and out of view as both he and the raft bobbed up and down in the huge swells. Every few minutes he would stop to catch his breath. He'd start out again when he got a good bead on the raft. He got within a few yards of the raft but couldn't close the gap. It kept drifting away from him. Finally, he gave it all he had and managed to get a hand on the rubbery surface. He pulled himself toward the raft and in the process swallowed a large amount of salt water. Balsey summoned all the strength he had and managed to pull himself inside the large raft. He looked but couldn't see any of the survivors. He was totally isolated. He did spot a large amphibious aircraft off in the distance. This aircraft also dropped a raft, but it was so far away that Balsey was sure it wouldn't be retrieved.

The combination of the fatigue and the salt water in his stomach made him queasy. He leaned over the side and vomited. Not wanting to be impaired by illness, he reached around the raft looking for the survival kit, hoping to find some sea sickness pills. He found a pouch hanging from one side of the raft and began rummaging through its contents. He spotted a small package of pills, but the label identified the pills as air sickness pills. Balsey took the useless pills and tossed them as far as he could. What he really needed was an Alka Seltzer. He tried burping away the gas and the sickness eventually subsided. He turned his attention back to the contents of the survival kit. He found two smoke flares. He grabbed one and removed the cap, but nothing happened. It was a dud. He tossed it into the water. He pulled the cap on the second flare; the puff of orange smoke it expelled was barely visible. He threw the flare overboard. He was digging through the survival pouch to see what other items it contained when he thought he heard the sound of a helicopter. He looked skyward and saw a helicopter approaching from the southwest.

Hugh swam toward the partially inflated raft. It was a difficult task as he was swimming against the wind and the waves. Adding to his difficulty was the life vest, which had been causing him problems almost from the time he had inflated it. The back panel tended to ride up his back, causing the vest to float away from his body. He lost sight of the raft several times in the rough seas. When he finally reached the raft, he found that it had completely deflated. His first thought was to try and tug the raft back to the slide. He grabbed hold of it and started swimming toward the slide but quickly tired. He saw the survival kit floating in a pouch attached to the raft. He ripped open the pouch and found a small hand-held air pump. He felt around the raft for an air valve to which he could connect the pump. He found air valves on each side of the raft. This particular raft had two separate inflation chambers, presumably to avoid full deflation if one side were to develop a leak. Hugh tried to thread the pump onto the valve. It was no easy task because the connector on the pump was rigidly attached. He had to keep the pump perpendicular to the raft. After some struggle, he managed to thread it on, but he was faced with another problem. The pump kept backfilling with water. The only way to make it work was for him to push himself underwater and pump with his hands and arms high above his head in order to keep the pump above the surface. Each time he would come up for air the pump would be forced back down into the water. He would then have to pump the water from the pump before he could get more air into the raft. Eventually, he got enough air into one side of the raft to give it some buoyancy. But when he tried to close the air valve so he could remove the pump, he found that the valve was rusted and unmovable. Hugh turned the raft around to check the other air valve. That valve turned normally, so he unthreaded the pump and connected it to the opposite side. His plan was to inflate the good side of the raft, then pump up the bad side, leaving the pump connected to that side to act as a plug, knowing that he could simply pump more air into the raft as needed. He finished pumping up the good side and clambered atop the partially inflated raft. He quickly sank into the water. There was barely enough buoyancy in the small four-man raft to keep him afloat.

Wilfred Spencer was alone in the water. From the wind against his face, he knew that he was being blown downwind from the main group of survivors. He had watched the civilian plane drop its two life rafts. Sometime later, he spotted the navigator sitting atop a flotation device. Wilfred was sure it was the navigator because he could see the pink life vest. He wasn't certain what Hugh was sitting on. It didn't look like a life raft. He also spotted a large group of survivors gathered in a circle around another flotation device.[*] He started swimming toward the survivors but stopped when he saw the Coast Guard aircraft drop a life raft. The raft landed about the same distance from him as the main group of survivors. Wilfred also knew the importance of a life raft in preventing hypothermia and decided to go after the

---

[*] When Wilfred learned later that the navigator had inflated the escape chute, he automatically assumed that what he had seen was the navigator sitting atop the escape chute. He assumed that the other survivors were gathered around one of the life rafts that had been dropped.

raft instead. He didn't get very far before realizing that reaching the raft was going to be more difficult than he first assumed. The life vest proved to be more of a hindrance than a help. No matter how hard he pulled on the straps the vest wanted to float away from his body. He felt that his clothes were hampering his progress, so he kicked off his shoes and removed his pants and set off once again for the raft. But before he could get to the raft, a Coast Guard helicopter came into view.

Rick Arnold saw the Coast Guard seaplane pass overhead. He watched as a bright orange object fell from the plane and hit the water. Rick's fist thought was that it was shark repellant. He couldn't imagine what else it could be. It was too small to be any kind of flotation device. He knew the Caribbean was notorious for its shark-infested waters. Maybe the pilot had seen sharks from the air and that was why they had dropped the repellant.* From that point on the fear of sharks was constant, especially when someone's feet or legs brushed up against his. Every few minutes he'd check his hand to see how badly he was bleeding.

Other passengers voiced their concerns about the possibility of sharks. Some made a conscious effort to distance themselves from passengers who were bleeding. The fact was that the plane had ditched in an area of the Caribbean known by sport fishermen as "shark gulch." They could not have gone down in a more dangerous location. While that fact would have done little to calm their fears, there was one bit of information concerning sharks that would have gone a long way toward alleviating their concerns: Sharks, as it turns out, avoid the surface in turbulent seas due to a lack of oxygen.

---

* Despite numerous attempts to develop such a repellant, none exists.

Unaware of this fact of marine biology, the survivors spent much of their time in constant fear of being attacked from below.

The fear of sharks made many of those around the escape slide question the actions of the crew. When the captain and navigator left the main group to swim toward the two life rafts, some of the passengers felt that they were only looking after themselves, especially when they didn't return with either raft.

It was also obvious to everyone that the co-pilot was safely atop the slide while they remained in the chilly water. It didn't help that he was also insisting that there wasn't room for anyone else and that any attempts to get on the slide might tip the whole thing over. Harry tried to ease the tension by making a joke about his watch, which he commented was still ticking (a reference to a popular television commercial at the time).

Tobias Cordeiro, who was in the water around the escape slide, probed Harry for details. "How far are we from land?" he asked.

"About thirty-five miles," Harry replied, demonstrating a degree of situational awareness prior to the ditching.

"How long will it take for a boat to get here?" Tobias asked.

"A couple of hours," Harry said solemnly.

Tobias hadn't contemplated rescue by helicopter. He could only picture boats racing to the scene. The planes circling overhead offered little comfort. Tobias prayed silently. He knew it would be dark soon. He wasn't sure how many of those in the water would last through the night.

Not long after this conversation, the first helicopter appeared off in the distance. A second helicopter was spotted minutes later. The rescue had begun.

Chapter 20

THE CLOSEST HELICOPTERS TO THE SITE OF THE ditching were the four CH-46 Marine helicopters that had departed off the deck of the *Guadalcanal*. They were approximately eighty miles away; about forty minutes flying time in ideal conditions. Major Dennis Beckman piloted the lead helicopter. Their initial vectors to the scene were provided by Helicopter Directional Control (HDC) aboard the *Guadalcanal*. HDC was the command center for helicopter operations. Beckman was told that the aircraft had ditched thirty-five miles out on the 080 degree bearing of the St. Croix radio beacon.* The four helicopters initially climbed to 1,000 feet but were forced to descend as they approached St. Croix due to deteriorating weather. Heavy rain and poor visibility eventually forced the four helicopters to separate into pairs. By the time they reached the general vicinity of the ditching they were as low as 200 feet.

---

* The information given to the crews was incorrect. They should have been told that the plane had ditched on the 080 degree radial of the St. Croix VOR.

John Barber was flying in EM-13 behind Major Beckman. He was sitting in his crew seat listening in on the intercom communication system (ICS). He and Vince Perron had already rigged up the hoist system and attached the rescue sling. This involved stringing the cable from the hoist mechanism located on the ceiling aft of the forward bulkhead through the combination pulley/guillotine mounted directly above the rescue hatch, more commonly referred to as the hell-hole. The hell-hole was a three-foot by three-foot opening in the bottom of the helicopter. Barber could hear pilots Art Nash and Bill Murphy complaining about not being able to locate the scene and wasting precious fuel in the process.

"Why the fuck doesn't he ask San Juan for a fix," a frustrated Art Nash lamented over the intercom, referring to the lead helicopter. Art was receiving the St. Croix radio beacon, though he still had no way of determining distance. They didn't know that the Coast Guard had dropped a radio beacon that would have led them directly to the scene.

Finally, Beckman was able to raise the Coast Guard HU-16. By this time, however, two helicopters had already arrived on the scene and a second Coast Guard helicopter was en route. With two aircraft circling and three helicopters performing rescues, Tom Blank, the On Scene Commander, determined that the weather was too poor to bring in more helicopters. He requested that the four Marine helicopters fly to St. Croix to await further instructions. The second pair of helicopters that had departed off the *Guadalcanal* was also told to land in St. Croix. A total of six Marine helicopters stood standby on the island of St. Croix, where preparations for treating the survivors had already begun.

Lt. Commander James Rylee and his crew had departed from the Roosevelt Roads Naval station some twenty-five minutes after the four Marine helicopters had departed off the *Guadalcanal*. They were soon confronted with the same poor weather conditions that the Marine pilots were dealing with. Rylee brought the helicopter down to four hundred feet to stay below the overcast. He tried using the heading hold on the autopilot, but when he let go of the pedals the helicopter wouldn't hold its heading. He also discovered that the radio altimeter wasn't working. The radio altimeter gives the pilot his height above the ground, or in this case, height above the water. Loss of either component meant the loss of auto-hovering capability. He would have to hand-fly the entire flight.

Approaching St. Croix, Rylee was told that a Coast Guard HU-16 Albatross was circling the scene. He tried contacting the Coast Guard aircraft using several UHF frequencies but was unable to establish radio contact. He did, however, pick up a Morse code signal on the guard frequency. He tuned his ADF to 243.0 and noticed that the needle was picking up a signal, so he started tracking toward the station. He was certain that it would lead him to the accident scene. He and Hartman kept their eyes peeled outside, looking for any sign of the survivors. At 17:20 (5:20 P.M.), Rylee came upon the accident scene. They were the first rescuers to reach the scene. The survivors had been in the water for just over an hour and a half.

The first thing Rylee and Hartman saw was the large group of survivors gathered around what looked like a life raft. They also saw a number of people floating independently from the main group. The scene was littered with debris: seat cushions, small pieces of metal, insulation, suitcases, articles of clothing, and a few larger pieces of a honeycomb material that were two to three feet in diameter. There were also bodies floating face down in the water. Lindley opened the side door of the helicopter and rigged up the hoist system. They had two methods of hoisting people into the helicopter: the standard rescue sling and the Boyd seat, also referred to as a rescue seat. The Boyd seat resembles a boat anchor with three sym-metrically spaced prongs designed to allow a person to sit on the prongs. The advantage of the Boyd seat was that two people could be hoisted up at the same time. Lindley first hooked up the rescue sling but changed his mind, thinking he could get more people into the helicopter faster with the Boyd seat.

The first person they came to was a lone male in a large life raft. Rylee maneuvered the helicopter directly over the raft and set up a hover at about fifty feet. Lindley leaned out the right side and lowered the rescue seat to the occupant in the raft. The rescue seat was imme-diately caught by the strong winds. The pendulum like motion of the seat made it impossible for the man inside the raft to grab hold of it. Lindley told Rylee to let down another twenty feet, hoping that the shorter distance would negate the effect of the wind. But as the heli-copter inched lower, the downwash from the rotor blades pushed the raft away from the helicopter. Normally, in a low hover situation like this one, Lindley would have had lateral control over the helicopter through the use of a joystick located at the rescue station. But the loss of the auto-hover meant that Lindley could not use the joystick to control the lateral movement of the helicopter. He had to give Rylee constant voice commands: left, right, forward, up, down, back. Lindley guided Rylee back over the raft, but the raft, with nothing to weigh it down, was tossed around like it was a child's bathtub toy. Before they could back off and make a third attempt, the raft folded in two, trap-ping the lone occupant. Lindley watched helplessly as the man strug-gled to extricate himself from the sandwiched life raft. Eventually, the man was able to free himself. He jumped into the water and swam a safe distance away. Seeing this, Lindley lowered the rescue seat into the water. This time the man had no trouble grabbing and climbing onto the rescue seat. As the survivor was raised toward the helicop-ter, Lindley noticed that the man was wearing epaulets; he counted four stripes. "I'm the captain," the man said as he was pulled inside. Lindley directed him to the cockpit so he could brief the two pilots. He then removed the Boyd seat and replaced it with the rescue sling, feeling that the Boyd seat was too dangerous to use in these conditions.

Rylee spoke briefly with the captain then maneuvered over a man and woman who were floating together in the water. The woman was holding onto the man, who didn't appear to be conscious. Lindley lowered the rescue sling and using hand signals was able to guide the woman into the sling. Upon entering the helicopter, the woman immediately expressed concern for her husband, who remained in the water. Lindley assured the woman that they weren't going to leave her husband behind. He leaned over the side to get a better look. Lindley told Rylee over the ICS that the man looked unconscious, adding that his eyes were closed and that he was leaning back in the water motionless.

"Do you want to go down after him?" Rylee asked.

Lindley was the more experienced hoist operator. He turned to Brazzell. "Will you go in?"

"I'll go," Brazzell said without hesitation. Brazzell had received rescue training prior to joining the VC-8 squadron, but it had been several years since his training, and it did not include training as a rescue swimmer. In fact, none of the men on the helicopter were experienced in performing rescues. Their main job at Roosevelt Roads involved the recovery of target drones. Before lowering Brazzell, Lindley removed the rescue sling and rigged up the Boyd seat once again. It was the only way to bring up two people at the same time. Brazzell, wearing his flight suit, helmet, civilian shoes, and a Mae West life preserver, sat down on the Boyd seat and was lowered to the water.

As soon as he made contact with the water, Brazzell made the decision to remain on the Boyd seat. The seas were too rough and the winds too strong to risk letting go. He used his hands and arms to paddle his way over to the unconscious man. Lindley had to let out just enough slack in the cable to prevent Brazzell from being injured by the Boyd seat, which would snap against him each time the cable became too taut.

As Brazzell neared the unconscious man, a wave washed over him and something hit him over the head. Out of the corner of his eye he caught sight of the object that had struck him; it was an aircraft tire. He shook it off and continued paddling. Brazzell knew as soon as he reached the man that the man was dead. His skin was already turning blue. He decided to try to retrieve him anyway. He maneuvered the Boyd seat under the man with the man's legs wrapped around Bill's waist. The man was so large that Brazzell couldn't get his arms completely around him. He held on as best as he could and signaled to Lindley to bring him up. They didn't get very far into the air before the large man slipped from Bill's grasp and fell back into the water. Bill turned toward the helicopter and gave Lindley a thumbs down signal to indicate that the man was dead. Lindley nodded then hoisted Brazzell back up to the helicopter. Bill, cognizant of the fact that the man's wife was in the helicopter, wasn't about to give up just yet. He started looking for something inside the helicopter that he could use to tie around the man. He plugged into the ICS to discuss the situation with Rylee.

"Is he alive?" Rylee asked.

"As far as I can tell," Brazzell said, "he's dead."

Jim made the decision to abandon any further attempts at retrieving the man. There wasn't time to waste trying to retrieve a dead man when there were other people in the water waiting to be rescued. He flew over the man one last time as he headed for another survivor. The woman whose husband was being left behind made no protests. She sat silently, staring off into space.

The next survivor they came to was another very large man who also appeared to be unresponsive. Jim could see that the man had stripped down to his underwear. He could also see abrasions on the man's head and face. He decided to over-fly him and head for the main group of survivors. The Coast Guard helicopter was already hovering over the main group, attempting to hoist two people in a rescue basket. Jim watched in disbelief as he witnessed the cable snap and the two men suddenly plunge back into the water. Jim's first thought was that the weight of the two men must have been too great, forcing the crew to sever the cable. He continued to hover as the Coast Guard helicopter next attempted to land on the water. It seemed like an impossible task to Jim, who was in the perfect position to watch the dangerous rescue attempt. He was certain that the Coast Guard crew and their passengers were about to join the very people they were trying to rescue. Finally, the Coast Guard crew gave up on their attempts to land on the water and left the scene, much to the relief of Hartman and Rylee. Jim maneuvered toward the raft. He was about to establish a hover when he heard the Coast Guard HU-16 calling him.

"Stand off! Stand off!" came the call from the HU-16. The pilot of the HU-16 apparently wanted Jim to stay away from the large group of survivors.

Jim knew that a second Coast Guard helicopter was in the area. He had heard him on the radio earlier. There was no way Jim was going to sit on the sidelines and watch as the Coast Guard rescued people. He turned down the radio and set up a hover about fifty feet off the water. "Start picking 'em up," he announced over the ICS.

"How many should we pick up?" Lindley asked.

"Pick 'em up until we can't hold any more," Rylee replied.

The first two pickups were the two men who were still clinging to the rescue basket released by the Coast Guard. They then moved to the main group of survivors. Lindley could see a man in uniform kneeling on the yellow flotation device. He lowered the sling, but it was quickly blown twenty yards downwind. Once again Lindley told Jim that they needed to be lower. Jim brought the helicopter down to twenty feet, less than half the distance of the recommended hovering altitude and only a few feet above the swells. Now Lindley could get the sling to the man in uniform. He gave a few hand signals to the crewman and got the first person into the sling. After that, the pickups went smoothly, one right after the other. Brazzell would pull the person inside and remove the rescue sling; Lindley would then lower the sling to the crewman, who would then help the next person. The survivors were brought up so quickly it was as if they were freshly caught fish being dragged aboard a fishing boat.

By this time Balsey had jumped into action and began assisting the two Navy crewmen by positioning people on the floor as they entered the helicopter. There were people sitting on the floor all along the sides of the helicopter. When there was no more space around the fuselage, people were placed wherever there was an empty spot.

Jim was doing all he could to maintain a steady hover in the howling winds. At one point he glanced down at his airspeed and read 39 knots, which meant that the winds were blowing that hard. Thirty-nine knots is equivalent to 45 mph. As difficult as the windy conditions made his task, there was one benefit: The strong winds provided additional lift and allowed him to carry more weight.

For the passengers still in the water, the windy conditions were compounded by the downwash from the rotor blades. At least one passenger sustained a facial injury from debris picked up by the swirling winds.

Eventually, they reached a point where there wasn't any more room inside the helicopter. Lindley announced over the ICS that they were full. Jim asked him to do a head count. A minute or two later, Lindley announced that they had twenty-six survivors on board.

Jim couldn't see what was going on behind him; his focus was on flying the helicopter. He assumed that they had picked up another seven or eight people. He couldn't believe that they had picked up that many survivors. "That can't be true," he told Lindley. "We can't hold that many. Count 'em again."

When Lindley came back with the same figure, Jim established radio contact with the HU-16. Jim's call sign was Saltspray 15. He informed the HU-16 that they had twenty-six people on board and wanted to know where he should take them. The HU-16 radioed back with instructions to proceed to St. Croix. Jim, who was enervated from spending the last hour and twenty-five minutes fighting the gusty winds, asked the HU-16 if 230 was a good heading for St. Croix.

"Saltspray 15, yes sir," the HU-16 replied. "That's a good heading."

Jim Rylee turned and headed for St. Croix. His only thought was to not screw up now. He knew he was overweight. He could feel it in the sluggish controls. The wind, which had helped him during the hover, was now making the overloaded helicopter difficult to handle. He climbed and increased the power, then handed over the controls to Hartman. The sooner he got to St. Croix the better.

Bill Shields and Carmond Fitzgerald arrived on scene within minutes of the Navy helicopter. Bill quickly assessed the situation. He saw the large group of survivors and the Navy helicopter. He also saw people scattered downwind of the main group. Shields knew that those being blown downwind were in the greatest jeopardy, so he flew downwind and circled back to begin his pickups.* There was a lot of chatter on the radios. ATC was on one frequency; the Skyvan was talking to San Juan Center, relaying communications from the HU-16; Carmond was talking to the RCC and the HU-16. Bill turned down the volume on

---

* A lone survivor in the water is more difficult to locate than survivors huddled together, especially in rough seas.

his radio so he could concentrate on the pickups. The only person he wanted to hear was the crewman in back working the hoist.

The HH-52A was equipped with both a rescue basket and a rescue sling. The rescue sling is the quickest way to get a person into a helicopter. Unfortunately, the rescue sling is often misused. The correct method is to back into the sling with the head and shoulders so that the sling can lock under the arms and the upper torso as the person is being lifted. Most people seeing the sling for the first time will stick their head and shoulders through the sling as if they're jumping through a hoop. This causes all of their weight to be distributed through the chest or stomach. If that person isn't in good physical shape, they will have difficulty holding that position for any length of time and will usually slip out of the sling before they reach the helicopter. For this reason, the rescue basket is the primary method used in a civilian rescue.*

The first pickup was a dark-skinned woman who at first appeared to be unconscious. Bill hovered directly over her and saw that she was moving. They lowered the basket to her and she managed to climb aboard. As she was brought inside the helicopter, she complained of internal pain and a lack of feeling in her legs.

They proceeded upwind and picked up a second straggler, a male. This person was wearing a uniform shirt but no pants or shoes. The person they picked up was the purser, Wilfred Spencer. They then proceeded upwind from the main group to pick up a lone individual in a partially inflated life raft. Navigator Hugh Hart was the third person rescued by the Coast Guard crew.[1]

Carmond's job during the rescue was to remain in communication with the On Scene Commander and to watch out for other aircraft.

---

* Most of the passengers rescued by the Navy helicopter used the rescue sling incorrectly. The helicopter was low enough to the water, however, that it didn't cause a problem.

He was also monitoring their fuel situation. He informed Bill that they only had enough fuel to remain on scene for another thirty minutes before they would have to head for St. Croix.

After picking up the man in the partially inflated life raft, Bill proceeded to the main group of survivors. The first person rescued from the main group was a woman who appeared to be injured. Several people in the water had to assist her into the basket. Once she was in the helicopter, Hugh and Wilfred carried the woman to an open spot on the floor. There were now four survivors on board the helicopter. Faced with a dwindling fuel supply, Shields told the hoist operator to start picking up two at a time.

The hoist system was rated to six hundred pounds. Shields hovered north of the slide and lowered the basket into the water. The hoist operator used hand signals to indicate that he wanted two people in the rescue basket. Two very large men swam toward the basket.

Seconds later the crew chief was heard over the ICS. "We've got a problem. The hoist is jammed! It won't go up any further!" The cable had started to unravel and was now binding the hoist system.

Shields, who had had a similar cable failure before, knew that he couldn't fly back to St. Croix with the two men dangling from the bottom of the helicopter. The cable could snap and send the two men hurtling through the air. They were going to have to shear the cable. He first tried to lower the basket to the water to allow the men to jump out, but the men were confused and wouldn't leave the basket. He told the crewman in back to prepare to cut the cable.

Shearing the cable is accomplished automatically by a knife located inside the housing of the hoist system. Both the pilot and the crew chief have the ability to activate the cartridge that operates the knife. Shields deferred the decision on when to shear the cable to the crewman in back, who was in a much better position to determine when the basket was close enough to the water to make the cut. The large swells, however, made it a difficult task. As soon as the basket appeared to be near the water, the swell would disappear and the basket would be left dangling fifteen feet above a trough. When the cable was finally sheared, the basket and its two occupants fell from a height of about ten feet. The two men clung to the basket not sure what had happened. Some of the passengers hadn't seen the helicopter crewman signal for two people and assumed that the men were being selfish. Everyone who witnessed the basket drop assumed the cable had broken due to excess weight.

With time running out, and no way of hoisting survivors into the helicopter, Shields tried a platform pickup. This is accomplished by attaching a metal platform to the door and then hovering close enough to the water so that the crew chief can assist people into the helicopter by hand. Shields made two attempts. Each time he neared the water, the swells, which were at times higher than the rotor blades, prevented him from staying long enough to make a successful pickup.[*] He finally decided that conditions were too dangerous for a platform pickup. He spotted the Navy SH-3A helicopter hovering nearby and decided to leave the scene.

Shortly after Bill Shields and Carmond Fitzgerald had departed from the Isla Grande airport, the duty officer placed a phone call to the unit's commanding officer, Charles Mayes. All of the standby crewmen had been dispatched to the scene. There was no one left to fly the second HH-52A. It was a Saturday and the duty officer was having trouble locating another crew. Charles Mayes volunteered to fly

---

[*] Most of those who were at the scene estimated the swells to be eight to ten feet high. Bill Shields claimed that when he was attempting to make the platform pickup that a few of the swells appeared to be above his rotor blades. The rotor blades sit some fourteen feet above the ground, which would indicate that at least some of the swells were up to fifteen feet high.

the second helicopter himself. When he arrived at the airport, he found the Operations Officer, Jim Brawley, already inside the helicopter making preparations to depart. When Jim saw his Commanding Officer approaching, he started to move over to the co-pilot seat, which on this helicopter was the left seat. Charles Mayes signaled for him to stay seated; he then jumped into the co-pilot seat. The third crewmember to climb aboard was an electronics technician. He didn't normally go out on rescues, but he was the only one left at the airport who knew how to work the hoist system.

Charles Mayes and Jim Brawley arrived on scene just as the Navy helicopter began picking up survivors from the main group. They spotted two people in the water upwind of the main group. Both appeared to be unconscious. Jim told the crewman to lower the rescue basket. Neither person made an attempt to get inside the basket. Jim decided to try a platform pickup. He had the same trouble trying to land in the rough seas as had Bill Shields. They abandoned their attempts and waited for the SH-3A to finish their pickups. As soon as Saltspray 15 departed the scene, they moved in and began bringing up survivors from the main group.

Operating the hoist system requires a degree of skill. The operator has to lean out of the helicopter and guide the cable with his right hand while his left hand works the toggle switch that operates the hoist. It can be a difficult task even in good weather. When the crewman in back said he was having difficulty controlling the basket in the strong winds, Charles Mayes left his seat and went in back to assist.

The HH-52A had a maximum gross weight of 8,400 pounds. With three crewmembers on board and full fuel, a full load would have been four passengers. After they picked up the sixth survivor, Jim Brawley expressed some concern that they might be overweight. Commander Mayes looked over Brawley's shoulders and saw that they had burned off a significant amount of fuel. He told Jim that he thought they could safely pick up one more. After the seventh pickup, the helicopter was so full they couldn't have picked up another person even if they had wanted to. They departed the scene for St. Croix, leaving three people behind at the slide.[2]

Tom Blank continued to circle the scene in the HU-16. When he got word that a number of pleasure craft had left St. Croix and were headed to the accident scene, he told his radio operator to have the boats return to St. Croix. He didn't want them interfering with the rescue. It's not known if the message got through or how many boats were involved. At one point in the rescue, a Cessna 150 arrived over the scene with the intention of taking photographs. The small two-place plane was much slower than the HU-16 and the Skyvan and quickly became a flight hazard. The pilot of the Cessna refused to leave until Tom Blank threatened to report him for interfering with a rescue operation.[3]

When the last helicopter departed the accident scene, there were still people in the water. There were three people at the escape slide and at least two more people who were either dead or unconscious floating nearby. It was a little after six P.M. The weather had improved, but now it was starting to get dark. Tom looked out on the horizon, hoping to see the six Marine helicopters headed his way. He had sent word for them not long after the Navy helicopter had left the scene.

Chapter 21

THE CREWS OF THE SIX CH-46 HELICOPTERS HAD not been very happy with the instructions from the Coast Guard HU-16 to land in St. Croix. In their minds, they were needlessly being kept away because of some inter-service rivalry. John Barber was one of those who disagreed with the order to land in St. Croix. But rather than waste time complaining about the situation, he set out to get his helicopter refueled. It was immediately apparent to Barber that it was going to take some time for the lone fueler to fuel each helicopter. Barber and Vince Perron, the extra crew chief who had hopped aboard as they refueled on the deck of the *Guadalcanal*, jumped out of the helicopter and approached the fueler. Vince Perron was a tall, strapping farm boy from Minnesota. While other guys had pinups taped to the inside of their lockers, Vince kept pictures of John Deere tractors and combines. "You're gonna fuel EM-13 first," Vince said threateningly to the fueler. The instructions Barber and Perron had received was that the Marine helicopters were going to be called out one at a time. They didn't want to be the last ones fueled. "Yes, sir," the fueler replied, looking up at the imposing figure staring down at him.

While the helicopters were being refueled, the pilots gathered inside the terminal to learn what they could about the ditching. When a Coast Guard helicopter landed with four survivors, several of the Marine pilots ran out to talk to the Coast Guard crew. Minutes later, two of the Marine helicopters were starting their engines. They departed St. Croix at 6:00 P.M.

Not long after the first two helicopters departed, Art Nash and Bill Murphy returned with news that they were next to launch. At 6:15 P.M., EM-13 and EM-15 headed out from St. Croix. The last two helicopters departed a few minutes later.

Twenty minutes after leaving St. Croix, Art Nash's voice came over the intercom. "Okay, keep your eyes open. We're coming up on the crash scene." Art could see the two helicopters that had taken off before him. The anti-collision lights on the top of each helicopter created a pulsating light that lit up the misty atmosphere of cloud, water, and spray.

Barber connected the pistol grip to the ceiling-mounted hoist control panel. The pistol grip was attached to a twenty-five foot cable that allowed him to operate the hoist remotely. He opened the hell-hole door and folded it backwards. He then took up his position lying flat on the door, looking straight down into the water. Randy Logan and Vince Perron served as an extra set of eyes. Vince stared out the gunner's window while Randy Logan stood in the doorway to the cockpit and looked straight ahead through the cockpit windows along with the pilots.

The first thing John saw was a small light. The light was attached to a life preserver, which was around the neck of a thin, elderly man still dressed in a business suit. "I got someone," John said over the intercom. "You're coming straight at him." John started giving Art directions.

"Okay, come forward, come forward, come forward...okay, slow down, slow down." But the helicopter didn't slow. It flew right over the man. "You just overshot him!" Barber yelled into the intercom.

"I have another one lined up," Art Nash said. Art had seen the first individual but the man looked unconscious, so he decided to go for the next person he spotted.

The second individual, however, didn't appear to be any more responsive than the first. Randy Logan, dressed in only his flight suit and wearing a Mae West life preserver, volunteered to go into the water after the man. After some discussion as to whether it was worth the risk, Randy got into the horse collar and Barber lowered him to the water. Randy immediately set to work getting the unconscious man into the rescue sling. It was dusk now and becoming harder for the pilots to find a reference point to use for hovering. Art Nash, who was the pilot in command, decided to hand over the controls to Bill Murphy, who had more experience flying the CH-46. It was a smart, unselfish decision by Art Nash.

Barber struggled to keep an eye on the two men in the water as they bobbed up and down in the huge swells. He gave constant instructions to Murphy — left, right, forward, back — to keep the helicopter from drifting away. Unlike the crews of the Coast Guard Helicopter and the Navy SH-3A helicopter, the pilots of the CH-46s couldn't see the hoist operation. They had to rely solely on directions from the crew chief.

Once Randy had the sling in place around the unconscious man he gave a thumbs up signal, indicating to Barber to raise the hoist. As John raised the hoist, he continued to keep one eye on Randy Logan, fearful that he could easily lose him and never find him again in the dark. John ran the hoist to the stop. The man was left dangling in the center of the helicopter, his feet barely clearing the hell hole. At this point he and Vince noticed that the man had stripped down to his underwear. There was nothing to grab onto to pull him inside. The flimsy life vest around his neck was of little help. Adding to the problem was the man's size. Barber guessed him to be well over 250 pounds. His skin was cold and clammy. He was dead weight. John let out some slack in the cable and with one hand pushed him toward Vince, who grabbed him and pulled him inside.

Vince removed the man's life vest and immediately started performing CPR. He did this despite the fact that the man's upper lip appeared to be gone. There was just a thin bloody strip where his lip should have been.[*] Barber meanwhile turned his full attention to retrieving Randy Logan, who by now was barely visible in the dwindling light. Once Randy was safely aboard, Barber closed the hellhole and started helping Vince by doing chest compressions. Alternately they would turn the man over and use a back pressure method of respiration, which involved applying pressure to his back, then pulling his arms and shoulders back in an attempt to clear his lungs of salt water.

While Vince and John were busy in back, Randy Logan gave Art Nash and Bill Murphy a quick assessment of what was happening. Art decided to fly immediately to St. Croix, where the man could receive medical treatment. He knew there were other helicopters in the area, plus by now it was so dark it was almost impossible to find a reference point for hovering.

Pilots Glenn Warren and Ned Lemoine were flying helicopter EM-07. They were the first to depart St. Croix and the first to arrive on scene. In back were Sergeant Gary Bockman, Lance Corporal William Schrader, and a Navy corpsman. Earlier in the day, twenty-year-old Bill

---

[*] There was some speculation after the fact that the man's lip could have been eaten by fish as he floated unconscious in the water.

Schrader had taken his final flight test to qualify as a crew chief. Bill had spent the day performing all of the duties of a crew chief while his examiner, a Sergeant Blankenship, looked on to make sure everything was done correctly. While John Barber and the three helicopters with him were doing troop back-loading, Bill Schrader's crew and another helicopter were put to work hauling supplies and equipment back to the ship. One of Bill's first tasks was to supervise an external lift of supplies. The supplies had been placed atop a large cargo net. Bill guided the helicopter over the load of supplies, giving the pilot instructions on altitude and direction. He then lowered a hook through the hell-hole to have it attached to the cargo net. With this accomplished, he gave the pilots instructions to slowly lift the supplies. When Bill was assured that they had a good lift, he instructed the pilots to return to the ship. The next task was to lower the supplies to a waiting crew on the deck of the *Guadalcanal*. Blankenship wanted to see another external lift, so he had Bill set up a jeep lift. The jeep lift was a bit trickier because if it isn't rigged up properly the jeep can shift after being lifted and throw off the helicopter's center of gravity. Bill hooked up the jeep without difficulty, and the pilots got in a little practice of their own, flying with the heavy jeep suspended beneath them. Rather than fly the jeep back to the ship, Blankenship wanted to have Bill oversee the loading of the jeep into the helicopter through the loading ramp. Bill performed the task without difficulty.

When the helicopter returned to the *Guadalcanal* later that afternoon, Bill was feeling confident. Everything had gone smoothly. As soon as the rotors stopped turning and the noise quieted down, Sergeant Blankenship stuck out his hand and congratulated Bill on becoming a crew chief. The pilots congratulated him also, then told him to put the bird to bed. Bill folded the blades, put on the protective covers, then had the helicopter parked along with the others on the side of the flight deck. He hadn't even made it off the flight deck to celebrate when he got word about the ditching. He saw the first four helicopters land and take on fuel. He had his helicopter pulled out of the pack. He was joined by Crew Chief Gary Bockman and a Navy corpsman. Bill performed another preflight and had the helicopter ready to go when pilots Glenn Warren and Ned Lemoine jumped in. Before departing, Bill and Gary grabbed some blankets and tossed them into the back of the helicopter. They didn't have time for anything else.

Warren and Lemoine departed the *Guadalcanal* along with another helicopter piloted by Captain Gordon Tubesing. The two helicopters were told to fly directly to St. Croix. The first four helicopters off the *Guadalcanal* were already on the ground in St. Croix when they landed.

Captains Warren and Tubesing weren't on the ground very long when they saw the Coast Guard helicopter land. After talking briefly with the two Coast Guard pilots, they were told to head out to the accident scene. Neither of their helicopters had been refueled. Both decided to go with the fuel they had, which was a little over an hour's worth.

The Coast Guard crew had briefed the pilots on where the plane had ditched, but both Warren and Tubesing had trouble locating the scene. Low ceilings and poor visibility forced the two helicopters to fly as low as 50 feet above the water. It was also becoming difficult to see due to the rapidly dwindling daylight. Glenn was concerned that if they didn't find the scene soon, they would have to return to St. Croix due to a lack of fuel.

The Navy corpsman was first to spot what looked like two or three people sitting in a life raft. Glenn wasted little time taking up a position directly over the slide. Bill Schrader and Gary Bockman prepared to lower the rescue sling. The first few attempts at lowering the rescue collar were unsuccessful. The swells made it difficult to judge the distance between the helicopter and the survivors. Just when it looked like the collar was in position, the person trying to grab onto it would disappear into a trough. The wind was also causing havoc, blowing the collar off center and out of sight.

Each failed attempt was followed by an update on the fuel status. "We've got less than twenty minutes of fuel," Ned Lemoine warned.

"Talk to me, Billy," Captain Warren said over the radio. "We're not leaving until we get 'em all." It was getting so dark that he was afraid that if they didn't get the three survivors now they wouldn't be recovered until the next day.

Bill Schrader had been a crew chief for a little more than two hours. He could count on one hand the number of hoists he had performed. As he peered down into the maelstrom below him, he could feel his stomach churning. He had felt some butterflies earlier in the day during his flight test, but this was different. This time there was no Sergeant Blankenship standing nearby to bail him out if he screwed up. This time the lives of three men rested squarely on his shoulders. Bill put aside his fears and focused on the task at hand. "We need to be closer to the water," he announced over the ICS. As the helicopter inched lower, he was able to judge the swells better. "Hold it right there," he said, sounding like a veteran crew chief. This time one of the men on the slide was able to grab and hold onto the rescue sling. The first pickup was a man with a beard. This was passenger Rick Arnold. He appeared to be suffering from hypothermia and was given a blanket. The second person rescued was a young male, later identified as passenger George Kellner. He was shivering uncontrollably. The Navy corpsman and Gary Bockman wrapped a blanket around him. When that didn't stop the shivering, one of the men in the helicopter lit a cigarette and put it in George's mouth. George gladly inhaled the warm smoke despite having quit smoking months earlier.

There was now just one survivor left on the slide. Bill lowered the sling but the man had difficulty grabbing onto it in the rough seas. The two pilots became increasingly concerned about their fuel status. The fuel burn increases significantly during a hover. Just when Glenn was about to pull out, Schrader announced over the ICS that he had the last man. The last person rescued was one of the pilots. Bill didn't know if it was the captain or the first officer. He didn't take time to ask. First Officer Harry Evans was the last person rescued.

"We got 'em," Bill said over the intercom as soon as the man was safely inside the helicopter.

With that, Glenn Warren turned the helicopter around and headed directly for St. Croix. There was some doubt as to whether or not they had enough fuel to make it. The two pilots kept a close eye on the fuel gauges, fully prepared to set down in the water or preferably a highway if necessary. Fortunately, they didn't have to. They landed with less than five minutes of fuel remaining.

Chapter

AT THE TIME OF THE DITCHING, THE NEWLY ELECTED Governor of the Virgin Islands, Melvin H. Evans, was waiting to take a flight on an Antilles Airboat from St. Croix to St. Thomas. Upon hearing news of the accident, he immediately canceled his plans and began coordinating efforts to arrange for medical attention for the survivors.[1] Governor Evans, a physician himself, drove to the Charles Harwood Memorial Hospital to alert the hospital staff and to pick up medical supplies and equipment before returning to the airport. He used a newly installed Civil Defense communication system to broadcast news of the ditching and to alert local authorities. Volunteers soon began showing up at the airport and at the hospital. Spectators filled the terminal and observation decks. Before the night was through, the crowd at the airport would grow to nearly a thousand people.[2]

The first helicopter to arrive in St. Croix was the Coast Guard helicopter piloted by Bill Shields and Carmond Fitzgerald. Two women were taken off the helicopter by stretcher and placed into waiting ambulances. Wilfred and Hugh didn't require immediate medical attention. Hugh's right knee was bothering him, but he could walk without assistance. Wilfred's only injury was a bruise on his forehead, which he had received from flying debris at the moment of impact. The two became separated in the rush of people. Wilfred was whisked away to a VIP room where someone offered him a pair of work pants. Wilfred accepted the pants gratefully. Now that he was safely back on solid ground he was embarrassed to be walking around in nothing but his shirt and Jockey shorts. Hugh was taken to another room on the second floor of the terminal building.

Captain Balsey DeWitt was one of twenty-six people rescued by the crew of the Navy Sea King helicopter. The fact that he was the first person rescued was a complete coincidence. Had it been up to him, he would have insisted on being rescued last. Balsey did all that he could after being rescued to assist the survivors as they were brought into the helicopter. He continued to show concern for the passengers as he sat in the helicopter on the way to St. Croix. One man complained that he was in a lot of pain. "Just hang on," Balsey told him. "We're headed to St. Croix. We'll be on the ground shortly." Balsey noticed an attractive young woman sitting next to him who had a large cut on her face. She was pressing her hand against her forehead. When she let off the pressure, her skin unfolded to reveal the magnitude of her injury. Balsey looked for something to use to temporarily hold the skin in place, but the woman insisted that she was okay.

Once they landed and had taxied to the terminal, one of the pilots turned to Balsey and told him to wait until the others had left. They had apparently gotten word that they were to keep the crewmembers separated from the passengers. Not long after everyone had exited the helicopter, Balsey was taken to a private room. It was too early at this point to know if there had been any casualties, but Balsey had a terrible sinking feeling in the pit of his stomach. He knew that they had left one woman's husband behind in the water. He suspected that there might have been people trapped inside the plane. How else could he explain the actions of the male passenger who had attempted to reenter the plane after Balsey had helped him onto the wing? Yet, as strong as his suspicions were, he still held out hope that he was wrong. But then he remembered the two little girls. He hadn't seen the children on the helicopter or at any time while he was in the water. He knew that they would have been the first ones rescued.

Balsey lowered his head and asked for a man of the cloth. He wanted to speak to a clergyman and didn't care what faith. Some time had passed when a man in plain clothes entered the room. Balsey looked but didn't see a collar on the man. When the man started asking questions about the flight, Balsey stopped him and asked if he was a minister. The man avoided answering and began anew with questions about the ditching. Balsey asked to see some identification. When the man hesitated, Balsey grabbed him by the arm and started to go through his pockets. The man backed off and took out his wallet. The first thing Balsey saw was a badge identifying the man as a member of the Press. Balsey told the reporter to leave the room, telling him to pass on word that the only person he wanted to talk to was a priest. "Will you talk to me later?" he asked. "Don't push it," Balsey said as he escorted him out of the room.

Eventually, Balsey did get to speak with a priest — a Father Gow from St. John's Anglican Church. Balsey told the priest that he had caused some people their untimely death. The priest did his best to console him, telling him to not question the actions of God. Together they prayed for those who had not survived.

Tobias Cordeiro had not been injured in the ditching, despite the fact that he had been sitting unrestrained on the life raft at the time of impact.* He was in the water around the slide when the first Coast Guard helicopter arrived. Tobias spotted Wilfred sitting in the helicopter. At least he knew that Wilfred was safe. Seeing Wilfred gave him some hope that maybe Margareth survived as well.

Tobias was eventually picked up by the second Coast Guard helicopter. He agreed to go only after he was assured that no injured passengers remained in the water. Once he landed at St. Croix, he immediately set out to look for Margareth. He squinted as he scanned the large crowd standing in front of the terminal building. He couldn't see very well due to the low light and the fact that he had lost his glasses in the water. When he didn't spot her, he asked some of the people on the ramp if anyone had seen the stewardess from the plane. No one had seen her. He was given a cursory examination, then led to a waiting room where he met up with Wilfred. A short time later, both he and Wilfred were taken to the Estate Carlton Hotel and Condominium complex in Fredericksted, St. Croix, where each was given a private room.

As soon as Wilfred Spencer got to his room, he called his wife Marlene. She was in tears. She had been informed of the accident by someone from ALM, but the person who called didn't have any details. "I'm in St. Croix," Wilfred told his wife. "I am together with Tito. Call his family and tell them that Tito is all right." Wilfred could still hear his wife trying to hold back the tears. "Listen," he said

---

* A special study conducted more than a year after the accident noted that none of the three aft-facing crewmembers received serious injuries, despite the fact that they weren't wearing their seatbelts. This was the result of the decelerative loads at impact being more uniformly distributed over their bodies. The study went on to say that, "...adequately stressed rearward-facing seats offer a form of maximum body support with a minimum of objectionable restraint. Economic considerations and passenger acceptance have been the major drawbacks in considering the implementation of this safety concept." (Special Study: Passenger survival in turbojet ditchings (A critical case review) NTSB-AAS-72-2.)

in a softened voice, "we have one problem. We are missing Margareth. Tell her family that we are looking for her but that she is not with us at this moment."

Harry Evans was the last person rescued. He had performed admirably as the ranking crewmember at the slide, organizing the rescue effort from the surface and assisting passengers into the rescue sling. Several of the rescuers would later single him out for his help in the rescue. By the time Harry landed in St. Croix, it was nearly dark. He was brought to a room where Balsey and Hugh had been waiting. All three placed calls home. Balsey also took a call from ONA. Bill Bailey was on the other end. Balsey talked to him briefly but was too emotionally drained to provide details about the accident.

Harry removed his wallet and started going through the soaked contents. He pulled out a fishing license and joked about having to replace it after just getting it a few days earlier. It was an awkward time for the three men. They could only guess at what repercussions lay ahead. Each of them replayed the events in their own minds, searching for what they might have done differently to change the outcome. No one talked about the accident. There would be plenty of time for that later.

At one point a reporter was allowed to speak with the crew. When the reporter mentioned to Balsey that several of the passengers had praised him for the "beautiful" job he had done in ditching the plane, Balsey responded by saying: "Not beautiful enough. People were lost."

Some time around seven or eight that night, after all the ambulances were gone and the rescue helicopters were no longer taking off and landing, the three crewmembers were driven to the same hotel and condominium complex where Wilfred and Tobias were staying. None of them had received injuries serious enough to require medical attention. Balsey didn't even ask for a Band-Aid for his hand, which was still stinging from the salt water. When they got to the hotel, they met briefly in Balsey's room. It was the first time since the accident that they felt free to discuss what had happened.

Harry was first to broach the subject. "We need to get our stories straight," he said, glancing up at Balsey and Hugh to gauge their reaction.

"We don't need to get anything straight, Harry," Balsey said. "You tell it just the way you saw it. We're a crew. We don't have to make up any Goddamn stories." That was the last time anything was said about the accident that night.*

Jeannie Larmony was one of the first people rescued from the slide. She was picked up by the Navy helicopter. Jeannie was fortunate to get one of the last spots on the canvas troop seat. Those who came after her were not so lucky. While the survivors were grateful to have been rescued, the ride inside the helicopter was an uncomfortable one. They had been packed into the helicopter so tightly that there was barely room to breathe. They were cold and wet and practically sitting on top of each other. Most were still wearing their inflated life vests, which restricted movement even further. Adding to their discomfort was the air inside the helicopter, which smelled of a malodorous combination of vomit, blood, wet hair, and damp clothes.

When they landed at St. Croix, they were immediately met by paramedics and other medical personnel. Photographers lit up the ramp with their cameras as the survivors were directed to waiting

---

* This conversation is the recollection of Balsey DeWitt. Harry Evans did not want to be interviewed for this book.

ambulances. Jeannie was one of the last people out of the helicopter. There was no ambulance waiting to take her to the hospital. There was only one hospital on St. Croix and what few ambulances they had were already in use. Fortunately, volunteers offered to drive the survivors to the hospital in their private vehicles. Two men volunteered to take Jeannie. They placed her in the back seat. It was a long, bumpy ride to the hospital. Jeannie felt every pothole in the road. Eventually they caught up with one of the ambulances. The main road to the hospital was a narrow two-lane highway. Not everyone on the island had heard of the accident. More than a few vehicles failed to give way to the ambulances, despite the flashing lights and sirens.

Jeannie had hardly made it through the front door of the hospital when she was approached by a medical team who quickly removed her clothing to check for injuries. Jeannie complained that her neck and back were hurting. The doctors put a collar around her neck and treated the injuries to her back before moving on to other survivors. Had they done a more thorough examination, they would have discovered that Jeannie also had two broken ribs. This would not be discovered until days later when her own doctor examined her upon her return to New York.

Jeannie learned from one of the nurses that there was a gentleman in a nearby room who had asked about her. It was Walter Hodge, the man she had spoken to while boarding in New York. Walter had some serious injuries of his own and was unable to get out of bed. He had remembered his brief talk with Jeannie and was concerned about her condition.

When Israel Kruger reached the hospital in Christianstead, his main concern was to find his wife. Like several other couples aboard ALM

980, Israel and Toby had become separated during the rescue. Other than blurry vision and a swollen ankle, Israel didn't seem to have sustained any serious injuries. Before he could inquire about Toby, the nurses rushed him into an examining room. When the doctor performing the exam felt around his ribs, Israel let out a yell. An x-ray revealed three fractured ribs. As soon as the doctors were finished wrapping him up, Israel set off to look for Toby.

The Charles Harwood Memorial Hospital was a small three-story building with approximately fifty beds. As news of the accident spread, several patients voluntarily gave up their hospital beds. Hundreds of volunteers lined up to donate blood. The survivors had been separated into groups of males and females. Israel found Toby in a room with several other women survivors. She was so glad to see him that she immediately stood up and embraced him. Israel winced in pain and pointed to his sore ribs. Toby had escaped the ordeal totally unscathed.

Emerson Ussery had only a few bruises from having been thrown against the bulkhead and into the cockpit door. He also had a sore back that had been giving him problems from the moment he first entered the water. The pain in his back was aggravated further when he was struck from behind by a rescue basket as he tried to assist another passenger in the water. Emerson was eventually picked up by the second Coast Guard helicopter.

Emerson lived on St. Croix and was well known. He was a major employer on the island, as well as a sponsor for numerous local events and charities. After landing in St. Croix, Emerson spotted Governor Melvin Evans, whom he knew, and headed toward him.

"Emerson, we got an emergency here," the Governor said as he hurried by, as if Emerson was getting in the way of the rescue operation.

"I can see that," Emerson replied. His back had stiffened to the point where he could hardly walk. He couldn't chase after the governor to explain that he had been on the plane. He spotted an airport worker and asked him if he would get him a cab. Emerson rode to the hospital in a taxicab. When he got to the hospital, he ran into the same problem again.

"Emerson, you're going to have to come back tomorrow," one of the nurses said as he limped into the hospital. "We got an emergency going on."

Emerson tried to explain that he had been on the plane but the nurse cut him off.

"Emerson, go home. We're too busy right now."

Emerson waited for the nurse to leave before walking down the hall to search for an empty bed. He took the first open bed he saw. Minutes later, a doctor entered the room. "Emerson, go home, goddamnit!"

Emerson was known as a practical joker. He tried to explain that he had been on the plane, but the doctor only looked exasperated and left. So Emerson got up again and searched for another room. This time he spotted a passenger whom he had helped in the water. Emerson took the open bed next to her. This time when the doctor and nurse came in to toss him out the woman spoke up on his behalf.

"He was on that plane," she said. "He helped me. You leave him alone."

Only then did Emerson get the medical attention he had been seeking.

Rick Arnold was determined to get Loretta out of the water first. She was obviously in pain. She had told Rick that she thought her back was broken. When the first Coast Guard helicopter arrived,

Rick told those around him that Loretta needed medical attention, and several people helped him load Loretta into the rescue basket.

Rick's only injury was to his hand, although he was feeling some discomfort in his back. After the injured passengers were taken out of the water, the sequence of those being rescued was random. Rick felt confident that he would be rescued and didn't feel a sense of urgency to be next into the helicopter. He was, however, growing concerned about the dwindling daylight. At one point, Rick and two others were the only people left at the slide. They didn't see any other survivors. Thinking that it might be too dark for the helicopters to return, Rick suggested that he and the other survivor in the water join the first officer on the slide. Harry agreed and helped Rick and the other passenger, a young man in his mid- to late twenties, onto the slide. The three of them sat atop the slide, pondering the possibility of having to spend the night in the rough seas. It was a frightening thought. The only positive sign was the two aircraft still circling overhead, which was a good indication that they hadn't been completely abandoned. Their moods improved when they heard a low-flying helicopter approaching from the west.

Rick was first in the sling. He used the opportunity to take one last glance at the accident scene, this time from the perspective of looking down from above. He still found it hard to believe what had happened and wanted to have a visual image to take with him. The first thing he noticed was the debris floating around: pieces of luggage, toilet paper, and other objects he couldn't identify. There was a discoloration of the water, a different shade of blue in and around the area where the plane had gone down. Other than the two people on the slide, he didn't see anyone else in the water.

Rick thanked the crewman who had helped him into the helicopter. He was cold and feeling waterlogged. He had been in the water nearly three hours. The crewman wrapped a blanket around him. Rick took a seat on the floor as the crewman turned his attention to rescuing the two remaining people on the slide.

Nothing was said during the brief ride to St. Croix. Like those rescued before him, his thoughts were filled with the events that had just taken place and the knowledge that he was safe.

When they landed at St. Croix, Rick saw a large crowd of people but no ambulances. He and the second passenger in the helicopter were taken to the hospital in a private car. Harry Evans stayed behind to join up with the rest of the flight crew.

Once at the hospital, Rick was ushered into a small examining room and given a hospital gown to wear. A doctor came by minutes later to check on him. The doctor was a large man with poor bedside manner. He performed a perfunctory examination and found the gash in Rick's hand. Rick looked on in horror as the doctor pulled out a large needle and thread and proceeded to stitch the wound without any preparation. Rick made a comment about wanting something for the pain. "You don't need anything," the doctor said in accented English. Rick let out a scream as the needle was thrust into his finger.*

After the doctor was finished stitching Rick's wound, Rick set out to find Loretta. He had already concluded that Gene hadn't survived. When he found Loretta, she was having an argument with one of the doctors over how best to treat her broken back. The doctor was suggesting a procedure that could have left her permanently paralyzed. Loretta was adamantly against it. Fortunately for her, she won the argument and was put in a brace instead.

That night in the hospital Rick was asked if he could take a phone call from a reporter. Rick answered the questions as best he could. By

---

* To this day, Rick has scars from where the large needle entered and exited his finger.

this time news of the accident had reached the states. Rick's parents were in the city to see a play. Somehow his parents got word of the accident and were able to hear the entire interview with Rick as it was broadcast.

Chapter 23

LINDLEY AND BRAZZELL HAD BEEN FORCED TO STAND after picking up their twenty-six survivors. The helicopter was so full there wasn't even room to crouch down. Lindley scanned the traumatized faces of the passengers as they sat huddled together inside the helicopter. Their wounds ranged from simple cuts and facial lacerations to broken bones. He noticed one man whose collarbone was protruding through his skin. The men in their business suits and the women in their dresses looked oddly out of place. Most of them had removed their shoes. Every now and then Lindley would take a peek outside to see how high they were. He tried to not show his concern. He could tell by the strained sound of the engines and the unsteady way the helicopter moved through the air that they were overweight.

A few of the women asked for blankets, but there were none to hand out. "They're getting mighty cold back here," Lindley announced over the ICS.

"Close the hole," Rylee told him. There was a large two-foot hole in the bottom of the floor where the sonar had been removed. The empty hole was now used for ventilation. Lindley closed the hole and the cold draft subsided.

At one point on the way back to St. Croix the quiet inside the helicopter was interrupted by laughter. Bill Brazzell turned to see a woman holding a roll of money wrapped with a rubber band. "I lost everything else but I managed to keep this," she said, shaking her head as if to indicate that she couldn't believe that the money had survived the ordeal. Neither Bill nor Lindley had seen the money on the woman as she was being hoisted into the helicopter. She was dressed in a brightly colored tropical print dress with spaghetti straps. There could have been only one place where she could have stashed the money. There was no way to tell how much she had managed to save, but judging from the size of the roll, it was a sizeable amount.

The light was fading fast as Rylee entered the traffic pattern at St. Croix. He landed on a taxiway and taxied to the main terminal building where he saw waiting ambulances and a large group of people milling about. As they were taxiing in, one of the survivors caught a glimpse of the large crowd and asked for a comb, not wanting to get caught unexpectedly by a photographer or television camera.

As soon as the helicopter came to a stop, Lindley opened the door and the passengers streamed out. One woman turned to Brazzell as she was leaving and offered an invitation to him and the rest of the crew to join her and her friends for a drink. Brazzell nodded his head toward the cockpit as if to indicate that they were still on duty.

By the time Jim Rylee unbuckled his shoulder harness and turned around all but one passenger had exited the helicopter. Balsey had stayed behind to personally thank the two helicopter pilots. Jim shook Balsey's hand then jumped out and tried to assist an elderly man to an ambulance. As he grabbed hold of the man, he realized that he was completely drained of energy. He signaled for Lindley who then assisted the passenger to the waiting ambulance. At one point, Jim was approached by a reporter. He brushed him aside after catching a whiff of the man's breath, which smelled of alcohol.

As the crowd of people subsided, Lindley and Brazzell noticed a large pile of life preservers lying on the floor inside the helicopter. They also spotted several life preservers lying on the ramp, the owners having waited until they were safely on terra firma before ridding themselves of the uncomfortable vests. Lindley and Brazzell scooped up the life vests and tossed them into the back of the helicopter. Jim Rylee had also removed a life vest from a female passenger as she lay on a stretcher. She obviously didn't need it anymore. Jim tossed the vest into the back of the helicopter along with the others. Each crewman would later take a few of the life vests home as souvenirs.*

With the survivors safely on their way to the hospital, Lindley secured the aft section of the helicopter and hooked up to the ICS. "Let's go home," he told Jim. Lindley and Brazzell sat in their crew seats. They were hooked up to the ICS, but no one said anything. They flew back to Roosy Roads with not a word being spoken.

John Barber and Vince Perron had kept up the CPR on their lone survivor all the way to St. Croix. At no time did they detect a heartbeat or a pulse. Upon arriving at St. Croix, Art Nash lowered the loading ramp and several paramedics rushed inside carrying a stretcher. By now the two men were totally exhausted. They sat back against the fuselage and let the paramedics take over. A doctor came aboard and placed a stethoscope against the man's chest. He listened

---

* When I interviewed Jim, he still had one of the life vests from that night.

for a few seconds then gave a thumbs up sign, indicating that he had detected a heart beat.

The other five helicopters landed minutes later. Only EM-07, piloted by Glen Warren and Ned Lemoine, had survivors aboard. It was dark now and the crews were not looking forward to having to fly back to the ship, where they would have to make a night landing on a rolling deck in bad weather. Fortunately, their concerns were alleviated when a man approached and said that he was working on finding rooms for the crewmembers. They would be spending the night on St. Croix.

While those details were being worked out, a number of marines headed inside to the airport bar. John Barber stayed behind. He still had to secure the helicopter. He tied down the blades and put on the protective covers. The adrenaline was still pumping, but his arms were so weak from doing the CPR he could hardly lift them above his head. His first thought after securing the helicopter was to call his fiancée to tell her about the rescue. He went inside and located one of the special phone booths used for calling the States. The call was taken by his fiancée's mother. John gave her a brief run-down on what had happened and said that he would call again later. He hung up and headed for the bar to hook up with Vince Perron and the rest of his crew.

John found Vince and Randy Logan sitting at the bar surrounded by other crews wanting to hear the details of their rescue. When Vince saw John, he cleared a spot for him at the bar and ordered him a rum and Coke. John learned a few drinks later, after his head began throbbing and the room began spinning, that the rum he was drinking was 151 proof. When a woman entered the bar later that evening looking for volunteers to donate blood, John and the others were politely turned down.

At one point, Vince was telling the others about his efforts to revive the man they had rescued. He casually mentioned that the man had eaten bean sprouts for dinner. "How do you know that?" someone asked. "Because he threw up while I was doing CPR," Vince replied.

There was a sense of celebration in knowing that they had possibly saved a man's life. They all saw the doctor give the thumbs-up sign. But each of them had their doubts. For one, the man never once responded to the CPR. Secondly, the section of the helicopter where the doctor had listened for the man's heartbeat was located directly beneath two turbine-powered engines that were still running. You couldn't hear yourself talk, let alone hear a heartbeat.[*]

After the unofficial "debrief" at the bar, the thirty-six men were taken to the same condominium complex where the ONA crewmembers were staying. The crews shared new three-bedroom luxury condominiums.[1]

Bill Bohlke flew in a loose formation behind the HU-16 for nearly two hours, relaying messages to and from San Juan Center. George Johnson, who was sitting in the co-pilot's seat, flew whenever Bill needed a break.

When they landed in St. Croix, it was dark enough that Bill needed his landing lights. As he taxied past the crowd in front of the terminal building, he spotted fifteen or twenty Army surplus stretchers laid out on the ramp waiting to be put to use. Sadly, Bill knew that the stretchers would go unused. He parked the Skyvan and thanked

---

[*] John Barber would not learn the fate of the man that he had helped rescue until some thirty-plus years later when I interviewed him for this book. Julius Eisenberg was pronounced dead on arrival at the hospital.

Paul Wikander, George Johnson, Andy Titus, and Gorge Stoute for their help. While the rest of the men were in a celebratory mood, George Stoute was tense and uneasy. He expressed concern over the fact that he was going to be late returning to the prison. The work release program had been a blessing for him; he didn't want to jeopardize losing the privilege. George was assured that he had no reason to be concerned. Once the prison officials learned the reason for his late return, they would surely understand. One of the men commented that George might even be entitled to a reduction in his sentence for his participation in the rescue. After all, he had risked his life to help drop life rafts to the survivors. They all agreed that if anyone should ask about the rescue they would make sure that George received recognition for his efforts. With that, they shook hands and went their separate ways. Paul Wikander agreed to take George back to the prison.

Bill left the Skyvan and walked up to the tower to talk to controller Jimmy Gingrich. After filling Jimmy in on what had taken place, he went looking for the flight crew. He was told that the captain and another crewmember were upstairs in the Eastern Airlines VIP room. Bill headed upstairs and introduced himself to Balsey and Harry, identifying himself as the pilot of the Skyvan. They talked briefly. Bill could tell that the two men were still shaken by their ordeal. He told them that he was available if they needed anything and then left to call his wife. When he got downstairs, someone asked him if he would take a phone call from a CBS news reporter. Bill took the phone call and talked to the reporter for several minutes. He mentioned George Stoute by name and told how George had risked his life. The phone conversation was later broadcast on the CBS radio network.

As soon as Bill finished talking to the reporter, he phoned his wife. She was still at her girlfriend's house. He gave her a quick rundown on the ditching, then asked how she was doing. She told him that the labor pains had intensified and her girlfriend was suggesting they go to the hospital. Bill rushed to the girlfriend's house. Before heading to the hospital, Bill decided to call their family doctor. By now news of the ditching had spread across the island. The doctor had been in touch with the hospital and had learned that there were no hospital beds. They had all been taken by the survivors. He suggested that they come to the hospital in the morning. A nervous Bill and Tuddy left for home, hoping that the baby would delay its entrance into the world for at least one more day.

While the rest of the rescuers were headed home or to luxury accommodations, the Coast Guard pilots were busy discussing the possibility of conducting a night search. The concern was that if there were any survivors still in the water, their chances for survival through the night were minimal. The biggest fear was sharks. But another concern was the difficulty of finding a lone individual in the open sea. The survivors were initially confined to an area of about thirty to forty yards wide and seventy-five yards long. By nightfall this area had expanded to well over two hundred yards in length. With each passing hour the search area grew larger. The decision was made to conduct a night search, using parachute flares dropped from an HU-16.

By this time, Bill Shields had already reported the loss of his hoist system. A new cable and basket were flown into St. Croix, but it was going to take several hours to replace the damaged cable. Shields discussed the situation with his commanding officer, Charles Mayes, who had been on the second Coast Guard helicopter. They agreed that while Bill would not be able to perform any rescues, he could still participate in the night search. If he spotted a survivor, he could direct rescue crews to the spot.

A little after 7:00 P.M., Bill Shields and Carmond Fitzgerald left St. Croix for the accident scene. The second Coast Guard helicopter followed minutes later. Tom Blank, who had acted as the On Scene Commander for the duration of the rescue, landed in St. Croix where they met up with another HU-16 crew scheduled to fly the night search. Tom and his crew then flew back to San Juan. They had flown a total of seven and a half hours. The captain of the USS *Guadalcanal*, which had arrived on scene just after sunset, became the On Scene Commander. The *Point Whitehorn* also arrived on scene after sunset. According to the deck logs for the *Point Whitehorn*, sunset occurred at 18:46 (6:46 P.M.). The crew of the *Point Whitehorn* was told to conduct a surface search independent of the *Guadalcanal*. The seas were too rough to conduct a coordinated search.

In order for parachute flares to be effective, they have to be dropped from an altitude of at least 1,000 feet. Fortunately, the weather had improved to the point where the HU-16 crew was able to climb to an altitude of 1,500 feet. The parachute flares are contained inside a canister about a foot in diameter and four feet long. The magnesium flares put out an extremely bright white light — bright enough that it could temporarily blind a person if he or she were to look directly at it. The same lead line used to toss out the life raft is attached to the top of the canister. The flare is forcibly tossed out and away from the aircraft by the drop master; the heat from the flare is sufficiently hot enough that it could damage the aircraft if it were to ignite too close to the plane. When the flare reaches the end of the lead line, the top of the canister is yanked off; the flare is ignited and the parachute deploys. The flare will then burn for up to three minutes, illuminating an area about the size of a football field. The illumination over water, however, is of little use unless there is something in the water to reflect back the light. Otherwise, the water remains dark, except for a few seconds as the flare descends closer to the surface.

The helicopters would scan the water as the flare slowly dropped to the surface. They flew at an altitude of 500 feet. If something was spotted, the helicopter would descend to as low as fifty feet to investigate, using a directional spotlight attached to the bottom of the helicopter.

Both the *Guadalcanal* and the *Point Whitehorn* were also using spotlights to search for survivors.

To an observer in the water, it would have been an eerie scene as they watched the flares drop slowly from a stygian sky. The light from the flares would have been punctuated by the momentary illumination of the helicopter spotlights as they moved in to investigate a suspicious reflection or item that had floated free from the aircraft. If there were any survivors that night, they most certainly would have witnessed the search, which would have been visible for miles. But they would ultimately have realized that they had drifted too far away from the accident scene to be found. Except for a couple of empty life rafts, nothing of significance was recovered that night.

There had been a total of sixty-three people on board ALM 980 — fifty-seven passengers and a crew of six. By the end of the day there were forty survivors, twenty-two missing, and one dead. The man that John Barber and his crew had rescued, passenger Julius Eisenberg, was pronounced dead upon arrival at the hospital.[*] Seven passengers were missing spouses, including Jim Razzi and Loretta

---

[*] I have found two separate references to Mr. Eisenberg. One reference indicated that his first name was Julius. A second reference indicated that it was Julien. I have chosen the more common Julius.

Gremelsbacker. Also among the missing were three married couples, the two little girls Jennifer and Kristin Caldwell and their father William Caldwell, and stewardess Margareth Abraham. She had last been seen shoving passengers into their seats just prior to impact.

Part Three

POSTFLIGHT

Chapter 24

SOMETIME BETWEEN TWO AND THREE IN THE MORNING on Sunday, May 3, a New York State Trooper approached a row of tents at a Girl Scout campsite with an important message to deliver. The individual the trooper was looking for was ONA Assistant Chief Pilot Ed Veronelli. Ed was at the campsite along with his daughter. Ed's mother had given someone at ONA the approximate location of where he was camping and, with that, the state trooper was able to locate Ed's car, parked a short distance from the campsite.

With only his flashlight to guide him, the trooper made his way down a narrow dirt path and stopped at the very first tent he came to. The startled occupants of that tent directed the officer a few feet away to where Ed Veronelli had pitched his tent. Ed learned of the accident after having been awakened by the trooper's flashlight. The news hit Ed especially hard. He had originally been scheduled to fly the May 2 flight.

There had actually been three pilots scheduled to fly the May 2 flight before Balsey. The first pilot was taken off the flight because his daughter had died in a tragic car accident. A second pilot had been assigned the trip but had to be taken off due to a scheduling conflict. Ed was then assigned the flight. As the weekend approached, Ed remembered the promise he had made to his daughter to go with her on the camping trip. Ed removed himself from the schedule and told scheduling to put a flight instructor on the flight, knowing that Harry Evans was going to be the first officer. Such were the workings of fate and chance.

Ed gathered his things and immediately left for home. He listened to reports of the accident over the radio as he made the hour-plus drive back to New Jersey. After a quick shower and a change of clothes, Ed left for ONA headquarters. He found the offices of ONA swarming with people. News of the accident had spread quickly. Managers from every department were there; crewmembers preparing for their flights stopped by for updates. The first few hours were marked by chaos and confusion. This was ONA's first accident. Everyone had questions: *Where did the plane ditch? How many survived? How many were still missing? How many were injured?* Adding to the chaotic atmosphere were the phones that never stopped ringing.

The one person everyone turned to for answers was Steedman Hinckley. Steedman had learned of the ditching not long after it happened. Upon hearing of the accident, he immediately left for New York along with his wife Ingrid and their daughter Annalisa. Steedman would later confide to family and friends that he had sought out a church that night to pray for the passengers and crew aboard the fateful flight.

Steedman gathered the department heads together and collectively they came up with a course of action. Their first priority was to save any and all records pertaining to the flight, such as weather documents, the flight plan, the load manifest, and maintenance records. Training records for the crews would have to be assembled. Steedman also suggested that they gather as much data as possible concerning the previous flights to St. Maarten. The task of notifying relatives of passengers on the flight was the responsibility of ALM and KLM in New York.

Steedman showed a genuine concern for the people involved in the accident, but he was also worried about how the negative publicity might affect ONA. Details of the accident were sketchy. Steedman decided he should fly to St. Croix, where he could make decisions based on first hand information. He made preparations to fly to St. Croix first thing Monday morning.

Octavio Irausquin was in Europe when he first learned of the ditching. He made immediate preparations to return to Curaçao. He also authorized the use of one of ALM's DC-9s to fly to St. Croix on Sunday. In addition to ALM and Dutch government officials, the plane also carried family members of the three crewmembers. Among the family members on the flight on Sunday were Wilfred's wife Marlene, Tobias's brother and sister, and Margareth's father and twin brother. Margareth's fiancé, Robby Schouten, was also on board.

Upon landing at St. Croix, most of those on the plane headed for the Estate Carlton Hotel where Wilfred and Tobias were staying. After a tearful reunion with family members, Wilfred and Tobias spoke briefly with several ALM officials.

Later in the day, Wilfred and Tobias met privately with Robby Schouten and Margareth's father and brother. The three were planning on renting a plane to conduct their own search for Margareth. Wilfred and Tobias gave them what little information they had and even pitched in a few dollars to help with the plane rental, but they had to admit that they hadn't seen Margareth since just before the plane hit the water.

Balsey, Harry, and Hugh had no family members in St. Croix to support them. Nor did they have access to the type of support programs that today's crews rely on after a serious accident or incident.[1] The three crewmembers spent much of their time in their rooms talking on the phone. Balsey spoke with his wife Edith and his mother. He also took a call from Ed Starkloff. Starkloff wanted to know if Balsey was up to answering questions. Balsey hadn't slept very well and wasn't ready for an inquisition just yet. But Balsey considered Starkloff a friend. He wasn't thinking about what he should or shouldn't do with regard to protecting his rights. He wanted answers himself.

Starkloff began by asking Balsey how much fuel he had at the beginning of the first approach. Balsey couldn't give him an answer. He hadn't had time to sort it all out yet. Starkloff asked a few more questions about fuel status but soon sensed that Balsey wasn't ready to answer specific questions about the flight. He asked Balsey if he was all right. He told him that he was coming to St. Croix, and that he would stop by to see him when he arrived, adding that if Balsey didn't want to talk about the accident that he'd still come to visit.

Later that afternoon, an ALM official took the three crewmembers shopping for clothes. They were still wearing their damp uniform clothes. It was Sunday and a storeowner had offered to open his store exclusively for the survivors of the ditching. The store carried mostly general merchandise; the clothing selections were limited. They all picked out pants, a few touristy shirts, and underwear.

The only footwear available was Converse tennis shoes. Harry Evans picked out a bright orange pair of high tops.

At the Charles Harwood Memorial Hospital in Christianstead, the passengers began to mingle in the halls of the hospital, comparing notes on their experiences and trying to make arrangements for flying back to New York. Emerson Ussery, who had had such a hard time convincing local authorities and hospital staff that he had been a passenger on the flight, handed out money to a number of distressed passengers.[2] He then called his family physician, who scheduled him for x-rays. The x-rays indicated that he had several crushed discs in his back. Later that day, he was fitted with a full body brace that he would end up wearing for nearly three months.

Bill Bohlke and his wife Tuddy arrived at the hospital early that morning. It didn't take long after Tuddy was admitted for word to get out that a pilot of one of the aircraft that had been circling the accident scene was at the hospital. Bill was soon swarmed by survivors with questions about what he had seen. They described what their husbands or wives had been wearing and asked if he had seen them. They were still holding out hope that there might be more survivors. Bill tried to explain that it was difficult to make out details from the air. In Bill's mind, everyone who had made it out of the aircraft had been picked up. He grew increasingly uncomfortable as more passengers approached him with specific questions about missing loved ones. Not wanting to be the bearer of bad news, and nervous over the prospect of becoming a father, Bill told his wife that he was going to the airport and to call if there was any news. Tamara Ann Bohlke was born a little after 4:00 in the afternoon on May 3, 1970. Bill arrived back at the hospital within minutes of the delivery.

The thirty-six marines who had been involved in the SAR on Saturday left the condominium complex early Sunday morning for the airport. Poor weather conditions forced them to delay their departure until after 9:00 A.M. The six helicopters flew to the accident scene and searched for survivors for a short time before returning to the ship. The *Guadalcanal* had remained in the search area overnight. Marine crews continued searching for survivors all that day, flying a total of fifty-seven sorties, totaling over eighty hours of flying time.[3] No survivors or bodies were recovered.

The Coast Guard cutter *Point Whitehorn* had remained in the search area overnight as well. The small boat had taken a beating in the rough seas. Most of the crew became sick.[4] They continued searching for survivors for the better part of the day. No bodies or survivors were found, though the *Whitehorn* did recover a number of items from the scene, including the rescue basket that had been cut from Bill Shields's helicopter; the four life rafts that had been dropped; as well as life jackets, seat parts, and other miscellaneous debris. A picture of some of the recovered items was published in the *Virgin Island Daily News* on Wednesday.

The search for survivors covered a wide area and involved numerous aircraft, helicopters, and ships. Low ceilings and poor visibility, however, hampered their efforts. If there were survivors still in the water, they would have seen the search aircraft flying overhead. But their prolonged submersion in the cool waters would have left them immobile, assuming they were still conscious. A person able to signal rescuers has a much better chance of being seen than an individual floating motionless in a rough sea. Despite the odds of finding anyone alive, the Coast Guard decided to continue the search at first light Monday morning.*

---

* Interviews with passengers indicated that at least forty-three people were known to have exited the aircraft. Forty-one survivors were recovered, leaving at least two people unaccounted for.

Chapter 25

IICK BAKER WAS AT HOME IN OXON HILL, Maryland when he first learned of the ditching of ALM 980. Dick was an investigator with the National Transportation Safety Board (NTSB). He received the initial call about the accident around 6:00 P.M. and was told to wait for further instructions. He had no way of knowing it then, but at the very time he was learning of the accident there were passengers and crew still in the water waiting to be rescued.

Dick was one of only four men at the time to hold the title of Investigator in Charge (IIC). The IIC is the senior investigator coordinating the investigative functions for the NTSB. This includes organizing the parties to the investigation, assigning individuals to investigative groups, dealing with the press, conducting daily briefings, writing preliminary reports, and providing updates to managers at headquarters.

Dick was informed later that evening that he was to head the investigation into ALM 980. He was told to fly to St. Croix to determine how many people were going to be needed for the investigation.

Normally, the IIC would round up the people on his on-call list and head to the scene of an accident immediately upon notification. If no commercial airline flights are available, the NTSB can utilize FAA aircraft to fly to the site of an accident. Dick decided to take the earliest commercial flight, which was a morning departure on American Airlines to San Juan, Puerto Rico.

Dick arrived in San Juan early Sunday afternoon. His first stop was the San Juan Air Route Traffic Control Center. Dick knew the accident involved a DC-9 and that it had ditched in the Caribbean due to fuel exhaustion. He was aware of the failed landing attempts in St. Maarten. He also knew that the aircraft belonged to Overseas National Airways, an airline that he had not heard of prior to the accident. That was the extent of the information Dick had received.

Accident investigators are taught to not speculate about the cause of an accident before all the facts are known. At the same time, it is human nature to speculate. On the surface, this accident looked like an open and shut case. The crew tried to land at an airport in marginal weather and after multiple landing attempts ran out of fuel trying to divert to their alternate. Dick Baker, however, had been investigating aviation accidents for a long time. He knew that there was seldom a single factor involved in an accident. Part of his knowledge came from personal experience. Dick had been involved in an aircraft accident himself. Ironically, the accident involved fuel exhaustion.

Dick Baker was a former naval aviator, having spent fifteen years on active duty and five years in the Navy reserve. He had flown a variety of aircraft for the Navy, including the turbine-powered F9F Panther, which he flew during the Korean War. The last few years of his military service, Dick flew helicopters. He also flew helicopters part time for a civilian company with the hope of getting a job when his military career ended. It was during this transition period when he was flying for both the Navy and for the civilian company when he had his accident.

Dick was flying over a densely wooded area of North Carolina in a civilian Bell helicopter when the engine suddenly quit. Dick and his lone passenger received only minor injuries, but the helicopter was severely damaged. At that time, the Civil Aeronautics Board conducted all investigations concerning civilian aircraft. Dick was eager to find out the cause of the engine failure and volunteered to assist the investigators. The first thing he and the investigators discovered was that the engine had quit due to fuel exhaustion. He had been flying the helicopter with an inoperative fuel gauge. Fuel records and flight time records, however, indicated that there should have been adequate fuel for the flight. Dick and the investigators combed over the wreckage searching for clues. Upon closer inspection, they discovered fuel stains running overboard from the fuel tank. They searched for the origin of the stains and discovered a loose fitting between the fuel tank and the engine, which allowed the fuel to leak out. Determining the cause of his own accident piqued Dick's interest in the process of accident investigations.

When he left the Navy in 1958, Dick was offered a job with the Bureau of Aviation Safety, a division of the CAB. He remained with the CAB as an investigator of both civil and commercial aviation accidents until 1967, at which time the NTSB was formed for the purpose of accident investigations.

At close to six feet tall and with a crew cut, Dick Baker wasn't that far removed from the naval aviator he once was. He was forty-nine but still looked and dressed much like he had two decades earlier, when Buddy Holly tunes ruled the airwaves and hair that touched the collar was considered long.[1]

One of Dick's first tasks when he arrived in San Juan was to determine which investigative groups were going to be needed. The NTSB uses a group methodology to conduct accident investigations. Each investigative group examines the accident from a specific viewpoint. Examples of the types of investigative groups include weather, human factors, Air Traffic Control (ATC), maintenance, operations, etc. The groups are comprised of individuals from various interested parties, including representatives of the airline, the aircraft manufacturer, the FAA and ALPA. The information derived from these separate groups forms the basis for the Board's overall conclusions.

It wasn't immediately apparent from the information that Dick had received what groups would be needed. For example, since there was no wreckage, did they really need a structures group? Dick decided that there was no need for a structures group, though one of the investigators was given the task of examining aircraft parts that had been recovered from the water. One group that should have been formed but was not was the maintenance records group. The oversight wouldn't be discovered until weeks later, giving ONA ample time to correct any deficiencies in the paperwork concerning the fuel totalizer and the work done on the fuel probes.

With the investigative groups identified, Dick called Washington to notify his go-team. The go-team was the name given to the individual investigators who would later head up the separate investigative groups. Team members began arriving in San Juan on Sunday evening. Dick and the rest of his team flew to St. Croix on Monday afternoon and set up operations at the airport. They also began the process of assigning individuals to the various investigative groups. The delay in getting the investigation teams in place hampered the investigation to a degree. By Monday, many of the surviving passengers had already left the island or were planning to leave the next day. Interviews with survivors were limited to the passengers on hand at the hospital or those still at the St. Croix airport. The investigators did manage to get written statements from a number of eyewitnesses who were on the ground at St. Maarten during the failed landing attempts. Those statements would later challenge the weather reports given to the crew by the controller at St. Maarten.

Ed Veronelli learned early Monday morning that he was to fly to St. Croix with Steedman. He hadn't even had time to go home and pack. He had to buy a suit jacket and some shirts on a stopover in San Juan. Accompanying Steedman and Ed on the flight on Monday morning were Steve Lang, a lawyer for an outside firm that represented ONA, and Assistant Vice President of Legal Bob Wagenfeld.

That evening after arriving in St. Croix, they had dinner with Balsey, Harry, and Hugh. They ate near the beach at a table as far from the crowds as they could find.[2] Condolences were expressed, but little was said about the accident. Steedman, in the presence of the two lawyers, was especially guarded in his comments. The pastel-colored shirts and tennis shoes worn by the three ONA crewmembers stood in stark contrast to the business attire worn by Steedman and the lawyers and only added to the awkwardness of the meeting.

On Tuesday, additional ONA managers arrived in St. Croix, including Ed Starkloff, Milt Marshall, and Ed Leiser, the Superintendent of Maintenance. That morning they met with the NTSB investigators and were assigned to different investigative groups. Ed Veronelli was assigned to the human factors group. The primary focus of the human factors group is crash survival analysis. One of Ed's tasks was to interview survivors at the hospital in Christianstead. This was Ed's first experience with an accident investigation, and he found the job unsettling. One passenger they interviewed was Gloria Caldwell, the woman who had lost her husband

and two little girls. When Gloria learned that Ed was with ONA, she asked him to leave the room and refused to answer any questions until he did. From that point on, Ed identified himself only if asked.

Ed listened carefully as passengers described seats being ripped from the floor and seatbelts failing. He heard complaints about passengers not having adequate warning prior to impact. He heard about difficulties with finding, opening, and donning life vests. Several passengers reported that the life vests were inadequate for the conditions that existed, claiming that the vests rode too high around their necks, restricting their breathing and funneling water into their faces. Some stated that the life vests failed to keep their heads above the water.[*]

The Coast Guard had recovered a number of life vests both from the water and from the Coast Guard helicopters used in the rescues. The vests were in fairly good shape. Some were still partially inflated. The lights on some of the vests were still working.[†] Dick Baker and several other NTSB investigators took a half dozen of the life vests to do some preliminary testing in a pool back at the hotel. They first wanted to see if the vests would right an unconscious person in the water. They discovered that they could only right themselves by using their arms and legs. Once they were righted, however, they didn't have any problems with the vests riding up their chests like many of the passengers had stated. But there were some major differences between their test conditions and the conditions that existed the day of the ditching. First, they were in a hotel pool in a controlled environment, and they had more than five minutes to properly don the vests. Secondly, they performed their tests wearing swimming trunks.

---

[*] Life vests have two inflation chambers. Normally, inflating just one chamber gives sufficient buoyancy. Inflating both chambers can cause many of the problems described by the passengers.
[†] The life vests contained small lights powered by self contained batteries. Some of the lights were salt water activated while others had to be manually switched on.

Had they been fully clothed, in salt water, and in rough seas, they might have reached some very different conclusions.[3]

Each morning the members of the various investigative groups met at the airport to discuss their findings from the previous day and to map out what needed to be done next. Dick Baker was to oversee the meetings. The progress meetings were an opportunity for the individual investigative groups to share information and additional leads.

By the end of his first day with the human factors group, Ed Veronelli had heard enough sad stories that he asked to be reassigned to one of the other investigation groups. He was subsequently reassigned to the ATC group. He left for San Juan on Wednesday to listen to the ATC tapes containing the communications between San Juan Center and ALM 980.

Part of Dick Baker's job was to do a cost benefit analysis on certain aspects of every investigation. When it came time to make a decision on whether to attempt a retrieval of the cockpit voice recorder (CVR) and the flight data recorder (FDR), Dick determined that the data that might be retrieved was not worth the cost of retrieval. The plane had ditched in waters that were five thousand feet deep.

The flight data recorder on the DC-9 was rudimentary compared to the digital flight data recorders found on today's commercial aircraft. The actual recording was done by a stylus that engraved traces of the recorded parameters on a continuously moving metal foil. The only flight parameters recorded were airspeed, altitude, heading, and g-loads. The engine and fuel readouts were not recorded. Still, it would have been useful to have the data to compare with the recollections of the crew with regard to the approaches at St. Maarten and the subsequent diversion. The FDR records the last twenty-five hours of flight and thus would have recorded the entire flight. The cockpit voice recorder would have been even more valuable, having captured the last thirty minutes of conversation inside the cockpit. This would have covered all three landing attempts and the ditching. Whether there was even technology available that would have made retrieval possible was never discussed, though Ed Starkloff was approached by a representative of a salvage company who offered to retrieve the aircraft for one million dollars. Starkloff politely turned him down.*

---

* If the recorders were recovered today, there is still some possibility that useful data could be retrieved.

Chapter

T HE STORY OF THE DITCHING WAS FRONT-PAGE NEWS
for the major papers in the Caribbean and
several papers in the U.S., including the *New York Times*. Early news
reports of the accident, however, were fraught with errors. Several
papers gave erroneous numbers for passengers who were listed as
either missing or dead. The *San Juan Star* on May 3 reported 37 rescued, 26 missing, and one dead.* Some papers reported that the
flight had originated in St. Maarten. A passenger list provided by
KLM contained several errors that were never corrected. The errors
included the names of passengers who were not aboard the flight
and numerous misspellings. Loretta Gremelsbacker was not listed on
any passenger list. Gene Gremelsbacker's sister, Ellen, who was supposed to have been on the flight but had canceled at the last minute,
was listed on the passenger list as Elly Gremelsbacker. Rick Arnold
was listed as Reginald Arnold. A number of papers reported that two

---

* The errors were attributed mostly due to an incomplete passenger list and the
fact that the crewmembers did not go to the hospital, and therefore were not
accounted for.

infants on the flight were missing. The reports were referring to Jennifer and Kristin Caldwell, whom most passengers remembered as being between the ages of four and five.

The story continued to draw wide attention in the Caribbean as the search for survivors continued. In the U.S., news coverage of the accident and the continued search for survivors was reduced to a few buried paragraphs in the *New York Times*. By Tuesday, the story of ALM 980 was pushed into obscurity by a much bigger story back home. On May 4, 1970, four students were killed by National Guardsman on the campus of Kent State University in Ohio. Reactions to that tragedy would occupy headlines for days.

The escalating tensions in the U.S. were of little consequence to Balsey, Harry, and Hugh. The three remained isolated from all that was going on around them. When Ed Starkloff showed up at the hotel on Tuesday, he called Balsey to tell him that it was best that they not talk. "There's a lot going on right now, Balsey," he said. "You better listen to your side and I'll take mine." It was an early indication of management's decision to distance itself from the three crewmembers. Ed Veronelli stopped by to talk, but Balsey steered the conversation away from the accident. Steedman's time was occupied with meetings with the FAA, Dutch officials, and representatives of ALM. Eventually, attorneys Steve Lang and Bob Wagenfeld met with Balsey to ask some questions. It didn't take long for Balsey to conclude that the lawyers weren't there for his protection but to protect ONA.

Balsey had legal representation through the pilots union. An ALPA attorney from Miami, John O'Brien, was assigned to represent the two pilots. John O'Brien, however, still hadn't arrived in St. Croix. In the interim, Balsey met with Milt Marshall, the ALPA MEC Chairman at ONA, and Tommy Ahern, another ONA ALPA representative. Their job was to advise pilots in situations similar to that

in which Balsey now found himself. But Milt Marshall, who sometimes referred to Balsey as "Mr. United," didn't care for Balsey. He
had protested Balsey's seniority number. He had filed complaints
against him. The two had a mutual dislike for each other. Milt
Marshall may have been there under the pretense of wanting to help,
but Balsey thought otherwise. He could see the satisfaction in Milt
Marshall's eyes. The two men told Balsey that if he wanted to get out
of the mess that he had created, he had better listen to them. They
were insensitive to Balsey's emotional state. When one of them made
a comment about people having been killed, Balsey's eyes welled
up. He knew at that point that he wasn't going to get any help from
ALPA, at least not at the local level. He later asked to have the two
removed from his case. Balsey would talk only to ALPA national.

There were several attempts by members of the news media to
talk with Balsey and the other two crewmembers. All three declined.
Those looking for answers may not agree with the reluctance of
flight crews to discuss their involvement in fatal accidents, but it is
always best to remain silent as the potential to incriminate one's
self is too great, especially in the immediate days following an accident when emotions can interfere with clear and rational thinking.

By Monday evening, the three crewmembers had yet to talk to
the investigators. They learned later that the delay was due to the
Dutch officials, who wanted the crew interviews conducted on Dutch
soil. The three kept to themselves as the NTSB and the Dutch
worked out their differences. They didn't have access to English language newspapers, which only added to their sense of isolation. They
did learn that there were still twenty-two people missing, a number
that weighed heavily on each of them.

The disagreements between the NTSB and the Dutch officials
were eventually resolved, and the crew met with investigators on
Tuesday afternoon, May 6. Representatives from both ONA and

ALM were present. Balsey was the first to be questioned. He was told that none of the information obtained during questioning could be used against him. He was asked if he had any objections to the FAA sitting in. Balsey felt that he had nothing to hide, so he allowed the FAA to be present. It was a decision that would later prove harmful to his career.[1]

Balsey was forthcoming in his answers to investigators. He went through the entire flight, careful to not overlook any details that might be important. He described the problems he encountered on his three failed landing attempts. He told them about the problems with the fuel totalizer. He mentioned not being able to find the St. Croix approach charts or the emergency checklist. He described his efforts to reenter the plane after exiting the cockpit.

The investigators were especially interested in hearing what Balsey had to say about his decision to continue to St. Maarten after initially starting a diversion to San Juan. The St. Maarten tower facility did not have the capability to record communications. The investigators had received conflicting statements from eyewitnesses on the ground at St. Maarten, indicating that the weather was below minimums at the time of the approaches. One eyewitness estimated that during one of the approaches the visibility was as low as ¼ mile in heavy rain showers. There were also unconfirmed reports that the St. Maarten tower controller might have been pressured to overstate the weather conditions by an influential resident who had been waiting for a passenger on the flight.[*] Balsey stated that he had been told that the ceilings were 1,000 broken, 5,000 overcast and visibility was 3 miles. He added that when he broke out on the first approach, the only place the weather appeared to be above minimums was directly over

---

[*] It's unclear whether the investigators were aware of this rumor. Dick Baker told me that he hadn't heard the rumor. Balsey claims that he first heard the rumor while in St. Croix.

the airport. But without a recorded transcript to back him up, it was his word against the tower controller's. Fortunately, days later a transcript of the conversation with the St. Maarten tower controller would turn up and confirm Balsey's account. While St. Maarten didn't record their communications, the tower at the Isla Grande airport, which shared the same tower frequency as St. Maarten, did have a recorder.*

One detail that was overlooked during questioning was the fact that the PA system wasn't working. It would be several months before investigators would discover this important piece of information.

After Harry and Hugh were interviewed, all three were asked to remain in St. Croix in case there were additional questions. They stayed on the island another two days. Upon arrival back in New York on Friday, they were ushered into a small briefing room at ONA's headquarters and told to not talk to anyone about the accident. They were asked to submit written statements and to have them completed by the following Monday. The company was sympathetic and almost apologetic when they told them that they would be off duty for the next thirty days while the incident was investigated.

The Monday after the accident, Bill Bohlke stopped by the hospital to see his wife and new baby girl. Once again, he was approached by survivors asking about missing loved ones. He didn't stay long before heading to the airport. That afternoon, two men came to see him. The two men were Robby Schouten and Margareth's twin brother Carol Abraham. They had heard that Bill had been involved in the rescue and wanted to know if he had seen Margareth. When Bill told

---

* While the initial conversation with ALM 980 concerning improving weather conditions was recorded, the communication between ALM 980 and the St. Maarten tower during the failed landing attempts was not recorded. The St. Maarten tower operator, Robert Seijkens, gave investigators a transcript that he assembled from memory for that portion of the flight.

them that he had not, they asked if he would be willing to fly them to the accident scene so they could conduct their own search. Bill agreed to take the pair up in a Piper Cherokee Arrow.

The weather on Monday was vastly different from the day of the ditching. The skies were crystal clear and devoid of even a wisp of a cloud. The sea was calm. They spotted a few items that looked like debris from the aircraft, but they saw nothing else. They searched for a solid three hours, flying various altitudes and headings. Bill let Robby and Carol make the decision on when to call off the search.

The next day Robby and Carol returned to the airport wanting to rent a plane for a second search. George Johnson, who had flown on the Skyvan with Bill Bohlke the day of the ditching, was the pilot.*

The Coast Guard continued to search for survivors on Tuesday as well. They had two helicopters and one fixed-wing aircraft in the area. The Coast Guard cutter *Point Whitehorn* was also involved in the search on Tuesday. No bodies or survivors were recovered, and subsequent searches were called off.

When Wilfred and Tobias returned to Curaçao on Tuesday, ALM held a press conference in which Octavio Irausquin praised the two flight stewards and Margareth for getting the passengers into their life vests prior to the ditching. Margareth was singled out for her sacrifice.

The survivors began leaving the hospital as early as Sunday, with several of them reserving hotel rooms as they made arrangements to fly back to New York. Six passengers were listed as critical; among them, Loretta Gremelsbacker, who had a broken back.

---

* Robby Schouten would eventually continue his search for Margareth on his own, chartering a small boat. He and the boat's captain searched a full two weeks before Robby finally gave up hope of finding his fiancée.

Rick Arnold left the hospital on Monday. He shared a hotel room with his brother Bob, who had flown to St. Croix to accompany him back to New York. On their return trip to New York on Tuesday, Bob gave Rick a Valium to relieve the stress of having to get back on an airplane so soon after the accident. Rick made the mistake of having a drink on the flight and, for better or worse, the combination of the Valium and the alcohol put him to sleep for most of the flight.

Three passengers were transported back to New York by stretcher. Special arrangements were made to accommodate the three on a Pan Am commercial flight. The flight engineer on the flight was Larry Phillips, who had been the flight engineer on Pan Am 454, the first aircraft on the scene. When he learned that three survivors of the ditching were on board, he introduced himself. He was greeted warmly by the survivors, who expressed how relieved they had been upon spotting the 727.[2]

One couple opted not to return to New York and instead negotiated with ALM to have it pay for a flight to San Juan, Puerto Rico. George and Martha Kellner, both in their mid twenties, had not been injured in the accident. They had been looking forward to having five days off in the Caribbean. They were obviously saddened over those who were injured and those who were still missing, but there was little they could do to change things. Martha was four months pregnant with their second child, and her husband was starting a new job the following week. There wouldn't be another opportunity for a vacation anytime soon, so they asked ALM to pay for a flight to San Juan and four nights at a resort hotel.[3]

Jeannie Larmony was one of a handful of survivors too injured to leave the hospital. Following her second day in the hospital, she was moved to another bed to free up her room for a woman with even more serious injuries. Jeannie found out later that the woman was the mother of the two little girls who had died in the accident.

Two weeks after the accident, Jeannie was asked if she was ready to go home. She was stretched out in a bed and unable to move. Her neck was in a collar; she ached from head to toe. Her back had taken such a beating from scraping against the air vents and the reading lights that she had to lie on a donut cushion to keep her back from coming in contact with the bed. She was told that she could be transported back to New York on a stretcher. There was no way Jeannie was going to fly back to New York tied to a stretcher. "When I feel like I'm able to sit up, then I'll go home," Jeannie said. She left the hospital a week later. Her son, Charlie, who worked for ONA, accompanied her on the trip.

Chapter 27

IN THE DAYS AND WEEKS FOLLOWING THE ACCIDENT, Balsey was asked to provide additional details regarding the ditching to investigators and ONA management. He answered questions by phone and made at least one trip to ONA headquarters to give a briefing there. He cooperated fully. Balsey was well aware of the uniqueness of the accident. It was the first open-water ditching of a commercial jet. There were countless questions from the NTSB investigators and the aircraft manufacturer: *What was the attitude of the aircraft when it hit the water? What was its speed? What was the configuration? How much damage was sustained? How long did the aircraft stay afloat? Did the aircraft sink tail first or nose first?*[*] (There was some speculation that the plane would have been brought down tail first by the weight of the two rear mounted engines.)

---

[*] Balsey gave the investigators the following details: He entered the water at 90 knots, with full flaps, and with the aircraft in a six degree pitch up attitude. He told the investigators that the aircraft remained afloat from between five to ten minutes. He also told them that he believed there was damage to the underside of the fuselage.

Despite the loss of life, the ditching was considered a success. Forty-three people were known to have exited the aircraft. There was some talk of having Balsey travel around the country to speak to other pilots about his experience as the first and only pilot to have ditched a commercial jet. Eventually the questions subsided and the attention shifted back to the facts surrounding the accident. It may have been a successful ditching, but it was a ditching that had become necessary only because the plane had run out of fuel.

Balsey spent much of his free time trying to re-create the flight on paper. He took copies of communication transcripts and overlaid position reports with known altitude, time, and fuel readings. He drew countless diagrams on plain paper or drafting paper, painstakingly going over every minute of the flight down to the last second before the ditching. He drew diagrams of his approach and three circles, plotting his altitude and computing distance flown and fuel burned. He became obsessed with trying to pinpoint what had gone wrong.

Following his thirty-day suspension, Balsey received word that the suspension was being extended. After that, he had less and less communication with the company. A friend in the maintenance department called to say that the maintenance log sheets for the DC-9 involved in the ditching had been destroyed, ostensibly to cover up information pertaining to improper work that had been done on the fuel probes. Balsey had been told that ONA had used unqualified mechanics on some of the work, and not all of the work was per the manufacturer's recommended procedures. The maintenance logs would have also shown numerous write-ups concerning the fuel totalizer giving erroneous indications.

Claims of the maintenance records being destroyed were never verified. Furthermore, destroying maintenance records to cover something up would have been totally uncharacteristic of ONA. In addition, one of the individuals handling maintenance records was Charlie Larmony, the son of passenger Jeannie Larmony. He certainly would not have been involved in any kind of cover up and would have been aware of any efforts to destroy the records.

Still, the NTSB had neglected to form a maintenance records group. Several weeks would go by before the regional accident investigator for ALPA, Louis McNair, inquired about the maintenance records. In a letter dated June 12, 1970, he questions why a maintenance records group was not formed, especially after the crew reported problems with the fuel totalizer.[1]

There was growing paranoia among some of ONA's pilots and mechanics regarding the investigation. Few people were aware of the verbal agreement between Steedman Hinckley and Octavio Irausquin to delay the installation of the auxiliary fuel tank. It was assumed by many that ONA had failed to meet the original April 1 deadline for installing the tank, and would ultimately suffer consequences if investigators were to discover this fact. Several pilots and mechanics would later claim that their phones were being tapped. Among those who suspected their phone conversations were being monitored were Hugh Hart and Ed Veronelli.

A month had gone by when Balsey received a call from Steedman. They had talked briefly several times since the accident. Steedman had shown genuine concern for his friend's well being. But this time the tone in Steedman's voice was strained. "Balsey," Steedman began matter-of-factly, "we can't speak anymore. The insurance company has advised me to cut off all communications with you. I just wanted to let you know." Balsey could tell that Steedman was uncomfortable making the call. "Don't worry about it, Steedman," Balsey said, reassuring his friend. "I understand." It would be some time before the two would speak again, and it would not be as employer to employee but as friend to friend.

In a letter dated June 15, 1970, Balsey was informed that he was being terminated. The letter was signed by Bill Bailey. An automatic appeal was filed by ALPA, but Balsey held out little hope for reinstatement. The loss of his job put him in an immediate financial bind. Balsey was his family's sole financial provider. He had a mortgage and car payments like everyone else.

Balsey's problems only worsened. On June 17, 1970, Balsey received a telegram from the FAA informing him that his Airline Transport Pilot certificate was being suspended until completion of the NTSB hearings, which were to be held in July. He was issued a commercial license, but the loss of his ATP made finding work as a pilot almost impossible. Balsey was thirty-seven years old and faced the very real prospect of being unemployed for a prolonged period of time — in the midst of a recession.

When Balsey received a letter from the NTSB telling him that he had to be in San Juan for the public hearings, he told them that he couldn't go. He said that he was out of work and didn't have the money. This forced the NTSB to subpoena him. The NTSB was now responsible for his costs.

Harry and Hugh hadn't fared much better than Balsey. Both were terminated. Harry had his ATP suspended, and Hugh had his navigator's license suspended.

Hugh Hart had additional problems to contend with. The day after returning home from St. Croix, Hugh went to see his personal doctor about his right knee. An x-ray of both knees revealed a bone chip in his left knee. The doctor decided to wrap the right knee and put the other leg in a cast. Hugh would end up wearing the cast for several months, making it impossible for him to seek other employment.

In contrast to the plight of the three ONA crewmembers, Wilfred and Tobias didn't have to worry about the loss of their jobs. The story of the ditching was major news in Curaçao and received front page coverage for several days following the accident. Wilfred, Tobias, and Margareth were praised for their actions. It was a sensational story that had a huge impact on the close-knit island community. Tobias and Wilfred became local celebrities recognized wherever they went. They each resumed flying after having three weeks off with pay.

One month after the accident, ALM honored Margareth and the twenty-two passengers who had perished by dropping a wreath at the site of the ditching. ALM Flight Attendant Supervisor Max Waas dropped the wreath from one of ALM's F-27 Friendship aircraft. Bill Bohlke was hired to fly a second aircraft with a photographer on board to capture the event. A picture showing Max Waas at the open door of the F-27 with the wreath in hand was published in a Curaçao newspaper.

Robby Schouten was so distraught over the loss of his fiancée that he decided to end his television show. He left Curaçao and moved to the Netherlands, eventually producing another television show that still runs today in Curaçao called *Far Away From Home Living With Us*. In the half-hour program, Robby interviews former residents of Curaçao, Aruba, and Bonaire who have moved to the Netherlands.

Margareth's family was equally distraught over her loss, especially her mother, who struggled over Margareth's death for many years. Not having Margareth's body left the family in a state of limbo. Margareth's mother refused to hold a funeral for her. She always held out hope that Margareth would someday walk through her front door. She would sit by the window staring out into space for hours at a time. She passed away ten years after the accident. Family members are certain that Margareth's death contributed to her mother's deteriorating health.[2]

The investigation into the ditching moved from the Caribbean to Washington a week after the accident. Investigators made several visits to ONA headquarters in New York, where they questioned those involved with the planning of the St. Maarten flights and reviewed training records for the crewmembers. The investigators were especially interested in learning when and if the crews had received emergency training concerning ditchings. When the investigators inquired about the emergency training given to the navigators, ONA had to admit that the navigators had not received any specific emergency training on the DC-9. Instead, a one page pilot bulletin had been issued to every DC-9 pilot that described the navigator's duties in a DC-9 emergency landing. The navigators, however, never received the bulletin.*

On May 14, the NTSB re-created the flight in a DC-9 simulator. The simulator, however, was programmed for different engines than those used on the subject aircraft and no meaningful results were obtained. To help determine what the fuel quantity should have been at various points in the flight, two fuel studies were conducted — one by the Safety Board and one by Douglas Aircraft. One interesting discovery from the fuel studies was the conclusion that the crew might have had adequate fuel to reach their planned alternate even after the failed landing attempts. Both fuel studies indicated that the plane should have had just over 2,100 pounds of fuel at the initiation of the climb from the St. Maarten radio beacon. Twenty-one hundred pounds was the amount of planned fuel considered necessary to reach the filed alternate of St. Thomas, which was 109 nautical miles from St. Maarten. St. Croix was a few miles closer. The NTSB listed several factors why they believe the plane ran out of

---

* ONA claimed that all pilots and navigators also received an update to their operations manual that explained the navigator's duties in a ditching. Hugh claims that he never received the manual update.

fuel before reaching St. Croix: unknown variables involving winds, weather, and track; the fact that the captain did not declare an emergency and request priority handling, which would have allowed him to climb sooner and thus burn less fuel; and the captain's decision to climb at a reduced power setting as opposed to a normal climb power setting, which would have resulted in a more efficient climb to altitude. There are a number of problems, however, with the Board's conclusions. The San Juan controller who took the handoff from St. Maarten testified that he would not have been able to clear ALM 980 higher even if it had declared an emergency, because of conflicting traffic. The Board also admitted that if the captain had climbed to a higher altitude immediately after leaving St. Maarten and had remained there, he would have opened up the possibility of running out of fuel at altitude, thus decreasing the chances of a successful ditching due to the weather and sea conditions.

The pilots and crewmen involved in the rescue of survivors from Flight 980 received varying degrees of recognition. Only one Marine helicopter crew received recognition. The crewmembers of EM-13, who rescued passenger Julius Eisenberg (who was later pronounced dead upon arrival at the hospital), all received medals. John Barber received a Navy Commendation medal. The crew of EM-07, who rescued the last three survivors, did not receive any commendations. It was an oversight that the crew wasn't particularly concerned about. They hadn't even known about the medals handed out to the crew of EM-13.* They were nearing the end of their six-month cruise and memories of the rescue faded quickly. The *Guadalcanal* returned to Morehead City, North Carolina at the end of May 1970.

---

* John Barber didn't receive his medal until after he left the Marines. It was mailed to him.

None of the Coast Guard crews involved in the rescue received commendations. One reason was that the Commanding Officer, Charles Mayes, had himself been involved in the rescue. He would have been the individual responsible for recommending commendations. It would have been inappropriate, however, for him to recommend himself for a commendation. He would later say that he regretted his decision to not request commendations for the other crewmembers. The Coast Guard crews, though, didn't perceive it as a slight. Performing rescues was their job. Both Bill Shields and Charles Mayes would be reassigned to other bases within weeks of the accident.

Jim Rylee and his crew were all formally recognized for their rescue of twenty-six survivors. It was at the time (and probably still is) the largest rescue by a single helicopter in Navy history. Commander Jim Rylee and Lt. (j.g.) Donald Hartman each received the Distinguished Flying Cross.* The Flying Cross, consisting of mounted propellers beneath red, white, and blue ribbons, is given for heroism or extraordinary achievement while participating in aerial flight. C.V. Lindley and Bill Brazzell each received Navy-Marine Corps medals.

---

* Don Hartman flew just one flight after the rescue before being permanently grounded for medical reasons.

Chapter

TWO AND A HALF MONTHS AFTER THE ACCIDENT, THE
NTSB held the public hearings into the ditch-
ing of ALM 980. The purpose of the public hearings is to provide a
complete and documented factual record of an investigation through
the testimony of witnesses. The facts obtained at the public hearings
supplement the on-scene and follow-up investigation of an accident.

The hearings were held in San Juan, Puerto Rico. It is a long-
standing practice of the Board to conduct the hearings in a location close to the site of the accident. There are several reasons for
this: the availability of eyewitnesses; the need to accommodate family members wanting to attend (most accidents occur near the departure or arrival airport); and the fact that it provides an opportunity
for the NTSB to address safety concerns in an environment where
the message is most likely to be heard.

The hearings were scheduled to begin on Tuesday, July 7 and continue through the ninth, with a preliminary conference to be held
on July 6. The purpose of the preliminary conference was to establish who would testify and in what order.

Balsey arrived in San Juan on Monday afternoon. That night, he met with his attorney John O'Brien. They were sitting at a table having dinner when they were approached by a well-dressed woman. O'Brien recognized the woman and told Balsey that it was Isabel Burgess, an NTSB lawyer and the chairperson of the hearings.

"Hi," Ms. Burgess said in a sanguine voice. "Is this Captain DeWitt? How are you this evening?"

Balsey had not been looking forward to the hearings. A day hadn't gone by since the accident that he hadn't thought about what he might have done differently to change the outcome. He had already talked to the NTSB investigators. He had spent countless hours rehashing all the grisly details for ONA, the aircraft manufacturer, and dozens of others. He had lost his job. And he had lost his license for doing the only thing he knew how to do. Now he was being told to present himself for cross-examination by a group of armchair quarterbacks. The last thing he needed was some NTSB lawyer trying to cozy up to him. "Madam, do I know you?" Balsey said, sounding irritated by the intrusion.

"Oh, I'm sorry. I'm Isabel Burgess. Do you mind if I sit down and ask you a few questions?"

"Well, Ms. Burgess," Balsey began, "I didn't come over and interrupt your dinner. If you don't mind, could you please go back to your table and I'll stay at mine. I'm quite sure that you'll have plenty of time to ask me questions tomorrow."

Isabel straightened up. "Does that mean you plan to testify?" The hearings were not a legal proceeding. Balsey had the option of not taking the stand. The penalty for not taking the stand, however, was possible jail time.

"I'm here by subpoena, Ms. Burgess, "Balsey said. "I haven't made up my mind whether or not I'm going to take the stand. So could you please kindly return to your table?" The next time Balsey would speak to Ms. Isabel Burgess would be from the witness stand.

The hearings were held in the Caribbean Suite at the Americana Hotel. Seating was provided for several hundred, though the room was seldom more than half full. The NTSB board sat behind a long table at one end of the room. Dick Baker and his investigators, along with representatives from ONA, ALM, ALPA, FAA, Douglas Aircraft, and the Coast Guard, sat at two tables on either side of the main NTSB table, forming a U shape. A witness stand was placed adjacent to the NTSB table. Each table was equipped with a single microphone. If someone at one of the tables had a question for a witness, he would either have to write the question down and have it read, or wait until the microphone could be passed to him.

The first witness to testify was Dick Baker. Dick talked about his initial notification of the accident and outlined the investigation to date. Next to testify was ONA mechanic George Chopay. George was chosen to testify before the flight crew because the Board wanted to establish the fact that the plane had no mechanical problems and had adequate fuel for the flight. They also wanted to establish that there had been no signs of fuel leakage.

Balsey took the stand next, looking thinner than most who knew him could remember. Dressed in a dark business suit and with his hair neatly trimmed, he appeared confident and unshakable. One investigator, Marty Spieser, a lawyer and the Operations Group Chairman, confided to Dick Baker that he was feeling ill over having to confront the former captain. He had to leave the room briefly to regain his composure before he could begin his questioning.

Those familiar with public hearings will readily admit that new information is seldom uncovered. The hearings usually occur months after an accident, and the majority of the individuals testifying have already given statements to investigators. The proceedings are designed more for the benefit of the public rather than as an investigative tool. But as Balsey was being questioned by Marty Spieser, one very important piece of information came to light that somehow

had been overlooked. It happened toward the beginning of the afternoon session. Balsey had just walked the spectators through the
entire flight up to the point where he was about to describe the
ditching when the following exchange took place:

Q. When you went to emergency power, would you describe what
emergency systems were available to you, especially in the area of
communications between the cabin and yourself in the cockpit?

A. I don't quite follow your question here at this time, Mr. Spieser.

Q. When you went to emergency power, was the public address
system available to you to communicate to the cabin?

A. The public address system from the cockpit to the cabin was
inoperative on this flight.

Q. I beg your pardon?

A. The public address system from the cockpit to the cabin was
inoperative on the flight.

Q. When did it become inoperative?

A. It was inoperative when I checked it at JFK.

The comment stunned the investigators, who had no prior knowledge of the inoperative PA system. There had been numerous reports
from passengers who claimed that there had been no warning prior
to impact, but the investigators assumed that the crew had simply
neglected to make an announcement. The disclosure of the inoperative PA made headlines the next day, though none of the papers
mentioned the fact that the PA was not a required item according to
the minimum equipment list (MEL), or that Balsey had tried to signal the crew by flicking the seatbelt sign off and on three times.

During a break in his testimony, Balsey was mobbed by reporters.
When one reporter stepped in front of him and shoved a microphone in his face, Balsey swiped the microphone away. "If you guys
start pushing me where I can't breathe, I'll make room. I don't want
anyone within three feet of me!" Balsey looked around at the startled

faces. They were mostly reporters for the local papers. When they didn't back off fast enough, Balsey raised his voice. "Do you guys understand English?" Balsey had a few more choice words with the group before forcing his way out of the room.

Over the course of the next few days, each of the remaining crewmembers was put on the witness stand. Hours of testimony were taken. The hearings were extended an extra two days to accommodate all twenty-two witnesses. The drama of the ditching and rescue was played out for the spectators through the testimony of the crewmembers, passengers, and rescuers. Press coverage of the hearings, however, was limited to the equivalent of sound bites, with reporters latching on to only one or two points from a select few witnesses. With Balsey, it was the inoperative PA. With Hugh, it was the lack of emergency training on the DC-9. When Harry was asked if he had received training for the flight, he answered that he had not. He added that he had requested additional training and had been told that he would be trained on the flight. The next day the headlines read: "Lack of Training Cited in Ditching." Ed Veronelli was particularly upset with that misrepresentation. Ed had gone out of his way to give Harry twenty-five hours of observer time before assigning him the trip. He tried to clarify that fact when he testified on Friday, but by the time he took the stand most of the reporters had already left.[*]

Also testifying on Friday was B. H. Thompson, a Douglas Aircraft engineer. He was brought in specifically to address the problem of the spinning fuel totalizer. After several hours of esoteric testimony related to the operation of the fuel quantity indicating system on the DC-9, Thompson speculated that the problem with the totalizer was

---

[*] Harry was referring to the fact that he hadn't received training on international procedures. He also hadn't received training on the LORAN. Ed Veronelli was aware of this and that was why he had paired Harry with an instructor.

most likely the result of water droplets on the fuel probes or a fault in the wiring. He testified that the sloshing of fuel inside the tanks was an unlikely cause for the spinning, though he admitted that Douglas Aircraft had never actually flight tested a DC-9 with fuel as low as that on ALM 980.

The last person to testify on Friday was Steedman Hinckley. It was late in the day, and except for the Safety Board and a few ONA employees, the room was mostly empty. Most of the spectators had left during the testimony of B. H. Thompson, the Douglas Aircraft engineer. Not even the most dedicated reporter was able to sit through his lengthy explanation of the fuel measuring system on the DC-9.

For Steedman, the accident had been a major setback. The negative publicity had weakened an already shaky financial picture. Declining revenues had forced him to sell off his interests in both the river boats and the cruise ships. His hotel venture was also threatened. Adding to his troubles was the knowledge that his decision to delay the installation of the extra fuel tank had played a role in the accident, albeit indirectly.

As he took his seat and faced the sparse crowd, Steedman appeared relaxed and at ease, as if he were getting ready to conduct one of his weekly safety briefings. The first hour or so Steedman answered questions related to the steps involved in getting the route approved by the CAB and FAA. The reporters who had left early hadn't missed much. It wasn't until Dick Baker took the microphone that things got interesting. Dick, reading directly from the lease agreement Steedman had signed with ALM, asked Steedman why the extra fuel tank had not been installed as agreed upon in the lease agreement. Up until this point, Steedman wasn't even sure if he would be questioned about the missing tank. ONA had given investigators everything they had requested, but the attorneys had advised against saying anything about the fuel tank unless specifically asked. Steedman gave a concerned look to Bob Wagenfeld, ONA's corporate attorney, who happened to be sitting at the examiners' table. When Wagenfeld indicated no objections, Steedman took a deep breath then proceeded to explain in detail why the tank had not been installed. He recounted the phone conversations he had had with Octavio Irausquin concerning the delays with Douglas Aircraft. He told the investigators that it had been his idea to delay the tank installation because of better-than-expected load factors. It was the type of damning information that could have only added to ONA's troubles. But with no reporters present, the story of the missing fuel tank went unreported. ONA dodged a bullet, thanks primarily to the long-winded testimony of one engineer.

With the questions concerning the extra fuel tank behind him, Steedman relaxed once again. Despite the obvious pressure he had been under the past several months, he hadn't lost his sense of humor. When he was asked if he was aware of any problems on the New York–St. Maarten flights prior to May 2, Steedman responded by saying that "Running an airline is a problem any way you look at it."

By Saturday, July 11, the last day of testimony, interest in the hearings had waned. Attendance by spectators had dropped off considerably. The only earth-shattering news to come out of the hearings thus far happened early on Wednesday morning when San Juan was rattled by an earthquake. Many of the hearing participants were forced to vacate their hotel rooms, fearful that the hotel might collapse. Robert Seijkens, the St. Maarten tower controller, jumped from his second floor balcony during the worst of the tremors. Those who witnessed the leap jokingly commented that he had jumped in an attempt to do himself in, so he wouldn't have to testify. He was in San Juan by subpoena.

By Sunday, the hearings hadn't garnered a single column of news coverage. The big story on Sunday was the crowning of the new Miss Universe, Marisol Malaret Contreras, a twenty-year-old secretary from Puerto Rico.

For Balsey, the close of the public hearings was the final chapter on the accident. There was nothing more that he could do or say. When ALPA approached him about his automatic appeal to his dismissal, he waived his right for a separate hearing and agreed to have his case heard along with that of Harry Evans. Balsey didn't even attend the hearing in which his dismissal was upheld. He put the accident behind him and moved on with his life. It would be more than thirty years before he would once again agree to talk about that fateful day.

The final NTSB report on the accident was issued March 31, 1971. The probable cause of the accident was stated as follows:[1]

> The Board determines that the probable cause of this accident was fuel exhaustion which resulted from continued, unsuccessful attempts to land at St. Maarten until insufficient fuel remained to reach an alternate airport. A contributing factor was the reduced visibility in the approach zone because of rain showers, a condition not reported to the flight.[*]

---

[*] This is the closest the NTSB would come to admitting that the crew may not have received accurate weather information from the St. Maarten tower operator. Rumors that the St. Maarten tower operator had been pressured into giving a better weather report than what actually existed were never pursued, even though testimony was given by a pilot who happened to be in the tower at the time, who stated that the weather was far worse than what was reported to the crew.

The Board also finds that the probability of survival would have been increased substantially in this accident if there had been better crew coordination prior to and during the ditching.

The final report also included a number of recommendations, some of which have been adopted and some which have not. The first recommendation was to have the words "warn passengers" inserted as one of the last items on the emergency landing or ditching checklist. This recommendation was adopted, and today all emergency landing checklists have similar wording for the crew to warn the passengers prior to any emergency landing. The second recommendation was to require that no passenger flight be dispatched without a working PA system from both the cockpit and the cabin. The FAA and the airlines argued that this requirement was unnecessary due to alternate means of communicating with the passengers, including the use of megaphones and bells as signals. As a result, as long as other means of communicating are established, a flight can legally depart without an operative PA from the cockpit.

The Safety Board also recommended that steps be taken to eliminate fabric-to-metal-type seatbelts. This recommendation was adopted. There were two recommendations for improving the access and usability of life vests and life rafts. While there has been much improvement involving life rafts, especially in the area of combination escape/slide rafts, little has been done to improve life vest usability. The life vests in use today are, for the most part, identical to those found in 1970. Lastly, the Board recommended that a VHF communications link between San Juan ARTCC and Juliana Tower be installed to improve voice communications between the two. This was accomplished soon after the report.

The following paragraph was also included in the report:

> There is no doubt that the ditching was accomplished under extremely adverse conditions. The captain demonstrated exceptional airmanship in the control of the aircraft, and the first officer and navigator greatly minimized the loss of life while awaiting rescue in the water. The effectiveness of three cabin attendants was reduced because of their lack of knowledge of what was happening, and the short preparation time available to them.

For the passengers and for family members of those lost, the accident would take its toll for years to come. A number of passengers and family members filed lawsuits. Every lawsuit was eventually settled out of court. The amount of the settlements depended on a number of factors, including the extent of the passenger's injuries; whether the suit involved the loss of life; and the aggressiveness of the respective lawyer. The average settlement was approximately $20,000 after lawyer's fees. The lowest settlement I found was to George and Martha Kellner, the married couple who had negotiated with ALM to have it pay for a stay in San Juan, Puerto Rico. They were originally offered just $3,000 each, which they rejected. The next offer was for $12,500 each. Their lawyer suggested that they accept the offer, stating that the insurance company had been keeping tabs on them since the accident. The insurance company knew about their trip to San Juan. It also knew that the couple's baby had been born without complications and that both had been on several airline flights since the accident.[2] The couple subsequently agreed to the $25,000 settlement.

The highest settlement I was able to uncover was to Loretta Gremelsbacker, who had lost her husband and also suffered a broken back. She agreed to a settlement of $1,250,000.[3]

Some passengers agreed to settlements that they would later regret. Walter Hodge and Jeannie Larmony are two examples. Both were unable to return to work as a result of the injuries they sustained in the accident. The money they received fell far short of compensating them for their loss of income. The same could be said for family members who had lost loved ones in the accident. The daughter of Jacques and Sylvia Urighere, who were both lost in the accident, settled for $50,000. The emotional stress to her and her family over the loss of her parents would linger for many years.[4]

Not all passengers pursued lawsuits against the airlines. Israel and Toby Kruger did not sue. Toby Kruger had worked as a legal secretary and didn't want to have to relive the accident in depositions and court appearances. They did, however, collect an insurance check for $135,000 for their lost jewelry.

Emerson Ussery wasn't looking for a large settlement, but he did have legal claims for a lawsuit. Besides his emotional pain and suffering, he also had physical injuries. He suffered a back injury that kept him in a full-body brace for three months. He couldn't claim loss of earnings, though, because he continued to work even with the brace on. His lawyer filed suit within three weeks of the accident, asking for $150,000. The suit was eventually handed over to a New York law firm that took the case on a 35% contingency fee. Emerson flew to New York to give a deposition. While he was there, his lawyer brought back a settlement offer of $10,000. Emerson scratched his head. "You guys are willing to settle for that?" he asked incredulously. He couldn't believe that they would settle for something that would net them a measly $3,500.

Emerson told his lawyers that if they were willing to accept $3,500 that was fine with him. He walked back into the room and told the lawyers for the insurance company that he would settle for $25,000 plus $3,500 dollars for his attorneys. The lawyers for the insurance company smiled and agreed to the settlement.

The investors who had given Emerson $350,000 in cash to take with him to St. Maarten lost their money. It remains in a briefcase at the bottom of the Caribbean Sea.[5]

Lastly, for the families of those still listed as missing, there will always be questions about that fateful day. For them there can never be a sense of closure. Most refused to have funerals. They have no burial site to visit. Unlike similar disasters today, there is no beach-side memorial. Even the exact resting place of the aircraft is unknown. For these people, it's hoped that the detailed account given here can at least offer some comfort by keeping alive the memories of those who were lost.

Chapter 29

THE TERM "DITCHING" IS NORMALLY DEFINED AS A controlled descent and landing on water. The emphasis here is that the aircraft is intentionally set down on water, and the crew has adequate time to prepare the passengers for a water landing.[1] Accidents involving aircraft that end up in the water unintentionally are known as "unplanned water contact" accidents. There have been numerous accidents that fit the latter category. Aircraft ditchings involving large transport category aircraft, however, are extremely rare.

One of the first forced water landings involving a commercial airliner occurred in 1956.[2] A Pan American Stratocuiser en route from Honolulu to San Francisco was forced to ditch in the Pacific after experiencing a runaway propeller.[*] There were no serious injuries thanks to a number of factors: For one, the crew had over five hours to prepare for the ditching. (The problem had been encountered at

---
[*] A runaway propeller is caused by a failure of the propeller governor, resulting in the propeller exceeding its RPM limits.

night and the captain elected to wait until daylight to ditch.) Secondly, a Coast Guard cutter was standing by to recover the passengers as they exited the aircraft and boarded life rafts launched by crewmembers. Lastly, the sea conditions were ideal, with only a light northeast wind and swells of only two feet. Despite the favorable conditions, the tail of the plane separated from the fuselage during the landing. Pictures taken by a passenger on the flight were later published by *Life* magazine, which also ran a story on the ditching.[3]

The advantage of having adequate time to prepare for a ditching was also demonstrated in the ditching of a Northwest Airlines DC-7 on October 22, 1962. The DC-7 was operating as a Military Air Transport flight from McChord Air Force Base in Tacoma, Washington to Elmendorf Air Force Base in Anchorage, Alaska. While cruising at 20,000 feet, the number two engine experienced a partial loss of power. The propeller subsequently oversped, and the crew was unable to feather the propeller. The captain alerted the steward and told him to prepare the cabin for ditching. The following preparations were made: all passengers were wearing life vests; the passengers were instructed to remove sharp objects from their persons; carry-on baggage, food trays, galley equipment, and other loose items were stowed out of the way so as not to impede the evacuation; the flight attendants demonstrated the brace position; passengers seated near the emergency exits were instructed in the operation of the exits as well as the launching of life rafts; and four twenty-man life rafts were repositioned near emergency exits with their static lines secured to nearby seats.

After informing the captain that the cabin was secured, the steward made a PA announcement instructing the passengers to assume the brace position. The plane was ditched shortly thereafter. Approximately forty-five minutes had elapsed from the initial notification. After impact, a total of six rafts were launched successfully by crewmembers and passengers. All ninety-five passengers and seven crewmembers escaped without injury. The success of this ditching was attributed to a number of factors: ideal weather conditions; crew familiarity with ditching procedures; ample time to prepare the passengers; and finally, the military passengers' receptiveness and responsiveness to instructions.[4]

Since the advent of modern day jet travel, there have been only a handful of ditchings involving a commercial jet. The first ditching of a commercial jet occurred on August 21, 1963. The accident involved a Russian Tupolev 24. The plane, which was operated by Aeroflot, was on a flight from Estonia to Moscow. On departure, the pilot could not retract the landing gear. The crew elected to divert to Leningrad because of fog at the departure airport. The plane ran out of fuel while circling over Leningrad waiting to land. The plane ditched in the nearby Neva River. There were no fatalities. The aircraft, with all fifty-two occupants aboard, was towed to shore.[5]

There would not be another ditching involving a commercial jet until May 2, 1970, when ALM 980 ditched in the Caribbean.

The next ditching involving a commercial jet occurred on September 11, 1990. A Boeing 727 operated by Faucett Peru ditched in the Atlantic Ocean off the coast of Newfoundland after the crew became lost on a ferry flight. The plane did not carry water survival equipment. The plane and the sixteen occupants on board were never found.[6]

The last and most recent ditching of a commercial jet occurred on November 23, 1996. The plane was a Boeing 767 belonging to Ethiopian Airlines. The aircraft had departed Addis Ababa, Ethiopia, and was en route to Nairobi, Kenya, when it was hijacked by three Ethiopian males. The hijackers ordered the pilots to fly to Australia, where they hoped to seek political asylum. The co-pilot was beaten and forced from the cockpit. The captain elected to fly south along the east coast of Africa rather than east across the Indian Ocean toward Australia. The hijackers ignored warnings from the captain that the plane was running low on fuel. When the engines quit, the captain attempted to reach the Comoro Islands. The hijackers struggled for control of the plane. The plane broke apart on impact some five hundred yards from the seaside resort of Galawa. Prior to the impact, the captain was able to make two announcements to the passengers. In the first announcement, he informed the passengers of their low fuel situation and advised them to prepare for an emergency water landing. Life vests were subsequently handed out by the flight attendants, who then helped the passengers don and secure the vests. The flight attendants briefed the passengers not to inflate their vests until they were in the water. Many passengers ignored this instruction. The second announcement came just before impact when the captain instructed the passengers to brace for impact. Of the 175 passengers and crew aboard, 123 died, including the three hijackers. Many of those who perished in the accident drowned as a result of not being able to exit the aircraft due to their life vests having been inflated prior to exiting the aircraft.[7]

A close look at these four accidents will reveal that ALM 980 stands alone in its uniqueness as the only open-water ditching of a commercial jet. The Aeroflot ditching in 1963 occurred in a river and did not involve the use of emergency equipment, or an emergency evacuation. The Faucett Peru accident was not a commercial airline flight. And finally, the Ethiopian hijacking accident occurred within swimming distance of a beach. It could also be argued that it was not a true ditching. Video shot of the accident shows the left wingtip striking the water first. The plane cartwheeled to the left and quickly broke into three large segments. It's not even clear who was at the controls when the plane hit the water.

In 1970, when ALM 980 ditched in the Caribbean, two-engine air-craft were not permitted to make extended over-water flights unless there was a suitable landing site within one hour's flying time. Today, two-engine aircraft routinely make extended over-water flights.* The chance of losing both engines is considered to be so remote that the airlines and the FAA consider it to be an acceptable risk. However, not only has it happened before, but there is one incident on record in which all three engines of a three-engine aircraft have failed. The flight was Eastern Airlines Flight 855. The Lockheed L-1011 departed Miami May 5, 1983 on a flight to Nassau, Bahamas. There were ten crewmembers and 162 passengers on board. While descending through 15,000 feet on their approach to Nassau, the crew noted a low oil pressure indication on the number two engine. The captain elected to shut down the engine and return to Miami, citing weather and traffic at Nassau as his reason for not landing there. On the return trip to Miami, the low oil pressure lights for both the number one and number three engine came on. All three crewmembers on board suspected faulty instrumentation, conclud-ing that the odds of losing oil pressure to all three engines were astronomical. Approximately fifty-five miles outside of Miami, while descending through 12,000 feet, both of these engines failed. The aircraft was now powerless and sinking toward the ocean at a rate of 1,600 feet a minute. Fortunately, the crew had started their Auxiliary Power Unit (APU) and was able to maintain electrical and hydraulic power. The captain called for the lead flight attendant and told her to prepare the cabin for ditching. He said nothing about how much time remained before the expected ditching. The flight attendant used the PA in the cabin to instruct the passengers on how to don

---

* Aircraft making extended over-water flights must carry water survival equipment.

their life vests and told them to prepare for ditching. Fearing that the ditching was imminent, the flight attendants hurried the passengers into their life vests and told them to assume the brace position. Some passengers were so panic stricken that they continued to scream throughout the emergency. Other passengers were so immobilized by fear that they were incapable of functioning and had to be assisted with their life vests. The panic in the cabin intensified when the flight engineer announced over the PA to prepare for ditching.

Back in the cockpit, the crew frantically tried restarting the number two engine. They managed to get the engine started just 4,000 feet above the water. They were twenty-two miles from Miami. The aircraft was able to climb and continue on to Miami, where it landed safely.

The postflight investigation revealed several problems related to the donning of life vests. Many passengers had difficulty removing the life vests from under their seats. Others struggled with the plastic packages in which the vests were stored. Passengers found it difficult to don the life vests while seated with their seatbelts fastened. Some had to undo their seatbelts and lean forward; others found it easier to stand. There were problems lowering the back flap of the life vests. Many of the passengers wore their life vests unsecured around their waists. More than one passenger inflated their life vest even after having been instructed not to. One passenger stated that he had inflated his life vest because he didn't want to find out in the water that it wouldn't inflate.*

The loss of oil pressure on all three engines was later determined to be a result of the omission of an O-ring seal on the master chip detector of each engine.[8]

---

* Life vests can also be inflated manually by blowing into an inflation tube.

Another dramatic near-ditching occurred on Aug. 24, 2001. Canadian-based charter airline Air Transat was operating an Airbus A330 on a flight from Toronto, Canada to Lisbon, Portugal. En route, the crew noticed a fuel imbalance. The crew crossfed fuel to correct the imbalance. Unknown to the crew was the fact that the imbalance had been caused by a fuel leak on the right engine. By the time the crew realized what was happening, it was too late. The plane subsequently lost both engines due to fuel exhaustion and began a powerless glide toward the water. Miraculously, the captain managed to glide the aircraft in for a power-off night landing in the Azores. All 304 people on board escaped without serious injury.[9]

The most recent ditching of a commercial aircraft, as of this writing, occurred on August 6, 2005. The plane was a Tuninter ATR-72 turboprop en route from the Adriatic port of Bari to the Tunisian resort of Djerba. The plane ran out of fuel and was forced to ditch in the Mediterranean off Sicily's northern coast. The plane broke apart on impact, but a large section of fuselage remained floating long enough for survivors to cling to it until rescued. Twenty-three of the thirty-nine people on board survived. Investigators determined that mechanics had inadvertently replaced the fuel gauge on the plane with one from an ATR-42, which is a smaller version of the ATR-72.

Statistics show that there are approximately twelve to fifteen aircraft ditchings a year, almost exclusively involving light aircraft. Examples include general aviation aircraft, banner pilots, fish spotters, ferry flights, and smaller commuter aircraft. There are 171 airports in the U.S. located within five miles of a body of water of at least one-quarter square mile in surface area.[10] The number worldwide is manyfold that of the U.S.

Today, passengers traverse the world's oceans giving scarcely a thought to the vast expanse of open water beneath them. Yet if history is any indication, it is only a matter of time before another commercial airliner finds itself at the end of an error chain that leads to another ditching. It's hoped that when that time comes, the lessons learned here will make a difference in the final outcome.

Epilogue

ALSEY DEWITT WAS THIRTY-SEVEN YEARS OLD AT the time of the ditching of ALM 980. He had accumulated over 12,000 hours of flight time. It was all he knew how to do. Balsey would never again pilot another aircraft. The FAA revoked his Airline Transport Pilot (ATP) certificate after the public hearings in San Juan. According to Balsey, the FAA cited improper pre-flight planning as one of the reasons for the revocation, pointing out that Balsey didn't have the appropriate approach charts for St. Croix.* Balsey claims that information pertaining to the missing St. Croix approach charts was only brought up during questioning in St. Croix, and he had been told that none of the information from that meeting with investigators could be used against him. Balsey could have elected to go through the lengthy process of retaking the various written and flight tests needed to re-acquire his ratings, but he didn't have the time, money, or drive. He turned his focus on dealing with his financial crisis caused by the loss of his job. He traded in two new

---

* The charts were most likely in the chart book but filed incorrectly.

cars for a less expensive one. He moved his family back to upstate New York and rented out his house in Hopewell Junction. The rental income on the house covered both his mortgage and the car payments. He then started work on building a new house with savings and some help from his family. His wife Edith went to work for a nursing home. Balsey worked part time, doing odd jobs. He also made money selling logs that had been cut down on land that he owned.

Balsey was working part time in a sporting goods shop when the principal for the local high school stopped by. They were talking about the upcoming school year when the principal mentioned that he had a mechanical engineering class but hadn't yet hired a teacher. Balsey had done some drafting work and had taken a few engineering classes, so he offered his services. Balsey went to work that fall. For the first time in many years Balsey was teaching again.

Balsey felt at home in the classroom. He eventually went back to school himself and earned a degree in mathematics, a subject he loved almost as much as flying. He also received a teaching certificate. Balsey taught mathematics at the local college and also for a short time at a nearby prison before retiring. Edith still works at the nursing home. They live in the home that Balsey built on his grandfather's farm.

Hugh Hart, who was the least culpable in the accident, and who was responsible for helping passengers in the water by inflating the escape slide, spent much of the next five years fighting his dismissal from ONA. Hugh was initially represented by a lawyer for the navigators union. A hearing held in August 1970 ended in a stalemate. Hugh then hired his own attorney. Thus began a long legal process that would drag on for nearly four and a half years before a final hearing with an arbitrator was arranged. The company agreed to pay Hugh a severance package of $25,000, equal to what the other navigators had received. ONA stopped using navigators in 1971. Hugh couldn't collect back pay because the company argued that since he was in a leg cast after the accident he could not have performed his duties as a navigator. Hugh bought a sailboat with his settlement, though he didn't live near water and the boat went unused. Hugh worked off and on in real estate.

Harry Evans was the only one of the three ONA flight crewmembers to resume his flying career. The FAA returned his ATP certificate after the public hearings. Harry went to work for a short time in Las Vegas, flying scenic tour flights over the Grand Canyon. From there he worked his way back up the ladder, obtaining type ratings on a number of jet aircraft.

Wilfred Spencer continued flying for ALM but never again felt comfortable in the air. Seven years after the accident, Wilfred decided that he could no longer perform his duties and maintain his health. He asked to be reassigned to a non-flying position. ALM agreed but stipulated that he be paid a wage equal to the position it was willing to offer him. The pay was substantially less than his purser pay. Wilfred saw a specialist who told him that he had a fear of flying. He spent two years on disability before ALM officially dismissed him.

During his time at ALM, Wilfred pursued his interest in union work, eventually holding a top position in the flight attendants union. After leaving ALM, Wilfred was elected to head one of the largest labor unions in Curaçao. As of this writing, he still works for the union on a limited basis.

Tobias (Tito) Cordeiro stayed with ALM another seven years before leaving to work for an insurance company. He eventually purchased a McDonald's franchise on the island of Aruba, where he lives. The success of that first franchise led to the purchase of a second restaurant. Tobias then expanded to Curaçao, where he currently operates four McDonald's franchises. Tobias lives in a beautiful house overlooking the Caribbean Sea. The spectacular view from his house is made even more stunning by the luscious flowers and trees planted and cared for by his lovely wife Mireya. They have two daughters — Marnia and Monica.

The Dutch Government formally honored Margareth Aleida Abraham by naming a plaza at the Curaçao International Airport in her name. She was also recognized by President Richard Nixon, who presented her family and ALM officials with a plaque that still hangs on a wall at the Curaçao International Airport. The plaque reads as follows:

> A citizen of the Netherlands Antilles and a Stewardess of the Netherlands Antilles Airlines, Margareth Abraham courageously sacrificed her life for others on May 2, 1970. As a DC-9 jet prepared for an emergency landing in the Caribbean Sea, Margareth assisted her Antillean and American passengers in donning life vests, calming fears, and readying themselves for the crash. Showing no concern for her own safety, Margareth died for the sake of the passengers entrusted in her care.

This act of selfless heroism will abide forever in the hearts of her aviation colleagues, her country-men, and her friends in the United States.

Richard M. Nixon

Steedman Hinckley succeeded in turning ONA into a premier charter airline. Financial pressures brought on by two economic downturns in less than five years, however, strained the company's resources. After selling off the river boats and the cruise ship, Steedman had to unload the hotel project as well. He continued to acquire new aircraft, but a string of unfortunate accidents cast a dark cloud over the company.

On June 20, 1973, a DC-8 was involved in an accident in Bangor, Maine. The flight originated in Tampa, Florida and was destined for Geneva, Switzerland via Bangor and Amsterdam, the Netherlands. During the takeoff-roll, the plane blew two tires on the right main landing gear. The captain aborted the takeoff. Fire erupted as a result of friction between the metal wheels and the pavement. The fire spread to the right wing and right side of the fuselage. Thirty-four of the 251 passengers on board were injured, three seriously. Most of the injuries occurred during the evacuation.[1]

The next accident occurred on November 12, 1975 and involved a DC-10 on a flight from JFK to Jeddah, Saudi Arabia. The aircraft ingested sea gulls in the number three (right) engine during takeoff. The Captain aborted the takeoff, but damage caused to the number three engine hindered his attempt to decelerate the aircraft. The tires blew, the landing gear collapsed, and the right engine caught fire.

Eventually, the entire aircraft was engulfed in flames. There were two serious injuries but no fatalities. The flight carried 139 passengers and crew, mostly ONA flight attendants who were being repositioned for a temporary crew base in Saudi Arabia.[2]

A few months later on Jan 2, 1976, a second DC-10 was destroyed in a landing accident in Istanbul, Turkey. The plane landed short. There were no fatalities.[3]

The last accident to befall ONA occurred in 1977. A DC-8 carrying a load of cigarettes to Africa landed some 2,200 feet short of the runway. The captain and flight engineer were killed. This accident was especially devastating to ONA. The captain, who was well liked and had been with ONA for many years, was only two weeks away from retirement. The cause of the accident has never been determined.[4]

The string of accidents tarnished ONA's image as a first-class airline. The airline was saddled with the undeserved nickname of "Often Never Arrives." Although few deaths resulted from the accidents, the financial hit the airline took from the loss of revenue, higher insurance premiums, and other related expenses, soured interest in the airline from its financial backers. Steedman was voted out of the CEO position in 1977.

Faced with an expected increase in competition resulting from airline deregulation, the board members of ONA decided to cease operations in early 1978. They concluded that ONA's assets and options on new aircraft were worth more if sold piecemeal than if kept together as an operating airline.

Shortly after the decision was made to cease operations at ONA, Steedman began work on starting up another airline. He once again found financial backers and started United Air Carriers. The new airline provided aircraft and crews to other airlines when those airlines needed extra capacity. Steedman purchased a couple of DC-8s to fill in for Saudi Arabian Airlines during the pilgrimage to Mecca. As he had done previously with ONA, Steedman hired people with whom he was familiar to help run and manage his new airline. He even called Balsey to see if he would be interested in flying again. Balsey turned him down, telling Steedman that he had been away from flying for too long and his heart wasn't in it anymore.

By 1980, Steedman had done well enough in Saudi Arabia that he had the capital and resources to start up ONA once again. He folded United Air Carriers into ONA and moved his operations back to New York. Bill Bailey was hired to help run the company. Steedman thrived on the challenges of starting and running a new company. He worked tirelessly, pursuing old and new customers. When Pan American Airlines went out of business, Steedman purchased the name National Airlines, which Pan Am owned. It's unclear from the record whether Steedman operated under the name National Airlines. Economic pressures brought on by a sagging economy forced him to liquidate yet again. The name National Airlines was sold to a company based in Las Vegas, Nevada. That company operated under the name National Airlines until it ceased operations in December of 2002.

Steedman died of cancer in 1996. He is survived by his wife Ingrid, his son George Fox Steedman Hinckley Jr., and his two daughters, Annalisa and Katherine.

Ed Veronelli remained with ONA until the company ceased operations in 1978. He resigned from his management position within a year of the hearings in San Juan. He wasn't comfortable with the infighting among ONA's upper management. When Steedman started United Air Carriers, he offered Ed the position of Director of Operations. The job required a move to Saudi Arabia. Ed didn't want to move to Saudi Arabia, especially when there were abundant opportunities in the newly deregulated airline industry. He turned Steedman down and went to work for Air Jamaica. Ed worked for several airlines during the turbulent early years of deregulation, eventually ending up at Continental Airlines. Ed retired in 2001 as an assistant chief pilot at Continental Airlines.

After the ditching of ALM 980, Octavio (Tawa) Irausquin arranged for Northeast Airlines to fly the New York–St. Maarten route using a Boeing 727. ALM suspended the flights in 1979 due to competition by American and Eastern Airlines. Octavio continued to modernize his fleet of aircraft, but geographical limitations restricted the overall growth of the airline. Octavio left ALM in 1983 and lived for a short time in Miami. He moved back to Aruba in 1984 to work with the government of Aruba in establishing a Civil Aviation Department. Aruba gained independence in 1986, at which time Octavio became the Director of Civil Aviation. Octavio was also instrumental in starting the first official airline in Aruba, becoming the president of Air Aruba in 1988. He remained in that position until he retired in 1993. Octavio lives in Aruba and works part time as an aviation consultant.

ALM had no other accidents while Octavio was president. It did, however, have a hijacking of an F-27 to Cuba. In 1997, ALM changed its name to Air ALM. The airline ceased operations shortly after the September 11, 2001 hijackings. The airline had been experiencing financial difficulties prior to the hijackings. The loss of revenue from the temporary suspension of some of its routes was enough to force the airline to close its doors. The airline's routes are now flown by several local and foreign carriers.

Three months after pulling passenger Julius Isenberg from the waters of the Caribbean, John Barber received orders for Vietnam. He had less than a year to go in the Marines. He could have spent his final months at New River, but he felt compelled to serve in Vietnam. His father had served as an Army Medic in the second World War, and he had an uncle who had gone ashore on D-Day. He felt a sense of duty. So he made a point of getting to know the people in the clerk's office. When orders came for a helicopter crew, John Barber was first to sign up. He left for the Marble Mountain Air Facility located five miles south of DaNang on August 3, 1970. He flew as crew chief on combat missions for five months while in Vietnam and received over twenty-one combat air medals. John Barber was discharged from the Marines on April 21, 1971. He was married six months later. He currently works as a fireman for the Boston Fire Department.

Jim Rylee was promoted to Executive Officer of VC-8 Composite Squadron one month after the ditching. It was the highest position he could obtain in the Navy without a college degree. Jim retired from the Navy a month later. He went to work flying helicopters for a petroleum company. Jim passed away in February 2004.

Bill Bohlke Jr. returned to his job with Trans Caribbean Airlines. That airline was later purchased by American Airlines. Bill remained with American Airlines until his retirement in November of 2005. At the time of his retirement, Bill was number three in seniority at American and was a senior captain flying international routes on the Boeing 777. Bill and his wife Tuddy still operate an FBO on the island of St. Croix.

After the ditching and rescue, Bill's dad initiated a campaign to have George Stoute released from prison. He petitioned prison officials and Governor Melvin Evans. His motivation was not entirely altruistic. George was a good mechanic, and Bill Bohlke Sr. needed a full time mechanic. The efforts paid off, and George Stoute was granted a pardon by Governor Evans for his participation in the rescue. Unfortunately, the law required that he also be deported. He was a free man, but he could no longer live and work in St. Croix. He returned to Barbados. His whereabouts today are unknown.

Endnotes

Chapter 1

[1] The requirement for the navigator was a contractual obligation enforced by the navigator's union and not a regulatory requirement.

[2] The term "flight attendant" was not in use in 1970. It is used here and throughout the book to avoid overuse of the words steward, stewardess, and purser.

[3] ONA DC-9 Operations Manual.

[4] St. Maarten, located in the northern Caribbean, holds the distinction of being the world's smallest land mass shared by two sovereign nations. The French rule a large portion of the northern island (twenty-one square miles), while the Dutch rule the southern part (sixteen square miles). Visitors and residents can travel to either part of the island without restrictions. The French side is known for its nude beaches, while the south is known for its duty-free shops, hotels, and gambling. Gambling is illegal on the French side. (From *Frommers Caribbean.*)

[5] The paint scheme on ONA's aircraft was white with a dark blue stripe that started narrow at the nose and expanded as it moved rearward, eventually encompassing the entire tail. The shortened "Overseas National" was used on the first jets to come on line.

[6] The two airlines were ONA and ALM, the official airline of the Netherlands Antilles. ALM, which at one time was a subsidiary of KLM, used KLM's facilities and employees when operating out of JFK.

[7] None of the people I've talked to can confirm this incident. Wilfred Spencer, who was the purser on the flight and the one who greeted people as they boarded, claims it never happened. According to Wilfred, had there been anything unusual with the boarding process, he would have certainly known about it. Emerson claims that the only flight attendant he encountered during this brief episode was Margareth Abraham.

[8] There is no way to independently verify this story. When I asked Emerson for a name of one of the investors so that I might verify his account, he declined, stating that

299

he wasn't supposed to have that amount of undeclared cash in the first place and didn't want to see anyone get in trouble over it thirty-plus years later.

[9] U.S. Department of Transportation.

[10] The problem of hijackings would reach its zenith in September 1970 with the attempted simultaneous hijackings of four European aircraft bound for New York City. One of the hijack attempts, an El Al Boeing 707 departing Amsterdam, was thwarted by a reinforced cockpit door and two El Al Sky Marshals. A fifth aircraft was hijacked three days later in what has been dubbed "Black September." The hijackings were carried out by the Popular Front for Liberation of Palestine (PFLP). Three of the planes were blown up by the hijackers a few days later. Fortunately, all of the hostages had been released. President Nixon was so impressed with El Al's success in stopping the hijacking attempt on their plane that he implemented his own Federal Sky Marshal program days later. Metal detectors, however, would not become commonplace at airports for another four years.

[11] Wilfred Spencer's testimony at the NTSB hearings in San Juan, July 1970.

[12] The plane had a maximum capacity of 28,535 pounds of fuel based on a fuel density of 6.7 pounds per gallon. The plane was fueled to capacity. After fueling, the fuel totalizer read 28,900 pounds, the excess resulting from a difference in fuel density. Prior to takeoff approximately 500 pounds of fuel had been burned off during taxi and by the operation of the auxiliary power unit (APU).

[13] Life rafts were not a required briefing item. Information about the life rafts could be found in the emergency briefing cards.

Chapter 2

[1] Steedman's full name was George Fox Steedman Hinckley.

[2] Steedman's father did not serve in a flying capacity.

[3] Exeter became coeducational in 1970.

[4] The term "Supplemental Carrier" refers to a charter airline.

[5] The primary financial backers were Louis Marx Jr., Charles Hickox, Neil McConnell, and Dan Lufkin. All were close friends of Steedman's. Louis Marx Jr., a member of the Marx Toys family, was a Princeton classmate of Steedman's. Steedman also invested $375,000 of his own money.

[6] Phone interview with Ingrid Hinckley. A secretary showed Ingrid the notation on the application a few months after Ingrid arrived in New York.

[7] Steedman's first wife was Judy Gonsczo. They had a son, George Fox Steedman Hinckley, Jr. Steedman's wife gained custody of their son after the divorce.

[8] Phone interview with Ingrid Hinckley.

[9] June 1967 Prospectus.

[10] 1968 Annual Report.

[11] 1969 Annual Report.

[12] In a wet lease, the cost of fuel is included in the lease.

[13] The Netherlands Antilles consisted of six islands: Curaçao, Aruba, Bonaire, St. Maarten, Saba and St. Eustatius. Aruba became an independent nation in 1986.

[14] St. Maarten is the Dutch spelling. The French refer to the island as Saint Martin. The main airport is on the Dutch side, so I have used this one spelling throughout the book.

[15] Steedman Hinckley's testimony at the NTSB hearings in San Juan, July 1970.

Chapter 3

[1] There were many people involved in the negotiations of the wet-lease agreement. For simplicity's sake, I mention only Octavio and Steedman.
[2] Steedman Hinckley's testimony at the NTSB hearings in San Juan, July 1970. Ingrid also accompanied Steedman on the flight to Curaçao.
[3] An NDB approach is a non-precision approach. It is a low-cost, low-maintenance means of providing guidance to an airport in instrument conditions. NDB approaches are common in remote locations.
[4] February 6, 1969 memo from Bill Bailey to all navigators.
[5] Steedman Hinckley's testimony at the NTSB hearings in San Juan, July 1970.

Chapter 4

[1] Book Sense online database.
[2] *New York Times*, May 2, 1970.
[3] Problems with fuel probes are ongoing even today. The union for one airline sent out the following warning to its pilot group in early January 2006: "[The airline] has reduced the frequency of draining the fuel sumps on MD-80's. This leaves additional water in the tanks. The additional water encourages increased microbial growth. This, along with age-related deterioration of the polyurethane coatings on the fuel gauge probes, has led to a few incidents where inaccurate fuel quantity readings have been noted. The worst case so far involved an aircraft flaming out an engine on approach to ORD with 3,000 lbs indicating in the tank."
[4] ONA was the launch customer for the cargo version of the DC-9. The plane had larger landing gear than the regular DC-9. It was determined much later that the larger landing gear and other reinforcements were the cause of the higher fuel burns. The fuel planning charts were subsequently adjusted. This occurred well after the ditching.
[5] The figures presented here are the averages for the first thirty flights, not the first dozen flights as indicated in the text. It is assumed that the numbers would have been very similar. Load factor refers to the percentage of seats occupied.
[6] Steedman Hinckley's testimony at the NTSB hearings in San Juan July 1970.
[7] April 30, 1970 letter from Paul H. Patten, Director Operational Engineering Douglas Aircraft Company to Mr. M. Starkloff.
[8] Carl Morgan's testimony at the NTSB hearings in San Juan July 1970. In later testimony, a figure of 4,300 pounds of fuel was indicated for this same flight. I've chosen the 3,400 lb figure because the same figure appears in testimony given by Ed Veronelli, who was also on the flight. Balsey denies landing with fuel this low.
[9] Ed Veronelli Pilot Bulletin #57-70.
[10] Ibid.
[11] The alternate fuel was computed as follows: En Route reserve (10% of flight time) 2,100 pounds; fuel to alternate (St. Thomas) 2,100 pounds; hold fuel at 1,500 feet (30 minutes) 2,200 pounds.
[12] Official NTSB report. NTSB-AAR-71-B. Total fuel capacity was 28,535 pounds based on a fuel density of 6.7 pounds per gallon.

Chapter 5

[1] While Bermuda is often referred to as a single island, Bermuda actually comprises many small islands, with several of the larger land masses interconnected by roadways.
[2] Several pilots I talked to commented on Balsey's reluctance to fly high.
[3] The nickname "cherub-faced assassin" came up several times in interviews with former ONA pilots.
[4] Ed Veronelli interview with author.
[5] Modern-day jet aircraft use both leading edge slats and trailing edge flaps to provide additional lift at low speeds. A zero-flaps, slats-only takeoff allows the aircraft to accelerate quickly, an advantage at high altitude airports.
[6] Ed was promoted to assistant chief pilot of the DC-9 fleet. Balsey's assistant chief pilot, Boyd Michael, was promoted to chief pilot. Boyd spent most of his time in Dayton, Ohio where ONA had a DC-9 crew base.

Chapter 6

[1] Harry Evans testimony at the NTSB hearings in San Juan, July 1970.
[2] Ibid.
[3] Ed Veronelli interview with author.
[4] Ibid.
[5] In addition to Military Airlift Command (MAC) flying, ONA had contracts with both the Air Force and the Navy transporting cargo between military installations in the continental United States. The contract with the Air Force was known as Logistic Air Support (LOGAIR). A similar but smaller contract with the Navy was called Quick Transport (Quicktrans). ONA also participated in Commercial Air Movements (CAMS) charters. These were usually short-notice charters involving the movement of military personnel.
[6] Harry Evans testimony at the NTSB hearings in San Juan, July 1970.
[7] Tom Murphy phone interview with author.
[8] Hugh Hart interview with author.

Chapter 7

[1] It's hard to say with any degree of certainty where everyone was sitting. Several passengers moved after boarding. The records for the flight have been either lost or destroyed. The seat assignments given here are based on passenger interviews and other sources.
[2] Ellen Gemelsbacker phone interview with author. Peggy Rumore phone interview with author. (Peggy is one of Gene's sisters.) Loretta Gremelsbacker, who has since remarried, did not want to be interviewed for this book.
[3] Rick Arnold interview with author.
[4] Jeannie Larmony interview with author.
[5] Israel Kruger interview with author.
[6] E-mail from Christina Razzi.
[7] Emerson Ussery interview with author.

Chapter 8

¹ Hats were required uniform items for both male and female flight attendants. The steward uniform resembled those worn by the pilots. Stewardesses wore a white blouse and a dark blue skirt cut to just above the knees. White gloves and a dark blue cap completed the outfit. It was the same uniform worn by the KLM stewardesses.
² E-mail interview with Robby Schouten. Interview with Margareth's brothers Robert and Carol Abraham.
³ Wilfred Spencer interview with author.
⁴ Tobias Cordeiro interview with author.
⁵ Kristina Linder's testimony at the NTSB hearings in San Juan, July 1970. It's unclear from her testimony whether or not she ever gave instructions indicating that ONA used three bells to signal an emergency. Two of the flight attendants with whom I've spoken, who were in the class, do not remember any discussion regarding more than two bells.
⁶ Johnson, Daniel A. *Just in Case: A Passenger's Guide to Airplane Safety and Survival.* New York: Plenum Press.
⁷ Kristina Linder's testimony at the NTSB hearings in San Juan, July 1970.

Chapter 9

¹ Weather Group Chairman's factual report. Hubert McCaleb, June 16, 1970.
² Bill Bohlke interview with author. ALM 980 passenger Emerson Ussery was one of Bill's students.
³ Ibid.
⁴ John Barber interview with author.
⁵ James Rylee interview with author.
⁶ Bill Shields interview with author.
⁷ Carmond Fitzgerald phone interview with author.

Chapter 10

¹ The story about the watch was told to me by Robby Schouten. Margareth's actions related to the watch are speculations by the author.
² The Juliana tower did not record radio transmissions. The Isla Grande tower, however, which used the same 118.7 tower frequency as St. Maarten, did record its transmissions. The interference Balsey reports having was traffic at the Isla Grande airport. The airport in St. Maarten was named Juliana after Princess Juliana of the Netherlands. Note: Times are shown in UTC (18:48 = 2:48 pm).
³ In the U.S., visibility is given in statute miles. St. Maarten, which was controlled by the Dutch, reported its visibility in nautical miles.
⁴ The goal of Crew Resource Management training is to improve the interpersonal communication, decision making, and leadership skills of aircraft crews.

Chapter 11

[1] Aircraft navigate through space by reference to a heading comprised of 360 degrees. A 090-degree heading would indicate an easterly direction. The words vector and heading are interchangeable.

[2] When landing on a wet runway, the regulations call for the landing distance to be increased by 115% of the dry runway landing distance. For example: dry landing distance 4,500 feet; wet landing distance 5,175 feet (4,500 * 115%).

[3] Wind speed is always given in knots (kts.). A conversion table is used to convert from kts. to mph.

[4] VASI (Visual Approach Slope Indicator) provides vertical visual approach slope guidance to aircraft during landing by radiating a directional pattern of high-intensity red-and-white focused light beams. (*Airman's Information Manual.*)

[5] A number of sources were used in recreating the repeated landing attempts at St. Maarten. These include the official NTSB report, communication transcripts, hearing testimony, the written statements from all three crewmembers, and interviews with the author.

Chapter 12

[1] The term "flame out" refers to a jet engine losing its internal combustion, resulting in engine failure.

[2] Horne, Thomas A. "Putting wings in the water." *AOPA Pilot*, July 1999.

Chapter 13

[1] Wilfred Spencer interview with author. Wilfred Spencer's testimony at the NTSB hearings in San Juan, July 1970.

[2] Johnson, Daniel A. *Just in Case: A Passenger's Guide to Airplane Safety and Survival*, Plenum Press, New York.

[3] Special Study: Passenger survival in turbojet ditchings (a critical case review) (NTSB-AAS-72-2.)

[4] Wilfred testified that he didn't remember a passenger helping him.

[5] Emerson Ussery interview with author. Emerson Ussery's testimony at the NTSB hearings in San Juan, July 1970.

Chapter 14

[1] The phrase "stay clean" refers to delaying the use of flaps or the gear, which would increase drag.

[2] Had the checklist been found and read, it would not have said anything about warning the passengers prior to ditching. While the emergency checklist in the plane did not call for a passenger announcement prior to ditching, the operations manual did. In part it read: Two minutes before ditching, or at 1,000 feet, one of the pilots will announce over the public address system, "Standby for Ditching," and prior to

touchdown the command, "Brace for impact," will be given. (Revision #42 ONA operations manual March 25, 1970.) Adding a similar statement in the aircraft emergency checklist was one of the recommendations of the NTSB.
[3] The official time of the ditching was 19:49, which was within one minute of Hugh Hart's earlier estimate of time to fuel exhaustion.
[4] The primary function of the stall vane transducer is to provide angle of attack data to the stall warning system.

Chapter 15

[1] Arthur Johnson's testimony at the NTSB hearings in San Juan, July 1970.
[2] Jacinth Bryanth's testimony at the NTSB hearings in San Juan, July 1970.
[3] Emerson Ussery's testimony at the NTSB hearings in San Juan, July 1970. Emerson Ussery interview with author.
[4] Special Study: Passenger survival in turbojet ditchings (a critical case review) (NTSB-AAS-72-2.)
[5] Ibid.
[6] Ibid.
[7] Emerson Ussery's testimony at the NTSB hearings in San Juan, July 1970. Emerson Ussery interview with author.
[8] Jim Razzi did not want to be interviewed for this book. He did, however, answer questions through his daughter Christina.
[9] Ibid.

Chapter 16

[1] Wilfred Spencer interview with author. Tobias doesn't remember this brief exchange.
[2] Harry Evan's testimony at the NTSB hearings in San Juan, July 1970.

Chapter 17

[1] I have found one reference indicating that the captain's last name was Pash. A second reference indicates that it was Prash. I have chosen to go with Pash after talking with the flight engineer Larry Phillips.
[2] Phone interview with Larry Phillips. Newspaper accounts from the *Miami Herald* and *San Juan Star*.
[3] Controller Alexander Sambolin, knowing that a possible emergency was brewing, decided to stay plugged into the console. Both he and Silvia could communicate with the aircraft. E-mail interview with Alexander Sambolin.
[4] Charles Silvia's testimony at the NTSB hearings in San Juan, July 1970. Alexander Sambolin's testimony at the NTSB hearings in San Juan, July 1970. Charles Saunders's testimony at the NTSB hearings in San Juan, July 1970.

Chapter 18

[1] In 1970, the AMVER database was maintained by a mainframe computer located in Washington, D.C.
[2] Use of the AMVER system to locate the *Guadalcanal* is the author's assumption. The ship may also have been located through other means.
[3] *Point Whitehorn* deck logs. Phone interview with Kenneth P. Borrego.
[4] When a pilot leaves his second radio tuned to the emergency frequency, he is considered to be guarding the frequency. Note: Military aircraft use UHF 243.0, which is double the civilian VHF emergency frequency of 121.5. There was also an emergency beacon inside the cockpit of the DC-9. Neither crewmember remembered to grab it before exiting.

Chapter 20

[1] Neither Hugh nor Wilfred remembers the other being on the same helicopter. The evidence, however, indicates that they were.
[2] Charles Mayes phone interview with author. Jim Brawley's written statement dated May 19, 1970.
[3] A DC-3 transiting the area also spent a few minutes circling the scene, but quickly left after determining that it could not offer any assistance.

Chapter 22

[1] Governor Evans was the first elected governor of the Virgin Islands. He took office in early 1970. The plane that he was planning to take to St. Thomas is the plane that later flew out to the scene.
[2] As reported by the *Virgin Island Daily News*.

Chapter 23

[1] Several days later, Major Dennis Beckman, who had signed for the rooms, was billed several thousand dollars for use of the condominiums. The condominiums at the Estate Carlton remain today. The hotel was damaged in a hurricane and no longer exists.

Chapter 24

[1] Most airlines today have a Critical Incident Response Program (CIRP) in place to help passengers and crewmembers deal with traumatic events. Comprised of peer volunteers and mental health professionals, CIRP teams help to identify and diffuse problems before they reach an acute state.

[2] Emerson claims to have handed out over a thousand dollars to passengers. None of the money was ever repaid.
[3] John Dullighan. Special report supplemental sheet. "Rescue of passengers from ditched airliner." May 4, 1970. One newspaper source indicated that the aircraft carrier *USS. America* also aided in the search for survivors. I have been unable to verify this account.
[4] Phone interview with Kenneth P. Borrego.

Chapter 25

[1] Dick Baker interview with author.
[2] Neither Balsey nor Hugh recollects having dinner with Steedman after the accident. My interviews with Ed Veronelli and Steve Lang indicate that they did.
[3] Gerrit Walhout phone interview with author. Gerry was the co-chairman of the human factors group.

Chapter 26

[1] According to Dick Baker, the FAA does have the right to sit in on crew interviews.
[2] Larry Phillips phone interview with author.
[3] Martha Kellner phone interview with author. The couple's luck changed (or continued, depending on how you look at it) when they arrived in San Juan. George Kellner had a lucky streak at the casinos and won a considerable amount of money at the tables.

Chapter 27

[1] Louis McNair letter to Dick Baker. June 12, 1970.
[2] Robert Abraham interview with author.

Chapter 28

[1] SA-420. Report number NTSB-AAR-71-8, March 31, 1971.
[2] Their daughter Catherine is now a successful stage and film actress.
[3] *New York Daily News.*
[4] Phone interview with G. Reuben Richards, the grandson of the Urigheres. The amount of the award listed here is his recollection and is not supported by documentation.
[5] Emerson claims that he was reimbursed for the two $150,000 cashier's checks that were lost. There is no way to independently verify his claims.

Chapter 29

[1] Air Carrier Overwater Emergency Equipment and Procedures. (NTSB/SS-85-02, June 12, 1985.)

[2] The book *The High and the Mighty* by Ernest K. Gann contained a number of eerie similarities to the actual ditching which took place three years after the book was published.

[3] Brean, Herbert. "Ordeal on Flight 943: The Last Five Hours." *Life Magazine* Dec., Vol. 41, No. 18: 29 October 1956.

[4] Douglas DC-7C, N285 Northwest Airlines, Inc. Ditching in Sitka Sound, Alaska, October 22, 1962, Civil Aeronautics Board.

[5] *Flight International Magazine.*

[6] *Planecrashinfo.com.* I have found different figures given for the number of people on this flight. Some references have indicated that there were as few as twelve and at least one reference indicated that there were eighteen people on board.

[7] *Airdisaster.com.*

[8] Eastern Airlines L-1011 May 5, 1983 NTSB/AAR-84/04 PB84-910404. Report date March 9, 1984. Note: There is also a case on record in which a four-engine jet lost all four engines. The flight involved a British Airways Boeing 747. The plane flew through volcanic ash. Once the plane descended below the plume of ash the crew was able to restart all four engines.

[9] NTSB.gov.

[10] Bertorelli, Paul. "Ditching Myths Torpedoed." *Aviation Safety* 1999. Air Carrier Overwater Emergency Equipment and Procedures. NTSB/SS-85-02, June 12, 1985.

Epilogue

[1] DC-8 Bangor, Maine 6/20/73 NTSB-AAR-74-1 Report date Feb 7, 1974.

[2] NTSB.gov.

[3] Ibid.

[4] I could not locate this accident in the NTSB database. Several of the former ONA pilots I spoke with mentioned this accident.

Sources

Newspapers

"40 of 63 on New York Jet Safe in Caribbean Ditching." *New York Times* 3 May 1970.

"Airlines Pressing for Cruise Ship Links." *New York Times* 3 May 1970.

"Better Seat Belts For Planes Asked." *New York Times* 26 Sep. 1970.

"Board Says 57 on Airliner Got No Warning in Ditching." *New York Times* 2 June 1970.

"BWIA Jet Airliner Hijacked To Cuba." *San Juan Star* 2 May 1970.

Combined Services. "Big Eruptions on Campuses Across Nation" *New York Daily News* 2 May 1970.

"Did ALM Pilot Change Mind." Virgin Islands Charlotte Amalie *Daily News* 6 May 1970.

"Dutch Antilles Jetliner Ditches Off St. Croix." Virgin Islands Charlotte Amalie *Daily News* 4 May 1970.

Dreyer, Martha. "37 Rescued, Brought to St. Croix." *San Juan Star* 3 May 1970.

Dreyer, Martha. "Rebels Ask Asylum." *San Juan Star* 2 May 1970.

Dreyer, Martha. "What Price My Dead Husband." *San Juan Star* 5 May 1970.

"Gov Evans Lauds Services Rendered by St. Croix Groups." Virgin Islands Charlotte Amalie *Daily News* 5 May 1970.

"Indifference Blamed On Jetliner Tragedy." Virgin Islands Charlotte Amalie *Daily News* 5 May 1970.

"Jetliner Ditches in Caribbean; 7 Dead, 20 Missing, 36 Survive." *Miami Herald* 3 May 1970.

Lidin, Harold J. "Pilot Had Asked Clearance to Land Here." *San Juan Star* 6 May 1970.

"Life Jackets, Debris Found From Ill-fated Jet." Virgin Islands Charlotte Amalie *Daily News* 6 May 1970.

Lindsey, Robert. "Lack of Training Cited in Ditching." *New York Times* 10 July 1970.

Lindsey, Robert. "Navigator in Ditching of DC-9 Scores Procedures." *New York Times* 9 July 1970.

Lindsey, Robert. "Pilot of Ditched Plane Testifies Public Address Unit Was Out." *New York Times* 8 July 1970.

Lindsey, Robert. "Plane Ditching Stirs Doubts at Inquiry." *New York Times* 11 July 1970.

Malone, James. "Miami Pilot: 'We Were Lucky to Find the Raft.'" *Miami Herald* 3 May 1970.

McFadden, Robert D. "Rescue Craft in Caribbean Seek 22 Missing From Ditched Plane." *New York Times* 4 May 1970.

Muniz, Luis. "Ditched ALM Plane Had Enough Fuel to Reach Land, Pilot Says." *San Juan Star* 8 July 1970.

Muniz, Luis. "Witnesses Testify at Hearing Into May 2 ONA Jet Ditching." *San Juan Star* 9 July 1970.

"ONA Hearings Emphasize Flight Crew's Training." *San Juan Star* 11 July 1970.

Onis, Juan de. "Nixon Puts 'Bums' Label On Some College Radicals." *New York Times* 2 May 1970.

"Pan Am Captain Aloft Aided Jet's Rescuers." *San Juan Star* 3 May 1970.

"Passenger List." *San Juan Star* 4 May 1970.

"Passengers ignored lifejacket warning." *Trinidad Guardian* 5 May 1970.

"Passengers on Board." *Miami Herald* 4 May 1970.

Perez, David. "Hearings on Ditched Plane Continues." *San Juan Star* 10 July 1970.

Perez, David, and Martha Dreyer. "Officials Seek Data To Find Plunge Causes." *San Juan Star* 4 May 1970.

"Plane with 63 crashes in Virgins." *Trinidad Guardian* 4 May 1970.

"Report on Fatal Crash Say passengers Not Warned." Virgin Islands Charlotte Amalie *Daily News* 9 July 1970.

"Search Continues For 21 Persons, But Hope Fades." Virgin Islands Charlotte Amalie *Daily News* 5 May 1970.

"Search for Survivors Hampered." *Miami Herald* 4 May 1970.

"Survivor Says Only One Exit Would Open." *San Juan Star* 4 May 1970.

"Survivor Tells of ALM Ordeal." Virgin Islands Charlotte Amalie *Daily News* 5 May 1970.

"Survivors Tell Terror Of Ditching." *Miami Herald* 4 May 1970.

"Volunteers Aid in Rescue." Virgin Islands Charlotte Amalie *Daily News* 5 May 1970.

Books & Periodicals

Air Disasters, Volume 1 Chapter 8. Fyshwick, ACT: Aerospace Publications, 1995.

Adair, Bill. *The Mystery of Flight 427.* Washington D.C.: Smithsonian Institution Press, 2002.

Bacon, Stevenson W. "The Last Flight of the Carib Queen." *Popular Mechanics* Dec. 1970.

Brean, Herbert. "Ordeal on Flight 943: The Last Five Hours." *Life Magazine* Dec., Vol. 41, No. 18: 29 Oct. 1956.

"ComNavAirLant Lauds VC-8 Rescue Crew." *Naval Aviation News* July 1970.

Esper, George and The Associated Press. *The Eyewitness History of the Vietnam War.* New York: Ballantine Books, 1983.

Fredrick, Stephen A. *Unheeded Warning.* New York: McGraw-Hill, 1996.

Gann, Ernest K. *Fate is the Hunter*. New York: Simon and Schuster, 1961.

Gann, Ernest K. *The High and the Mighty*. New York: William Morrow & Co., 1953.

Horne, Thomas A. "Putting Wings in the Water." *AOPA Pilot* July 1999.

Jampoler, Andrew C.A. *Adak: The Rescue of Alfa Foxtrot 586*. Annapolis, Maryland: Naval Institute Press, 2003.

Johnson, Daniel A. *Just in Case: A Passenger's Guide to Airplane Safety and Survival*. New York and London: Plenum Press.

Pomerantz, Gary. *Nine minutes, twenty seconds*. New York: Crown Publishers, 2001.

Ryan, Cornelius. "One Minute to Ditch! The untold human story behind the headlines." *Collier* 21 Dec. 1956.

"SH-3A copter crew rescues 26 from Caribbean." *Mira Que Pasa* 8 May 1970.

Official NTSB documents

"Air Carrier Overwater Emergency Equipment and Procedures." NTSB/SS-85/02. June 12, 1985.

Blank, Thomas E. "Written statement provided to NTSB." May 1970.

Bohlke, William, Jr. "Written statement provided to NTSB." May 1970.

Brawley, James W. "Written statement provided to NTSB." May 6, 1970.

Fitzgerald, Carmond C. "Written statement provided to NTSB." June 18, 1970.

Graves, Francis X. "ATC Group Factual Report of Investigation." Docket No. SA-420.

Greauz, Georges. "Written statement provided to NTSB." May 21, 1970.

Hartman, Donald G. "Written statement provided to NTSB." May 1970.

McCaleb, Hubert. "Weather Group Chairman's Factual Report of Investigation." Docket No. SA-420. Exhibit No. 5A. June 16, 1970.

Nold, Elwell K. Jr. "Written statement provided to NTSB." Exhibit No. 3A. May 9, 1970.

Pash, William F. "Written statement provided to NTSB." May 15, 1970.

Ransom, Bill. "Written statement provided to NTSB." May 9, 1970.

Rylee, James E. "Written statement provided to NTSB." May 1970.

Shields, William F. "Written statement provided to NTSB." May 1970.

Speiser, Martin A. "Operations Group Chairman's Factual Report of Investigation." Docket No. SA-420. File No. 1-0001. Exhibit No. 2A.

Sweet, Walter. "Structures Group Chairman's Factual Report of Investigation." Docket No. SA-420. Exhibit No. 7A. May 26, 1970.

Vliestra, J. "Written statement provided to NTSB." May 1970.

Walhout, Gerrit J. "Human Factors Group Chairman's Factual Report of Investigation." Docket No. SA-420. Exhibit No. 6A.

Miscellaneous reports

Bertorelli, Paul. "Ditching Myths Torpedoed." *Aviation Safety* 1999.

DC-8 Bangor, Maine 6/20/73 NTSB-AAR-74-1 Report date Feb. 7, 1974.

FAA Communication Transcript. "San Juan Center; Isla Grande Tower" Docket No SA-420. Exhibit 3C.

Fisher, Lloyd J. "Factors Affecting Ditching of New Transport Airplanes." NASA Aircraft Safety and Operating Problems NASA SP-270. May 1971.

Johnson, Richard A. "Study on Transport Airplane Unplanned Water Contact." U.S. Department of Transportation. Feb. 1984.

Overseas National Airways Annual Report to Shareholders for 1967.

Overseas National Airways Annual Report to Shareholders for 1968.

Overseas National Airways Annual Report to Shareholders for 1969.

Overseas National Airways Annual Report to Shareholders for 1970.

Steenblik, Jan W. "CIRP: First Aid for The Psyche." *Air Line Pilot* magazine Apr. 2001.

"The Supplemental Airlines: A Report by the National Air Carrier Association." 1966.

Web Sites
Airdisasters.com
Equipped.org
NTSB.gov
ONACrew.com
Planecrashinfo.com
Popasmoke.com

Interviews
Abraham, Carol. Interview. December 2001.
Abraham, Robert. Interview. December 2001.
Arnold, Rick. Interview. October 2001; phone interview. January 2002.
Baker, Dick. Interview. March 2001.
Barber, John. Interview. July 2001.
Beckman, Dennis. Phone interview. January 2003.
Blank, Tom. Interview. July 2001.
Bohlke, Bill, Jr. Interview. November 2001; phone interview. December 2001.
Borrego, Kenneth. Phone interview. July 2001.
Brazzell, William. Interview. August 2001.
Cordeiro, Tobias (Tito). Interview. December 2001.
Crouthers, Jay. E-mail interview. July 2001.
DeWitt, Balsey. Interviews: July 2001, January 2002; phone interview. January 2002.
Dullighan, John. Phone interview. August 2001.
Fitzgerald, Carmond. Phone interview. July 2001.
Flavell, George. Phone interview. January 2002.
Gremelsbacker, Ellen. Phone and e-mail interviews. July 2001.
Hamilton, Jim. Phone interview. January 2002.
Hart, Hugh. Interview. May 2001; phone interview. July 2001.
Hartman, Donald. Phone interview. January 2006.

Hartog, Astrid den. E-mail interview. September 2001.

Hinckley, Albert. Phone interview. June 2002.

Hinckley, Ingrid. Phone interviews: March 2002, June 2002.

Hinckley, Steedman, Jr. Phone interview. July 2002.

Irausquin, Octavio (Tawa). Phone interview. March 2003.

Johnson, George. Phone interview. January 2002.

Kellner, George. Phone interview. January 2006.

Kellner, Martha. Phone interview. February 2003.

Kruger, Israel. Interview. November 2001.

Lang, Steve. Phone interview. March 2003.

Larmony, Charlie. Phone and e-mail interviews. December 2001.

Larmony, Jeannie. Interview. November 2001.

Lemoine, Ned. Phone interview. January 2003.

Lindley, Calvin. Interview. August 2001.

Logan, Randy. Phone and e-mail interviews. September 2003.

Mayes, Charles. Phone interview. January 2003.

Murphy, Tom. Phone interview. January 2002.

Nash, Art. Phone interview. September 2001.

Phillips, Larry. Phone and e-mail interviews. December 2001.

Razzi, Jim. E-mail interview. December 2002.

Richards, Gary. Phone interview. February 2003.

Rumore, Peggy. Phone and e-mail interviews. July 2001.

Rylee, James. Interview. May 2001.

Sambolin, Alex. Phone interview. October 2005.

Schouten, Robby. E-mail interview. February 2006.

Schrader, Bill. Phone interview. February 2002.

Shields, William. Interview. May 2001.

Spencer, Wilfred. Interview. December 2001.

Ussery, Emerson. Interview. October 2001; phone interview. December 2001.

Veronelli, Ed. Interview. January 2002.

Walhout, Gerrit. Phone interview. August 2001.

Warren, Glen. Phone interview. January 2003.

Wikander, Paul. Phone interview. December 2001.

Wise, Margaret. Phone interview. July 2002.

Credits

Front and Back cover Ocean Wave Microsoft.

Back Cover U.S. Marine Corps photograph by Corporal Matthew D. Kell.

Book Design by 1106 Design *www.1106design.com*

Figure 1. Mapping Solutions *www.mapmakers.com*

Figure 2. ONA DC-9 Operations Manual.

Figure 3. Mapping Solutions *www.mapmakers.com*

Figure 4. Mapping Solutions *www.mapmakers.com*

Figure 5. Photograph courtesy Balsey DeWitt.

Figure 6. Picture originally appeared in a Curaçao newspaper.

Figure 7. Photograph courtesy Hugh Hart.

Figure 8. Photograph courtesy Christina Razzi.

Figure 9. Photograph courtesy Emerson Ussery.

Figure 10. Photograph courtesy Israel Kruger.

Figure 11. Photograph courtesy Jeannie Larmony.

Figure 12. Photograph courtesy Rick Arnold.

Figure 13. Photograph courtesy Peggy Rumore.

Figure 14. ONA Annual Report.

Figure 15. Official Coast Guard photograph.

Figure 16. Official Coast Guard photograph.

Figure 17. Defense Visual Information Center, Riverside, California.

Figure 18. Photograph courtesy Jim Rylee.

Figure 19. Photograph courtesy John Barber.

Figure 20. Photograph courtesy Bill Shields.

Figure 21. Official Navy photograph courtesy Bill Brazzell.

Figure 22. Photograph courtesy John Barber.

Figure 23. Photograph courtesy Tom Blank.

Figure 24. Photograph courtesy Bill Shields.

Figure 25. Photograph courtesy Carmond Fitzgerald.

Figure 26. ONA Annual Report.

Figure 27. Photograph courtesy Tawa Irausquin.

Figure 28. Photograph courtesy Dick Baker.

Figure 29. ONA Publication.

Figure 30. Photograph courtesy Ed Veronelli.

Figure 31. U.S. Navy photograph by Lt. Dan Kneisler.

Figure 32. Defense Visual Information Center, Riverside, California.

Figure 33. Defense Visual Information Center, Riverside, California.

Figure 34. Photograph by author.

Figure 35. Photograph by author.

Figure 36. Photograph by author.

Figure 37. Photograph courtesy Alex Alberto.

Figure 38. Photograph courtesy Alex Alberto.

Figure 39. Photograph courtesy Robert Abraham.

Figure 40. Photograph courtesy Bill Bohlke Jr.

Figure 41. Photograph courtesy Michel Drenthe.

Author photograph by Brian Brinkley.

Acknowledgments

THE IDEA FOR WRITING THIS BOOK CAME ABOUT DUR-
ing a training class as a new pilot for TWA.
Our class of eight new hires was given the task of watching videos
on a number of topics, such as weather radar and hazardous mate-
rials. While these were important and necessary topics, I'll be the
first to admit that it was a struggle to keep my eyes open once the
lights were turned off. This all changed when the instructor shoved
in a videotape about an aircraft that was forced to ditch in the
Caribbean Sea.

There was nothing special about the video. It was mostly narra-
tion over crudely drawn graphics. But I remember sitting there as
if I were watching a Steven Spielberg blockbuster. The other pilots
were equally engrossed.

That night, I logged on to the Internet and started searching for
more information. I was certain that someone must have written a
book about this flight. But I found little information and no book.
I decided that I wanted to know more about the accident and, more
importantly, more about the people who were affected by this

tragedy. Thus began a five-year odyssey that would take me across the country and eventually to the southern reaches of the Caribbean.

During my research for this story, I discovered that there had been attempts by other authors to tell this story. Unfortunately for them, these attempts were made before the advent of the Internet. It was through the Internet that I was able to track down the numerous people involved in this story. I used e-mail to interview people as far away as Germany, Curaçao, and the Netherlands. Others, like the granddaughter of Jeannie Larmony, found me through my web site after they did an Internet search on the accident.

While my name graces the cover of this book, it was truly a collaborative effort. I won't mention everyone who contributed to the book here. Their names can be found elsewhere in the text. I would, however, like to single out a few individuals. First, I'd like to thank the crewmembers of ALM 980 who agreed to be interviewed: Balsey DeWitt, Hugh Hart, Wilfred Spencer, and Tobias (Tito) Cordeiro. A few individuals went out of their way to accommodate me by insisting that I stay in their homes rather than pay for a hotel room. Balsey and his wife Edith did so on two occasions. Bill Bohlke and his wife Tuddy graciously offered me a room in their house overlooking the Caribbean Sea. And Jim Rylee and his wife Donna, whom I interviewed on the thirty-first anniversary of the accident, provided a room in their home. Sadly, Jim passed away before he had a chance to read the manuscript.

I would like to thank the following readers who gave me valuable feedback during the early drafts of the manuscript: my wife Lynn Corsetti, Albert White, Jim and Barbara Hamiliton, Jerry Castellano, and Jeff Darnell. Lastly, a special thanks to editor Kathleen Marusak, who helped shape the manuscript from its earliest stages and kept me from embarrassing myself.

About the Author

E MILIO CORSETTI III IS A PROFESSIONAL PILOT AND author. His work has appeared in both regional and national publications including the *Chicago Tribune*, *Multimedia Producer*, and *Professional Pilot* magazine. A graduate of St. Louis University, Emilio has been covering aviation and space topics for more than fifteen years. This is his first book. For more information about the author and this book, please visit the author's web site at *www.EmilioCorsetti.com*.